MW00388721

Irasshai: Welcome to Japanese Teachers' Guide

Answer Keys and Resource Guide to the *Irasshai* Series

K. Negrelli, K. Suzuki and S. Suzuki

Irasshai is produced and operated by Georgia Public Broadcasting.

Printed by Booksurge Publishing, 7290-B Investment Dr., Charleston, SC 29418.

Copyright © 2009 by Georgia Public Telecommunications Commission. All rights reserved.

No part of this work may be produced or transmitted in any form or by any means, electronic or otherwise, including photocopying, or by any information storage or retrieval system without the prior written permission of Booksurge Publishing and Georgia Public Broadcasting, Education Division, *Irasshai* unless such copying is expressly permitted by federal copyright law. Address inquiries to *Irasshai*, Georgia Public Broadcasting, Education, 260 14th St., N.W., Atlanta, GA 30318.

Printed in the U.S.A.

ISBN: 1-4392-2668-7
EAN: 9781439226681

INTRODUCTION

Contents and Organization of the Teachers' Guide

This guide is designed for teachers and self-study learners using the *Irasshai* series. The series consists of two textbooks, *Irasshai*: Welcome to Japanese, Volumes 1 and 2, two corresponding workbooks, *Irasshai*: Welcome to Japanese, Workbook, Volumes 1 and 2, and the 138 video lessons available for online viewing or as a complete DVD set.

This teachers' guide is composed of four sections for each volume:

Suggested Activities – offering a variety of ways to expand on the content and make full use of the textbook, workbook and video lessons, the suggestions provided here are all optional but can be implemented to ensure in-depth lesson plans for every lesson.

Workbook Answer Keys – the workbooks were designed to provide supplemental practices that assist in the learner's development of a beginning level of proficiency in listening, speaking, reading and writing Japanese, as well as an understanding of Japanese culture. This teachers' guide provides answer keys to the three sections of each workbook:

Assignments - corresponding to the lessons in the textbook, they are divided into two parts, based on a pace of one lesson every two days. It is suggested that each part of the assignments be completed each day following the video lesson and interactive activities. While there is a variety of assignments, such as memorizing vocabulary, reviewing the notes of the lessons, and preparing for interactive activities, emphasis is placed on assignments involving reading and writing Japanese.

Particle Practices - these practices reiterate the explanations and example sentences found in the textbook. They provide periodic review of the usage of particles and offer further opportunities to demonstrate command of Japanese grammar.

Reading and Writing Practices - these supplementary practices complement the assignments and particle practices. They allow for reinforcement of basic vocabulary and grammatical patterns and enable students to gradually progress towards more personalized, creative writing tasks.

Flashcard Templates – students can use these templates to copy and make their own *hiragana, katakana,* and *kanji* flashcards. *Hiragana* and *katakana* are introduced in Volume 1, and a total of 70 *kanji* are covered in Volume 2. Copied onto cardstock paper, these flashcards can be used in class games and activities, as well as independent study or review of these characters.

Culture Matrices – these charts offer a lesson-by-lesson list of cultural topics introduced, and provide suggestions for supplemental online activities that enhance the cultural topics raised in each lesson.

Acknowledgements
The authors would like to thank Ms. Tomoko Aeba, Ms. Lisa Coppenbargar, Ms. Akiko Davis and Ms. Yoko Takeuchi for their contributions and efforts in the development of this teachers' guide. We are also indebted to Ms. Jennifer Barclay, who provided us with the fun, contemporary artwork of the cover, and Mr. Nick Bess, whose expertise enabled its final layout. We would also like to express deep gratitude to Ms. Lisa Hannabach, who single-handedly reviewed, revised, and re-constructed the many components of this guide and was instrumental in pulling it all together into a tight, neat package.

Table of Contents

Volume 1
Suggested Activities

General Suggested Activities
Additional Suggested Classroom Activities

General Suggested Activities

A. When beginning a new lesson:
   1. Make sure that your students know the topic and objectives for the lesson. They are listed at the beginning of each lesson.

     Ex.)   SEMESTER 1
              TOPIC: Introductions and greetings

LESSON 1

OBJECTIVES

At the end of this lesson you will be able to:
- ☑ Introduce yourself
- ☑ Greet someone for the first time
- ☑ Address people by name
- ☑ Pronounce common Japanese names

   2. Have your students make vocabulary/expression cards for the lesson – Write the lesson number in a corner so that they will know in which lesson it appears. On one side, write the vocabulary word, its part of speech, and its usage in a sentence. On the other side, write the English equivalents, as in the example below. Students can use the cards at any time they want to review the vocabulary words. They can also use them to test each other in pairs or in small groups.

     Ex.)

Front	Back
L1 **desu** (verb) (Ex.) Ken desu.	L1 **am, are, is** (verb) (Ex.) I am Ken.

   3. Distribute the **video checksheet** for the lesson to your students before you show the video lesson. Allow them to stop the video or watch it again as necessary. Have your students go over the answers to the video checksheets in class.

   4. Make sure that your students read all the notes such as **VOCABULARY NOTES, KEY GRAMMAR POINTS,** and **CULTURE NOTES**.

   5. Make sure that your students do the *INTERACTIVE ACTIVITIES*, one of the most valuable parts of the lesson.

   6. Check or have your students check answers to workbook assignments with the **Workbook Assignment Answer Keys**, included in this guide.

   7. Prior to the **A.I. (Audio Interaction)** session for the lesson, have your students preview the **A.I. pages**. The A.I. session should give them a chance to show what they have learned in the lesson.

B. When reviewing:
   1. *Hiragana / Katakana*:
     a. **Flashcard templates** are available in this guide and on our website: www.gpb.org/irasshai - **"for students" - student notebook - R+W Support column - Flashcard Templates**. Have your students cut out the card for each individual character. They can be used for learning and reviewing the characters individually as well as for review by a group of students. Lay out the cards on a large flat surface. One student will read out one of the cards, and other students can race to find the card. If it is the correct card, the student can keep it. At the end, count the number of the cards each student has.

b. For those who want to go over **how to read the basic *hiragana* and *katakana***, reference charts are available in both the textbooks and workbooks. Interactive charts are available online at www.gpb.org/irasshai - **"for students"** - **student notebook** - **R+W Support column** - ***Hiragana* Chart** / ***Katakana* Chart**. If you click on a character, you will hear its pronunciation.

c. **Writing Practice Sheets** for both *hiragana* and *katakana* are available in the workbooks as well as online at www.gpb.org/irasshai - **"for students"** - **student notebook** - **R+W Support column** - **Writing Practice Sheets**. Click on the lesson number to find the practice sheet of *hiragana* or *katakana* that you want to review.

2. Vocabulary:
For review, use the vocabulary cards that your students have made so far. They can work in pairs or groups. If they want to work in groups, divide the class into two groups or more. Choose a student from one group to act as the questioner. The questioner will say a word/expression in English and the other group will have a representative write the Japanese equivalent on the board. After giving 10 questions to the group, other students of the first group will check the answers. After that, switch the groups to do another set of 10 questions.

3. Particles:
Use the **Particle Practice Sheets** to review the particles that your students have learned so far. Each practice sheet covers the corresponding group of lessons covered on each test. They are best used right before the test. It might be helpful to re-read all the notes regarding the particles from the lessons in the textbook before they start the practice sheet.

4. Before the test: **Practice Test**
The practice test should play an important role in students' preparation for a test. A day or two before the scheduled Practice Test day, make a copy of the test **checklist** and **practice test** for each student to take home and complete as homework. On the Practice Test day, have students switch their practice tests with a partner and go over the answers together in class. When done, return the practice tests and go over the items on the checklist. Ask the class to review the items that they do not understand. Have them write down what they need to review and focus on these items at home.

C. When exploring general cultural topics regarding Japan:
Please refer to the **Culture Matrices** in this guide or online at www.gpb.org/irasshai
- **"for facilitators"** - **culture matrix 1** / **culture matrix 2**
- **"for students"** - **student notebook** - **Resources column** - **Culture Matrices**
You will find suggested topics for online research as well as topics and activities which can be found within **i-*irasshai***, www.gpb.org/irasshai - **"for students"** - **i-*irasshai***. Look for the provided key words under "Guidebook (Index)."

3

Additional Suggested Classroom Activities

Lesson 1

Roomaji	Japanese Names	*Meishi*	*Gairaigo*
Pronunciation of Japanese vowels Pair/Group Work	**CULTURE NOTES: Japanese names** Class Work	**CULTURE NOTES: Meishi** Project	**EXPANDING YOUR VOCABULARY** Discussion
Have students practice pronunciation using the *roomaji* side of *hiragana* flash cards.	Have students list some Japanese names they already know. Make sure that they know how to pronounce them in Japanese.	Have students make their own *meishi* in English and practice introductions with peers using the *meishi*. They can go over the rules for exchanging *meishi* and practice exchanging them.	Have students discuss *gairaigo* English speakers have from other languages (ie., déjà vu, etc).

Lesson 2

Syllabary and Syllables	Title Suffixes	Particles: *-ne, -yo*	Greetings
WRITING JAPANESE: Hiragana Pair/Group Work	**CULTURE NOTES: Sensei** **i-*irasshai* (online):** teachers Discussion	**KEY GRAMMAR POINTS** Discussion	**i-*irasshai* (online):** etiquette-greetings; welcome
Have students use the vocabulary cards that were previously made and figure out how many syllables each word/expression has.	Using i-*irasshai*, have students learn more about and discuss the differences in the use of title suffixes between the U.S. and Japan. (select the guide book (index) and click on the topic listed above).	Have students review particles.	Using i-*irasshai*, have students learn about, read and listen to more greetings (select the guide book (index) and click on the topics listed above).

Lesson 3

Classroom Commands	Greetings	Body Language	*Gairaigo*
VOCABULARY: ___-*o kaite kudasai* **Useful Expressions** (L1 A.I. page) Discussion	**i-*irasshai* (online):** greetings (activity)	**CULTURE NOTES** Discussion	**EXPANDING YOUR VOCABULARY** **i-*irasshai* (online):** *gairaigo* (activity)
Have students review the polite commands using [verb] + *kudasai* forms.	Using i-*irasshai*, have students learn more about greetings and expressions (select the guide book (index) and click on the topic listed above).	Have students discuss the differences between body language and body contact in Japan and the U.S.	Using i-*irasshai*, have students learn more about *gairaigo* (select the guide book (index) and click on the topics listed above).

Lesson 4

Numbers 1~10	Grades
VOCABULARY Pair/Group Work	**KEY GRAMMAR POINTS** **CULTURE NOTES** Discussion
Have students make cards with the Arabic numerals 1~10 on one side and Japanese numbers in *roomaji* on the other side and practice.	Have students discuss the differences between the U.S. and Japan regarding school levels. Have them practice converting grades in U.S. schools into those in Japanese schools.

4

Lesson 5

Particle: -wa	Question Words
KEY GRAMMAR POINTS: *-wa* Discussion	**KEY GRAMMAR POINTS:** **Nan-nen-sei?** **Doko?** Discussion
Have students review the function of the particle *-wa*. They can also review the other particles that they have learned so far, *-yo* and *-ne*.	Have students review how to make questions using a question word, and discuss how different Japanese question forms are from English.

Lesson 6

Ja nai desu
KEY GRAMMAR POINTS Discussion
Have students review how to make the negative form of the verb *desu*.

Lesson 7

Nan-sai	Numbers 10~99	Japanese Holidays
KEY GRAMMAR POINTS: **Nan-sai?** Discussion	**VOCABULARY** Pair/Group Work	**CULTURE NOTES** Discussion
Have students review how to make a question using *nan-sai* and go over other question words (*nan-nen-sei, doko*) from Lesson 5.	Using any two of the number cards from 1~9, form two-digit numbers. Students can practice saying the numbers.	Have students discuss the different ages for celebrations in Japan and the U.S.

Lesson 8

Honorific Prefix: *o-*	Particle: *-no*	Introductions
VOCABULARY NOTES: **Honorific prefix *o-*** Discussion	**KEY GRAMMAR POINTS:** **The particle -no** Class Work	Presentation

Have students review the honorific prefix *o-*. "*O-ikutsu desu-ka?*" is more formal than "*Ikutsu?*" What other phrases have we learned so far that have different versions of formality? *Doozo yoroshiku o-negai-shimasu / Doozo yoroshiku* (Lesson 1), *Ohayoo gozaimasu / Ohayoo* (Lesson 2)	Have students review the usage of the particle *-no* and other particles previously learned.	Using the following script, students can practice how to introduce themselves:
		    Hajimemashite. [Name] desu.
		    Gakkoo-wa [school name] desu.
		    [School name]-wa [Location] desu. [Grade]-sei desu.
		    Doozo yoroshiku.

Lesson 9

Kore~Sore	Question Form
VOCABULARY NOTES and **KEY GRAMMAR POINTS:** **Kore / Sore-wa ___ desu.** Pair Work	**KEY GRAMMAR POINTS:** **___ -wa nan desu-ka?** Class Work
Have students put the vocabulary cards for this lesson in an empty bag. Have a student pick one card from the bag and, showing the class the English side only, ask "*Kore-wa nan desu-ka?*" The others answer in Japanese, "*Sore-wa ___ desu.*" When all of them are done, put them back in the bag and switch roles.	Have students review how to make a question using *nan* and other question words: *nan-nen-sei* (Lesson 5), *doko* (Lesson 5), *nan-sai* (Lesson 7).

Lesson 10

~de ~to iimasu
KEY GRAMMAR POINTS Discussion
Have students review how to ask and tell what something is called in a language. They can also review other

particles that were previously introduced.
~wa nihongo-de nan-to iimasu-ka?
Pair Work
Have students put the vocabulary cards from Lessons 9 and 10 together (office supplies). In pairs, one asks, "*~-wa nihongo-de nan-to iimasu-ka?*" looking at the English side. The other answers, "____ *-to iimasu.*" When half of the cards are done, switch roles.

Lesson 11

Granting and Refusing a Request	Japanese Writing
CULTURE NOTES Discussion	**WRITING JAPANESE** **i-*irasshai* (online):** textbook-how to open one and read it (activity)
Have students review how to grant and refuse a request and list some important points.	Using i-*irasshai*, have students review the Japanese writing system and do the activity to learn how to open and read a textbook (select the guide book (index) and click on the topic listed above).

Lesson 12

Kore, sore, are, dore	Particle: *-no*
KEY GRAMMAR POINTS: kore, sore, are, dore Class Work	**KEY GRAMMAR POINTS: -no; Adjective + noun** Discussion
Place one bag near group A, one bag near group B, and one bag far from both groups A and B. Group A collects one notebook, pencil, red/blue pen, eraser, a sheet of paper, stapler, etc. Group B makes a list of the items and decides their locations. Group A asks group B, "*~-wa dore desu-ka?*" and group B answers, "*Kore/Sore/Are desu.*" Group A will place each item into the appropriate bag.	Have students review the usages of particle *-no*. Is *-no* also used between an adjective and noun? Have them explain why.

Lesson 13

Dame / Ii	Particle: *-yo*	Discipline / School Uniforms
VOCABULARY NOTES Discussion	**KEY GRAMMAR POINTS** Discussion	**CULTURE NOTES** **i-*irasshai* (online):** school uniforms; school greetings; duckboard; school shoes-changing (activity); shoe cabinet; school locker
Have students review how to express approval and disapproval. They can also review another usage of *ii* when asking for permission.	Have students review how to use sentence-final particles including *-ka* and *-ne*.	Using i-*irasshai*, have students read and listen (select the guide book (index) and click on the topics listed above).
Comics	Blackboard	Long (or double) vowels
CULTURE NOTES: Popularity of comics (*manga*) **i-*irasshai* (online):** comic books – manga	**i-*irasshai* (online):** blackboard	**WRITING JAPANESE** Discussion
Using i-*irasshai*, have students learn more about *manga* (select the guide book (index) and click on the topic listed above).	Using i-*irasshai*, have students learn more about Japanese schools (select the guide book (index) and click on the topic listed above).	Have students review how to write the second vowel of double vowels.

Lesson 14

O-negai-shimasu
VOCABULARY NOTES: O-negai-shimasu Discussion
Have students review the usage of this expression. Why is the same phrase used when people meet for the first time?

Ja, mata	Double Consonants
VOCABULARY Discussion	**WRITING JAPANESE** Discussion
Have students review and discuss when and with whom to use	Have students review how to write double

this expression. Ask them if they have learned any other informal expressions before.	consonants and how to pronounce them.

Lesson 15

Particles: -no and -to	Honorific and Humble Forms	*Dare-no desu-ka?*
KEY GRAMMAR POINTS Discussion	**CULTURE NOTES** Discussion	Class Work
Have students review the particles -no and -to and other usages of the particle -no.	Have students review and discuss the difference between honorific and humble forms and their usages.	Group A collects a pen from each member and puts all of the pens in a bag. Then they will give the bag to Group B. Each member of Group B picks a pen and guesses whose pen it is by asking, "*Kore-wa ~ -san / -kun-no pen desu-ka?*" If it is guessed correctly, give it back to the owner and give the bag to another member. When there are no pens left in the bag, switch groups and do it again.

Lesson 16

Kono, sono, ano, dono	Family Relationship Terms
KEY GRAMMAR POINTS Discussion	**CULTURE NOTES** Discussion
Have students review the set of *ko-so-a-do* words from this lesson and discuss the difference between them and *kore-sore-are-dore*.	Have students review the set of family relationship terms and discuss the difference in language usage between English and Japanese.

Lesson 17

Namae	-chan
VOCABULARY NOTES Discussion	**VOCABULARY NOTES** Discussion
Have students review the set of vocabulary of *o-namae ~ namae* and discuss their usage.	Have students review the title suffix *-chan* and its usage together with other title suffixes (*-san*, *-kun*, and *-sensei*).

Lesson 18

Questions	Particle: -mo	Counter: -nin
KEY GRAMMAR POINTS: **Imasu/imasen** **-ga** Discussion	**KEY GRAMMAR POINTS:** **-mo** Discussion	**KEY GRAMMAR POINTS:** **Counters** **Number + -nin** Discussion
Have students review how to form questions regarding family members.	Have students review how to use the particle *-mo* and other particles learned so far.	Have students review the counters for people and other counters learned so far.

Lesson 19

Addressing Family Members
CULTURE NOTES Role Play
Have students review how to address family members. They can work in groups of five or more. Have them create a family of five or more members and decide which person will be which family member. Have them practice calling each other according to the rules.

Lesson 20

Arimasu/arimasen	Particle: -no
KEY GRAMMAR POINTS Discussion	**KEY GRAMMAR POINTS** Discussion
Have students review how to form sentences using	Have students review how to use -no in the

arimasu and *arimasen* and the differences between *arimasu* and *imasu*.	sentence, "___ -*no desu*." They can also review the notes from Lesson 15.

~-ga arimasu-ka? Kono ~-wa ~-no desu-ka?
Class Work
Have one student ask the class for an item (ie. a pen, pencil, etc.) by saying "[item]-*ga arimasu*?" and collect as many as possible. A second student goes up to the items, picks one and asks, "*Kono* [item]-*wa* [person's name]-*no desu-ka*?" If wrong, that person responds with "*Iie, chigaimasu*." If correct, that person answers, "*Hai, soo desu*." and retrieves it. The second student should continue until the owner is found. Then third and fourth students go up and repeat the question pattern until all items are gone.

Lesson 21

Ko-so-a-do words	Adjectives
KEY GRAMMAR POINTS **EXPANDING YOUR VOCABULARY** Group Work	**KEY GRAMMAR POINTS** Discussion
Have students do the following procedures: 1. Review *koko, soko, asoko* and *doko* and other *ko-so-a-do* words. 2. Make cards of *gairaigo* items. 3. Three students, A, B and C, will sit apart from each other. Each student will have four *gairaigo* item cards. 4. Other students will go to Students A, B and C to find out who has which item by asking "___-*ga arimasu-ka*?" If the answer is "*Hai, arimasu*," they will write down what A, B and C have. Have them list all of the items. 5. Divide the questioners into two groups and seat them near Students A and B. Group 1 asks Group 2 where the first six items are by asking "___-*wa doko desu-ka*?" Group 2 will answer "*Koko/soko/asoko desu*." Check their answers with their own information. 6. After finishing the first six items, the other group asks about the last six items.	Have students review all of the adjectives they have learned so far.
	Writing Long Vowels
	WRITING JAPANESE Discussion
	Have students review how to write the long vowels. They can also refer to the notes from Lesson 13.

Lesson 22

Classroom Commands	*Kedo*	*I*-adjective
CLASSROOM COMMANDS WITH KUDASAI Class Work	**VOCABULARY NOTES** Discussion	**KEY GRAMMAR POINTS** Discussion
Have the class make a list of commands and write them down on a piece of paper. Then, have one student give a command to the class and have them respond. Let other students take turns being the leader.	Have students review the word *kedo* and discuss its function and how to use it in a sentence.	Have students review *i*-adjectives and their functions. Have them make sentences using *i*-adjectives.

Juku	Particle: -*o*
i-*irasshai* (online): school	**WRITING JAPANESE** Discussion
Using i-*irasshai*, have students learn more about *juku* (select the guide book (index) and click on the topic listed above).	Have students review how to write the particle -*o*. They can also review how to write the particle -*wa*.

Lesson 23

Midori-no	Particle: -*no*	*Nan-ban*	Telephone
VOCABULARY NOTES Discussion	**KEY GRAMMAR POINTS** Discussion	**KEY GRAMMAR POINTS** Discussion	**i-*irasshai* (online):** telephone, telephone directories (activity), and telephone numbers (activity)
Have students review the word *midori* and discuss the difference in its	Have students review the particle -*no* when reading telephone numbers and	Have students review questions using the word	Using i-*irasshai*, have students learn more about telephones (select the guide book (index)

8

function from other color words in *i*-adjective form.	other functions of the particle *-no*.	*nan*.	and click on the topics listed above).

Lesson 24

Telling Time	Small *hiragana*	Time
KEY GRAMMAR POINTS Discussion	**WRITING JAPANESE** Discussion	**i-*irasshai* (online)**: time zones (activity)
Have students review how to say each hour from 1:00 to 12:00 and discuss which numbers they should pay extra attention to.	Have students review the differences in pronunciation and writing small and regular size *hiragana*.	Using i-*irasshai*, have students do the activity on time (select the guide book (index) and click on the topic listed above).

Lesson 25

-pun / -fun	Counters	The Importance of Being on Time
KEY GRAMMAR POINTS Discussion	**KEY GRAMMAR POINTS** Discussion Class Work	**CULTURE NOTES** Discussion
Have students review how to say each minute and discuss which numbers take *-pun* or *-fun* and the differences in pronunciation and writing.	Have students review all the counters and forms of numbers. Have them make questions using each counter and answer them.	Have students discuss the difference in time consciousness between Japan and the U.S.

Lesson 26

Jugyoo	Particles: *-kara, -made*	Particle: *-o*	Television
VOCABULARY NOTES **i-*irasshai* (online)**: English class; English class (video)	**KEY GRAMMAR POINTS** Discussion	**KEY GRAMMAR POINTS** Discussion	**i-*irasshai* (online)**: television-*terebi*
Using i-*irasshai*, have students learn more about *jugyoo* and its meaning and about English classes in Japan (select the guide book (index) and click on the topics listed above).	Have students review particles and their usages.	Have students review the particle *-o* and its function. Have them pay attention to how to write it in *hiragana*.	Using i-*irasshai*, have students learn more about television (select the guide book (index) and click on the topic listed above).

Lesson 27

Time Word	Particle: *-ni*	*-masu / -masen*	Whispered Vowels
VOCABULARY NOTES **KEY GRAMMAR POINTS** Discussion	**KEY GRAMMAR POINTS** Discussion	**KEY GRAMMAR POINTS** Discussion	**PRONUNCIATION** Discussion
Have students review the time words *asa*, *hiru*, and *yoru* and their usages.	Have students review the particle *-ni* and its function. They can also review other particles.	Have students review verbs in non-past, polite and negative forms.	Have students review whispered vowels. They can refer to related notes from Lessons 1 and 5.

Lesson 28

Daily Schedule
Interview Class Work
1. Have students write their own schedule for the day using the <u>chart</u>* on the next page. 2. After completing the chart, have them interview their classmates.   Questions: a) School: *Gakkoo-wa nan-ji-made desu-ka?*

b) Part-time job: *Arubaito-ga arimasu-ka?* (If "yes") *Arubaito-wa nan-ji-kara nan-ji made desu-ka?*

c) Watch TV: *Terebi-o mimasu-ka?* (If "yes") *Terebi-wa nan-ji-kara nan-ji made desu-ka?*

d) Study: *Benkyoo-wa nan-ji-kara nanji-made desu-ka?*

e) Go to bed: *Yoru, nan-ji-ni nemasu-ka?*

f) Get up: *Asa, nan-ji-ni okimasu-ka?*

After interviewing each person, fill in the blanks of the <u>interview sheet**</u> below. After each person interviews four people, stop interviewing.

3. Have the class leader gather information and write it down on the board. Have the class try to make comments on the schedules.

<u>Typical comments on schedules:</u>

To the people who do multiple things in a day: *~-san / -kun-wa isogashii desu-ne.*

To the people who go to bed late at night: *~-san / -kun-wa yoru osoi desu-ne.*

To the people who get up early in the morning: *~-san / -kun-wa asa hayai desu-ne.*

To the people who study long hours: *~-san / -kun-wa sugoi desu-ne.*

* Chart: Daily Schedule

Schedule	School	Part-time job	Watch TV	Study	Go to bed	Get up
Time	~	~	~	~		

**Interview Sheet: Daily Schedule

Name			
School			
Part-time job			
Watch TV			
Study			
Go to bed			
Get up			

Lesson 29

Gairaigo	*Ocha* (Green Tea)
EXPANDING YOUR VOCABULARY Class Work	**i-*irasshai* (online):** tea drinking (quiz) tea making (activity)
Have students familiarize themselves with the *gairaigo*. If they wonder whether or not Japanese people have certain foods or drinks that they do not see in the list, have them create questions to ask their A.I. teacher during their AI session. For example, if a student wants to know if their A.I. teacher eats tacos, s/he can ask "*~-sensei-wa* "tacos"-*o tabemasu-ka?*" (Students must be prepared to explain the food if the A.I. teacher asks "*~-wa nan desu-ka?*") If she says "yes," then s/he can ask "'Tacos'-*wa nihongo-de nan-to iimasu-ka?*"	Using i-*irasshai*, have students learn more about how to make and drink tea (select the guide book (index) and click on the topics listed above).
Breakfast	
Class Work: Breakfast Survey	

1. Have students interview their classmates about their breakfasts. Use the <u>interview sheet*</u> below.
   Questions: Asa, tabemasu-ka? Asa, nan-ji-ni tabemasu-ka? Nani-o tabemasu-ka? Nani-o nomimasu-ka?

2. After interviewing three people, have them report the information. (ie., ~-san / -kun-wa asa ~-o tabemasu / nomimasu.)

3. Have the class leader write the results on the blackboard using the <u>report form**</u>on the next page. Decide what kind of breakfast items are the most popular among the class.

*Interview Sheet: Breakfast

Name:	Name:	Name:
Breakfast: yes / no	Breakfast: yes / no	Breakfast: yes / no
Time:	Time:	Time:
Food:	Food:	Food:
Drink:	Drink:	Drink:

<table>
<tr><td colspan="2"><u>Report on Breakfast</u></td></tr>
<tr><td>Do you eat breakfast?</td><td>Yes: No:</td></tr>
<tr><td>Food:</td><td>Cereal ( ), Toast ( ), Bagel ( ), Oatmeal ( ), Biscuit ( ),
Pancakes ( ), Grits ( ), Eggs ( ), Sausage ( ) Bacon ( ),
Others (   )</td></tr>
<tr><td>Drink:</td><td>Coffee ( ), Tea ( ), Juice ( ), Water ( ), Milk ( ),
Cola ( ), Others (   )</td></tr>
</table>

Lesson 30

Japanese Breakfast	Japanese Dishes; Coffee Shops
CULTURE NOTES Project	**CULTURE NOTES** **i-*irasshai* (online):** noodles, soy sauce, *sushi* – what is it? (optional video), *sushi* chef, *tempura*, toaster and breakfast, *udon,* coffee, coffee house dishes, coffee shop menu, and coffee shop sign
Have students read and learn about Japanese breakfast, then come up with questions to ask their A.I. teacher during the A.I. session. Q: ~-sensei-wa asa, ~-o tabemasu / nomimasu-ka?	Using i-*irasshai*, have students learn more about Japanese dishes and coffee shops (select the guide book (index) and click on the topics listed above).

Japanese Dishes

CULTURE NOTES

Class Work: Food Survey

1. Have students ask their classmates if they eat certain things and write down who eats what on the board using the <u>interview sheet</u>* below.
2. Have the class practice making sentences to report what they found out.
   ie., ~san/kun-wa ~-to ~ (-to ~)-o tabemasu kedo, ~ (-to ~)-wa tabemasen.
3. Have students check off each ingredient that is used in the five Japanese dishes listed in the <u>chart</u>** below. Then, have students ask each other who would or would not eat these dishes.
   Q: ~-san / -kun-wa [a Japanese dish]-o tabemasu-ka?

* Interview Sheet: Food Survey

なまえ name				
やさい vegetables				
たまご eggs				
にく meats				
さかな fish				
ごはん rice				

** Chart: Japanese Dishes

Ingredients	やさい	たまご	にく	さかな	ごはん
てんぷら					
すきやき					
すし					
さしみ					
やきとり					

Lesson 31

Politely refusing food and drink offers	*Itadakimasu.* *Gochisoosama deshita.*	Japanese Food Culture: How to Use Chopsticks
CULTURE NOTES Pair Work	**CULTURE NOTES** Discussion	**i-*irasshai* (online):** chopsticks – how to use
After having students read the notes	Have students discuss the	Using i-irasshai, have students learn

and review the phrases, pair students up to practice the dialogue using the food/drink vocabulary cards from Lessons 29 and 30.	difference in set phrases before and after eating between Japan and the U.S.	more about Japanese food culture (select the guide book (index) and click on the topic listed above).

Lesson 32

Ii desu.	*Gairaigo*	___-*wa doo desu-ka?*
VOCABULARY NOTES Discussion	**EXPANDING YOUR VOCABULARY** Pair Work	**KEY GRAMMAR POINTS** Pair Work
Have students review the usage of the phrase "*ii desu*" (Lessons 11 and 13).	1. For each *gairaigo*, have students ask their partner, "*~-wa eigo-de nan-to iimasu-ka?*" 2. After finishing the last *gairaigo*, let them ask their partner, "*Tabemono-wa dore desu-ka? Nomimono-wa dore desu-ka?*"	Have students name some restaurants in town that everybody knows. Have them ask each other for their opinion on food in those restaurants. Q: "[name of a restaurant]-*no* [name of the food]-*wa doo desu-ka?*" A:"*Totemo oishii /oishii /maamaa /anmari (oishikunai) desu.*"

Food and Restaurants
CULTURE NOTES **i-*irasshai* (online):** moist towel (quiz), noodle restaurant –menu items, restaurant phrases (activity), *sushi* ordering (activity), tea-*agari* (quiz), tipping (quiz)
1. Have students read the culture notes and discuss the differences in customs at restaurants between Japan and the U.S. 2. Using i-*irasshai*, have students learn more about Japanese restaurants (select the guide book (index) and click on the topics listed above).

Lesson 33

Food Culture; Dining Etiquette	-*masen-ka?*
CULTURE NOTES **i-*irasshai* (online):** Chopsticks – Don'ts, Etiquette – how to eat *sushi* and *sashimi* – how to eat (video); Food (fake) – Is it real or fake? Discussion	**KEY GRAMMAR POINTS** Discussion and Pair Work
1. Using i-*irasshai*, have students learn more about how to eat with chopsticks and table manners (select the guide book (index) and click on the topics listed above). 2. Let students discuss the differences in these topics between Japan and the U.S.	Have students review the usage of -*masen-ka?* as an invitation form. Pretend that they have invited their partner to dinner at their house. They offer him/her some food and drinks. They should remember how to accept and refuse politely.

Lesson 34

Dates
KEY GRAMMAR POINTS Discussion and Pair Work
1. Students can read the notes and discuss the difference between stating months and days of the month in English and Japanese. 2. Have students fill in the following chart* with the appropriate pronunciation for the certain time words. 3. Using the Month-Day board and number cards,** students can pair up, create a date and ask their partner what the date is. (ie. March 18th) Q: Nan-gatsu nan-nichi desu-ka? A: San-gatsu juu-hachi-nichi desu.

* Chart: Month and Day

Month	April	July	September
(pronunciation)	-gatsu	-gatsu	-gatsu
Day of the Month	14th	17th	19th
(pronunciation)	juu -ka	juu -nichi	juu -nichi

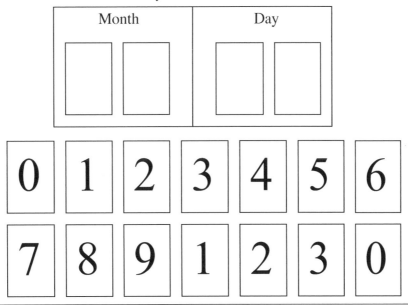

** Month-Day Board & Number Cards

Review: Counter Words
COUNTERS WE HAVE LEARNED
Discussion and Pair Work
Have students go over the counters they have learned using the summary box. Have students work in pairs, ask their partner a question using a counter word and have his/her partner answer the question. ie. Q: ~-san / -kun-wa nan-sai desu-ka?   A: #-sai desu.

Lesson 35

Gairaigo	*-masu* form	*-ni narimasu*
VOCABULARY: other words you will hear **i-*irasshai* (online):** *gairaigo*	**KEY GRAMMAR POINTS** Discussion	**KEY GRAMMAR POINTS** Discussion and Pair Work
Using i-*irasshai*, have students listen to more *gairaigo* and do the matching activity (select the guide book (index) and click on the topics listed above).	1. Have students review all verbs in their non-past, polite and negative forms. 2. Have students list all time words / phrases that can be used with verbs in future tense (ie. *ashita* = tomorrow; *go-ji-ni* = at 5:00; *kyoo* = today, etc.)	Review ages with students. Then have them practice the pattern by talking about various family members (Name of person-*wa* ~years old-*ni narimasu*).

Lesson 36

Writing *Kanji*	Blood Types
WRITING JAPANESE Discussion and Class Work	**CULTURE NOTES** **i-*irasshai* (online):** population, crowds, and blood types
1. Have students review information on the Japanese writing systems in Lesson 11. 2. Have students practice writing birthdays of friends/family in *kanji*, as in the example sentence below the additional practice chart.	Using i-*irasshai*, have students read more about blood types (select the guide book (index) and click on the topics listed above).

Lesson 37

-*kara*, -*made*	Holidays; Festivals	Christmas; New Year's; National Holidays
KEY GRAMMAR POINTS Discussion Class Work	**CULTURE NOTES** Discussion and Project	**Online Resources** *i-irasshai* (**online**): big bell
1. Have students review the usage of -*kara* and -*made* in Lesson 26. 2. Using -*kara* and -*made*, have students make sentences about your school's spring, summer, winter and Thanksgiving breaks.	1. Have students find out more about and discuss traditions around Japanese festivals. 2. Students can make a yearly calendar: cut and paste any festival photos from any website. Use them as the "picture of the month" for a yearly calendar. Write the dates of famous festivals and their respective cities on the specific festival dates.	1. Have students use various search engines to research traditional New Year's foods and read more about holidays in Japan. Have them print out photos and make posters with captions. 2. Using i-*irasshai*, have students watch the video on ringing the big bell (select the guide book (index) and click on the topic listed above).

Lesson 38

____-*ga hoshii desu (ka).*	Vocabulary (Nouns) Review
KEY GRAMMAR POINTS Game	**VOCABULARY** Class Work
Make groups of three to five. The first student starts out with the statement, "*Tanjoobi-ni XX-ga hoshii desu.*" The next person repeats this sentence but also adds another item (using XX-*to* YY)-*ga hoshii desu.* Each following person does the same, adding to the list. The game continues until someone cannot remember all the items mentioned. Start a new game using new items, adding adjectives (*atarashii, ookii, aoi*, etc.) where possible.	Going one lesson at a time from Lesson 25, have students look up any vocabulary that can be inserted in the blank: ____-*ga hoshii desu* (ie. Lesson 35: *purezento*; Lesson 33: *misoshiru*; Lesson 32: *nomimono, sandoitchi,* etc. Remember, they can only be <u>nouns</u>). In two columns, have students list the top five things they would want: A) for their next birthday and B) as an after-school snack. Randomly call on students to read their top sentence from each of the two columns.

Lesson 39

Vocabulary (Days of the Month) Review	Grammar Review
VOCABULARY: L34 Game	**GRAMMAR: Lessons 34-38** Game
Have students make two sets of cards, one with the days of the month in *hiragana* (ie. *tsuitachi*), the other with the days of the month in English (ie. the first). Mix the cards and turn them face down. Using the cards for the first ~ tenth, students can play a memory game (by turning two cards over and trying to make a pair). The winner is the one with the most pairs. (For a more challenging game, add more days of the month cards (ie. 11th ~ 15th, then 16th ~ 20th, etc.)	Divide the class into two teams. Each team compiles the key grammar points from Lessons 34 ~ 38 and writes each one on an index card (ie. Lesson 34, #1: -*gatsu*). Below each grammar point, they must also write a task related to that point (ie. for Lesson 34, #1: -*gatsu*: "Recite all even numbered months.") Tasks must be reasonable and manageable yet challenging. Each team puts their cards in a bag and gives the bag to the other team. Team members take turns pulling a card from the bag and completing the task on the card. Members of the opposite team decide if the task is done successfully, and if so, a point is awarded. The team with the highest score wins.

Lesson 40

Shimasu
VOCABULARY NOTES Project
Either draw or cut out pictures from magazines representing the *gairaigo* words. Have students make two collages with the pictures on one page, half of a page being things they DO, the other half being things they

DON'T do. Talk about their collages using ___-o shimasu. or ___-o shimasen.	
The -*masu* form	Place-*ni ikimasu.*
KEY GRAMMAR POINTS Discussion	**KEY GRAMMAR POINTS** Game
Re-read the information on the -*masu* form of verbs in Lessons 27, 33 and 35.	Make groups of three to five. The first person starts out with the statement "[some place]-*ni ikimasu.*" The next person repeats this sentence but also adds another place using "[place] –*to* [place])-*ni ikimasu.*" Each following person does the same, adding to the list. The game continues until someone cannot remember all places mentioned.

Lesson 41

Grammar Review
GRAMMAR: Lessons 37-40 Class Work

1. Using the pattern "[TV show]-*wa #-ji kara #-ji made desu.*" have students talk about their favorite TV shows. Then, ask others if they watch that show (ie. [TV show]-*o mimasu-ka?*)
2. Make smaller groups if the class is large. Each student is given three index cards on which s/he writes A) a TIME word, B) a VERB with an appropriate ACTIVITY (noun), and C) a person. Put the cards in three bags: A, B and C. Each student then picks a card from each bag and makes a sentence using the chosen words. Sentences can be true or silly, but all must be grammatically correct.
3. Have students prepare short essays based on the example sentences below on three topics: 1) a birthday, 2) a lunch break or 3) today/tomorrow. Have them memorize their essays. In two teams, one member from each team randomly picks a number (1, 2 or 3) from a bag. S/he must recite his/her essay. The member that recites his/hers most fluently earns a point for his/her team.
    ie. 1. Watashi-no tanjoobi-wa ___desu. (Moo sugu desu.) ___sai -ni narimasu. Tanjoobi-ni ___-to ___-ga hoshii desu.
        2. Hiru yasumi-wa ___-ji kara ___-ji made desu. Kyoo, ___-o tabemasu. ___-o nomimasu.
        3. Kyoo/ashita-wa ___gatsu___ desu. ___yoobi desu. Watashi-wa ___-o ___masu.

Particle: –*to* (with)	Review (L. 31 ~ 41)
KEY GRAMMAR POINTS Project	*Irasshai* **website**: for students - student notebook - Resources column - Choose Your Lesson - Japanese I 41 - Nan-to iimasu-ka? Parts 1 and 2
Have students bring in photos of themselves with friends or family members. Attach the photos to a poster board and write captions for the photos. (ie. [Person]-*to* [place]-*ni ikimasu.* [Person]-*to* [object]-*o shimasu / mimasu / tabemasu,* etc.)	Have students follow the instructions on the website and work individually or in small groups.

Lesson 42

Tanoshii	*O-shoogatsu*
VOCABULARY NOTES Discussion	**CULTURE NOTES** **Online Resources** **i-*irasshai* (online):** New Year celebration Discussion
Have students think about activities that interest them. Make sure they choose only nouns (ie. a movie, tennis, shopping, party, etc). Have them put the words into a sentence structure: [Noun] + -*wa tanoshii desu.* and present it in front of class. ie. *Tenisu-wa tanoshii desu.*	Have students use various search engines to research Japanese New Year's activities and cuisine, and hold a discussion on the differences in preparation for festivities between Japan and the U.S. You can also have students learn more about New Year's using i-*irasshai* (select the guide book (index) and click on the topics listed above).

Lesson 43

Particle: *-ga*	Visiting a Japanese Home
KEY GRAMMAR POINTS **Question word + ga** Discussion	**CULTURE NOTES** **i-*irasshai* (online):** door – closed door (quiz), doors – *fusama*, doors and windows – *shoji*, etiquette – gift, etiquette – sitting, gift (quiz), house – removing shoes (activity), table – *kotatsu*, table (quiz), *tatami* and *tatami* mat (quiz), *tatami* mats (activity), *tatami* room – removing shoes (activity), *tatami* room – seating order (activity), and Western-style room (quiz)
Have students review the usage of the particle *-ga* and other particles previously learned. (Lesson 26 - PARTICLES)	Using i-*irasshai*, have students read more about visiting a Japanese home (select the guide book (index) and click on the topics listed above).

Lesson 44

Visiting Japanese Home	Visiting Japanese Home
CULTURE NOTES: **Japanese bathing etiquette** **Toilet room etiquette** **Being a guest in a Japanese home** **Online Resources** Discussion	**CULTURE NOTES** **i-*irasshai* (online):** bath (quiz), bathroom drain, baths, bed, bed making etiquette – bathtub, and toilets
Have students use various search engines to research and hold a discussion on the differences between American and Japanese house settings and manners.	Using i-*irasshai*, have students read more about visiting a Japanese home (select the guide book (index) and click on the topics listed above).

Lesson 45

Time Expressions and Action Verbs	Vocabulary Review
KEY GRAMMAR POINTS Game	*Irasshai* **website**: for students - student notebook - Exercises column - Match *Roomaji* with English
Have students make cards with time expressions, such as *fuyu-yasumi* (winter break), *O-shoogatsu* (New Year's), days of the week, times of the day, etc. Face them down on a table. One student picks up a card and the student next him/her asks him/her, "[Time]-*ni nani-o shimashita-ka*?" The one who picked up the card answers, "*Sukii-ni ikimashita*." or other appropriate activity.	Have students review vocabulary that they have learned.

Lesson 46

Ongaku	Time Expression, place, and *ikimasu*
VOCABULARY Class Work	**KEY GRAMMAR POINTS** Game
Using the sample dialogue below, have students ask each other's preferences in music. A: Ongaku-o kikimasu-ka? B: Hai kikimasu. / Iie, kikimasen. A: Nani-o kikimasu-ka? B: <u>Kurasshikku</u>-o kikimasu.	Have students make two kinds of cards, one with Time Words and the other with Place Words. Example: Time Words: *hachi-ji, juu-gatsu, kinoo, kyoo*, etc. Place Words: *gakkoo, mooru*, etc. Have students place the cards face down in two stacks. One student picks one Time Word card and one Place Word card. Then, s/he will make a sentence putting these two words in the pattern: [Time]-*ni* [Place]-*ni ikimasu*, being careful to add, where necessary, the particle *-ni* which indicates time. Variation: Use the same materials and same procedures. One can ask a question, such as "*Kinoo mooru ni ikimashita-ka*?" The other can answer, "*Hai, ikimashita*." or "*Iie, ikimasen deshita*."

Kikimasu Japanese Media	
VOCABULARY NOTES:	
i-*irasshai* (online): library, magazines (quiz), movies, music – *hoogaku* and *yoogaku,* newspapers, novels, radio (or stereo), television – *terebi,* and VCR	
Using i-*irasshai,* have students read more about Japanese media (select the guide book (index) and click on the topics listed above).	

Lesson 47

Particle: *-de*	*Doko*; Plain Form of Verbs
KEY GRAMMAR POINTS Presentation	**KEY GRAMMAR POINTS** Pair Work
Have students think and write about their future plans and present them to the class. Examples are listed below. 1. [Place]-de arubaito-o shimasu. 2. [Place]-de [school subject]-no benkyoo-o shimasu. 3. [Place]-de shigoto-o shimasu. 4. [Place]-de [Object]-o mimasu. 5. [Place]-de [Object]-o shimasu.	Have students make plans with their partner by following the sample dialogue below. A: <u>Shuumatsu</u>, nani suru? B: <u>Eiga-o miru</u>? A: Doko-<u>de miru</u>? B: <u>ABC Eigakan</u>-wa doo? Vocabulary bank: *kaimono, paatii, terebi, anime,* etc.

Lesson 48

Particle: *-ni*	Day of the Week	*Hiragana* Review
KEY GRAMMAR POINTS: **Day of the week + *-ni* . . . + verb** Discussion	**KEY GRAMMAR POINTS:** **Nan-yoobi** Class Work	*Irasshai* **website**: for students - student notebook - Exercises column - Match *Hiragana* with *Hiragana*
Have students review the usage of particle *-ni* and other particles previously learned.	With all students looking at a year-long calendar, have individual students ask "[holiday]-*wa nan-yoobi desu-ka*?" Have students respond chorally or individually.	Have students review *hiragana* by matching cards.

Lesson 49

Kanji: days of the week	Review (Lessons 42 ~ 49)
WRITING JAPANESE Game	*Irasshai* **website**: for students - student notebook - Resources column - Choose Your Lesson - Japanese I <u>49</u> - Nan-to iimasu-ka? Parts 1 and 2
1. Make cards with *kanji* of the days of the week, Monday through Sunday. One student chooses one *kanji* card and asks other classmates, "*Nan-yoobi desu-ka?*" One has to answer, "[Day of the week]-*yoobi desu.*" 2. Make cards with a) *kanji* days of the week, b) the English meanings and c) the readings. Mix up all cards and lay them face down. Have students play a concentration-type game, where they pick three cards and must match the *kanji* with its equivalent meaning and reading.	Have students follow the instructions on the website and work individually or in small groups.

Lesson 50

School Subjects	
EXPANDING YOUR VOCABULARY Pair Work	
1. Have students write down the classes they have in Japanese. 2. Have students work in pairs to ask each other what kind of classes their partner has. A: Nan-no jugyoo-ga arimasu-ka? B: ~-to ~-to (....) ~-ga arimasu.	

Languages	Days of the Week	The Japanese Writing System
VOCABULARY NOTES Pair Work and Class Work	**KEY GRAMMAR POINTS** Pair Work	**WRITING JAPANESE** Discussion

1. Have students practice pronouncing names of different languages and stating their English equivalents.
2. Have them work in pairs to ask each other whether or not his/her partner knows some languages.
   A: ~go-ga wakarimasu-ka?
   B: Hai, wakarimasu. OR Iie, wakarimasen.
3. Have them report to the class by saying that "~-san / -kun-wa ~go-ga wakarimasu."
4. Have the class leader write down the names of the students and the languages they know.
5. Have one student ask the question "[a phrase]-wa ~go-de nan-to iimasu-ka?" to find out how a particular phrase is said in different languages.
	1. Have students list things to do or events to go to on each day of this week.
	2. Have students work in pairs to ask each other their plans for the week. The underlined parts can be changed.
	(Ex.)
	A: Nani-o shimasu-ka?
	B: <u>Eiga-ni ikimasu.</u>
	A: Nan-yoobi-ni <u>ikimasu</u>-ka?
	B: <u>Moku</u>-yoobi-ni <u>ikimasu.</u>
		1. Have students write down all the particles they have learned so far and example sentences using them.
		2. Have them convert the sentences into *hiragana* if not already done so.

Scheduling of Classes in Japanese Secondary Schools	*Katakana*
CULTURE NOTES **i-*irasshai* (online)**: school, school schedule, school seating (quiz), teachers **Online Resources** Discussion	**WRITING JAPANESE** Class Work
Using i-*irasshai*, have students learn more about Japanese schools and classes (select the guide book (index) and click on the topics listed above). Also have students use various search engines to research these topics. Have students discuss their findings and daily life in Japanese high schools.	Have students read the vocabulary words from GAIRAIGO and figure out their English equivalents. Answers: [**Objects**] computer, fax, notebook, pen, spoon, and TV [**Activities**] tennis, golf, date, meeting, part-time job, party, and skiing [**Food**] hamburger, cake, pizza, orange juice, milk, cola, and spaghetti [**Places**] America, California, France, Spain, restaurant, and studio [**People**] classmate(s), a girlfriend, a boyfriend, Smith, Brown, Amanda, and Tom [**Other**] zero, dollar, test, Christmas, class, group, and gas

Lesson 51

Muzukashii, *Kantan* and *Omoshiroi*
VOCABULARY Pair Work

1. Have students ask each other which school subjects are difficult, easy and interesting.
(Ex.) Q: Nan-no jugyoo-ga muzukashii desu-ka?
     A: [School subject]-ga muzukashii desu.
2. If there is more than one teacher teaching the same subject, let them discuss which teacher's class is difficult, easy and interesting.
(Ex.) Q: Dono-sensei-no suugaku-no jugyoo-ga kantan desu-ka?
     A: [Teacher's name]-sensei-no-ga kantan desu.
3. Discuss the books that they have read or movies that they have watched and have them ask each other which book or movie is interesting.
(Ex.) Q: Dono hon-ga omoshiroi desu-ka?
     A: [Book title]-ga omoshiroi desu.

School Subjects	Long Vowels in *Katakana*
i-*irasshai* (online): art class, biology lab, chemistry class, computer lab, English class, gym, home economics, language lab, music class, swimming Discussion	**WRITING JAPANESE** Class Work
Using i-*irasshai*, have students learn more about classes and classrooms in Japanese schools and discuss the differences between them and those in the U.S. (select the guide book (index) and click on the topics listed above).	Have students look at the *gairaigo* and underline the letter which makes a long vowel. (Ex.) konpyuutaa, nooto, supuun, deeto, miitingu, paatii, sukii, etc.

Lesson 52

Likes and Dislikes
KEY GRAMMAR POINTS Class Work

1. Have students name five movie stars and let a class leader write them down on the blackboard.
2. Have one student ask other students if s/he likes one of the movie stars.
   A: ~-ga suki desu-ka?
   B: Hai, daisuki/suki desu. OR Iie, anmari suki janai/kirai desu.
   (*daisuki*: 5 points, *suki*: 4 points, *anmari suki janai*: 2 points, and *kirai*: 0 points)
   Let the leader write down the total scores for each movie star and decide who is most popular.
3. Repeat the activity with different categories: TV programs, songs, video games, etc.

Lesson 53

Supootsu	*Yakyuu*
VOCABULARY **Online Resources** Discussion	**CULTURE NOTES** **Online Resources** Discussion
Have students use various search engines to research sports in Japan and discuss in class.	Have students use various search engines to research and answer the following questions: 1. Which sports are played professionally in Japan? 2. Is there Little League baseball in Japan? 3. Are there foreign players on Japan's professional baseball and soccer teams?

Lesson 54

Taiiku-no hi	*~masen-ka? ~mashoo!*
VOCABULARY **Online Resources** Discussion	**KEY GRAMMAR POINTS** **CULTURE NOTES** Pair Work (Weekend Plans)
Have students use various search engines to research Sports Day in Japan.	Let students make weekend plans. Have each pair make three sets of 5 cards: (1) sports they want to play, (2) places they want to go and (3) restaurants they would like to eat at. Have them put all the cards together, shuffle them and place them facing down on the table. One student, B, picks up one card, looks at it, puts it down, and tells the other student, A, its category only. Student A thinks of one of the cards in that category and starts the dialogue. Use the dialogues* below:

*Dialogues

[sport]
A: Kin-yoobi-ni (a sport)-o shimasen-ka?
[If it is the same sport that B saw on the card.]
B: Hai, shimashoo! Nan-ji-ni shimashoo-ka?
A: #-ji-wa doo desu-ka?
B: A, ii desu-ne.
[If it is not the same sport that B saw on the card.]
B: ~-wa chotto. . . (the sport)-wa doo desu-ka?
A: Ee, ii desu-yo! Jaa, #-ji-ni shimasen-ka?
B: Hai, soo shimashoo!

[place]
A: Do-yoobi-ni (a place)-ni ikimasen-ka?
[If it is the same place that B saw on the card]
B: Hai, ikimashoo! Nan-ji-ni ikimashoo-ka?
A: #-ji-wa doo desu-ka?
B: A, ii desu-ne.
[If it is not the same place that B saw on the card.]
B: ~-wa chotto. . . (the place)-wa doo desu-ka?
A: Ee, ii desu-yo! Jaa, #-ji-ni ikimasen-ka?
B: Hai, soo shimashoo!

[restaurant]
A: Nichi-yoobi-ni (a restaurant)-de tabemasen-ka?
[If it is the same place that B saw on the card.]
B: Hai, tabemashoo! Nanji-ni ikimashoo-ka?
A: #-ji-wa doo desu-ka?
B: A, ii desu-ne!

[If it is not the same restaurant that B saw on the card.]
B: ~-wa chotto. [the restaurant]-wa doo desu-ka?
A: Ee, ii desu-yo! #-ji-ni ikimasen-ka?
B: Hai, soo shimashoo!

Lesson 55

Japanese Traditional Sports
CULTURE NOTES **i-*irasshai* (online)**: sword fighting – *kendo* **Online Resources** Discussion

1. Have students use various search engines to research *kendo* and *judo* in Japan. Also have students use i-*irasshai* to learn more about *kendo* (select the guide book (index) and click on the topic listed above).
2. Have students answer the following questions:
  a. What are the features of traditional Japanese sports?
  b. What are the characteristics of *karate*?

Lesson 56

Joozu~Heta	*Kedo~Demo*	*Sorekara~To*	*Karaoke*
VOCABULARY NOTES Discussion	**KEY GRAMMAR NOTES** Discussion	**KEY GRAMMAR NOTES** Discussion	**CULTURE NOTES** **i-*irasshai* (online)**: karaoke machine
Have students re-read the notes and discuss the difference between Japan and the U.S. in expressing one's own skills.	Have students re-read the notes and discuss the differences in usage between *kedo* and *demo*.	Have students re-read the notes and discuss the differences in usage between *sorekara* and *to*.	Using i-*irasshai*, have students learn more about *karaoke* and listen to a sample (select the guide book (index) and click on the topic listed above).

Lesson 57

i-adjectives and *na*-adjectives	Japanese Traditional Music Instruments	Review
KEY GRAMMAR POINTS Class Work	**CULTURE NOTES** **Online Resources** Discussion	*Irasshai* website: for students - student notebook - Resources column - Choose Your Lesson - Japanese I 57 - Nan-to iimasu-ka? Part 1 and Part 2
Have students re-read the notes and discuss the difference in function between *i*-adjectives and *na*-adjectives.	Have students use various search engines to research Japanese traditional music instruments and discuss them in class.	Have students review vocabulary words and sentence structures that they have studied so far by doing the activities.

Nani-ga dekimasu-ka?	Reading katakana ア〜ト
Class Work: Show and Tell (in Japanese)	**OBJECTIVES** Card Game
Have students bring something to class that is related to what they are good at. Let each student stand in front of the class and tell what it is, what they can do, and some additional info. [Sample Script] Kore-wa boku-no doramu-no *stick*-desu. Boku-wa doramu-ga sukoshi dekimasu. Doramu-wa tanoshii desu. Mainichi doramu-no <u>renshuu</u> (practice)-o shimasu. (These are my drum sticks. I can play the drums a little. Playing drums is fun.	Work in pairs. Each student has one set of 20 *katakana* flash cards (ア〜ト). Both of the students shuffle the cards. Student A spreads the cards out with the *katakana* sides up on the table. When student B reads the *roomaji* part of a card, student A picks up the card. If the *katakana* can take two dots (*dakuten*), student A also needs to pronounce it with two dots. For example, if student A picks up キ, s/he needs to say *gi* (ギ) after saying *ki* (キ). Repeat it until all of the cards are gone. Then, switch roles.

I practice drums every day.)	

Lesson 58

Place-*no tenki-wa doo desu-ka?*	Writing *katakana* タ～ト, ダ～ド
Ame desu.	Review of ア～ゾ
KEY GRAMMAR POINTS	**OBJECTIVES**
Pair Work	Class Work: Writing Practice
1. In pairs, students make two lists of the same city names (ie. their hometown, Washington DC, Chicago, etc). Each student then draws a weather symbol (sun, rain, clouds, snow, bad weather) next to each city name, without showing their partner.	In teams of three or four, one member from each team goes to the board. A designated "reader" reads a *gairaigo* word from the list, and each team
They then guess the weather that their partner put down by asking Q: [city]-*wa* [weather] *desu-ka?* and responding A: *Hai, soo/~desu.* or *Iie, ~ ja nai desu.* They get only 1 guess for each city, and if they are wrong, they then ask Q: *~no tenki-wa doo desu-ka?* and their partner responds A: *~ desu.* based on the symbol s/he has drawn. The person who guesses right on the first question most wins. 2. Variation: same activity as above, this time using past tense. (Ex.) Q: [city]-*wa* [weather] *deshita-ka?* And responding A: *Hai, ~deshita.* or simply "*Iie*". If they guess wrong, they then ask Q: *~no tenki-wa doo deshita-ka?* and their partner responds A: *~ deshita.*	member at the board must write the English equivalent of the *gairaigo* word. The first one who writes the English equivalent correctly earns a point for his/her team. All other team members are judges. (Word list: *Shikago* [Chicago], *keeki* [cake], *tesuto*[test], *chiizu* [cheese], *sooseeji* [sausage], *sutajio* [studio], *deeto* [date], *gitaa* [guitar], *saizu* [size], *kukkii* [cookie], *guddo aidea* [good idea].

Lesson 59

The Negative of *i*-adjectives
KEY GRAMMAR POINTS
Pair and Group Work: Card Game and Class Survey

1. Students make their own sets of cards with an *i*-adjective on each card. With a partner, they go through their cards reading the *i*-adjective and its negative form. The student who goes through all cards fastest and most accurately wins.
2. On the back side of the above cards, students write the English meaning. With a partner, looking at the English meaning, students give the *i*-adj. in the affirmative (-*i desu*.) and the negative (-*ku nai desu*.). The student who goes through all cards fastest and most accurately wins.
3. Using the cards made in #2 above, students work in teams of four or five. Using one set of cards, one student picks a card and makes an affirmative and a negative sentence using that adjective. S/he keeps the card if both sentences are grammatically correct. The winner is the one who has the most cards. (Ex.) Watashi-no kuruma-wa furui desu. Kono jisho-wa furuku-nai desu.
4. Similar to the Class Poll Sheet* below, each student comes up with 3-4 nouns which they ask the class about. For example, the question is "*Rekishi-wa omoshiroi desu-ka?*" Those that agree raise their hand, saying "*Hai, omoshiroi desu.*" The questioner tallies the number. Those that disagree say "*Iie, omoshirokunai-desu.*" The questioner tallies that number. If students are unsure, they answer "*Wakarimasen.*" Results can be written on the board.

* Class Poll Sheet

noun	is ~	is not ~	not sure
Ex. れきし	おもしろい: 6	おもしろくない: 3	わかりません: 0
konpyuutaa	はやい:	はやくない:	わかりません:
うち	ふるい:	ふるくない:	わかりません:

[Other possible questions] Japanese: difficult? PE class: fun? Burger King's hamburgers: delicious? house: big? tomorrow: busy?

Reading *katakana* ナ～ノ、ン Review of ア～ド
OBJECTIVES
Concentration Card Game
As can be done at any point in the *katakana* learning schedule, students can make their own flashcards (or print out and use the cards provided online), one *hiragana* and the other *katakana*. They can then play a

matching game in pairs or small groups matching the correct *hiragana* to its *katakana* partner.

-*do*; *Nan-do?*	Celsius ~ Fahrenheit
KEY GRAMMAR POINTS Pair Work: Card Game and Class Work: Internet Activity	**CULTURE NOTES** **Online Resources** i-*irasshai* (online): thermometer - Fahrenheit vs. Celsius Class Work: Internet Activity
1. Have students make their own sets of 10-15 flashcards that have a temperature (0-100 degrees) on each card. They can pair up with a partner, swap cards and read the temperatures. Whoever gets through all the cards the fastest pairs up with another winner until the last two competing are the two fastest and most accurate in the class. These two compete in a championship round. 2. Using the internet, have students look up weather and temperatures in cities around the world. They can report (or write on board) "[city]-*wa ~do desu.*" and add a comment such as *"Yuki / ame / hare desu."* or *"Samui / atatakai / atsui / suzushii desu."*	1. Have students use various search engines to research sites which give metric-system conversions. 2. Input various temperatures and see the difference between various temperatures in Fahrenheit and Celsius. 3. By exploring other links, find the weather in various cities throughout Japan and report to the class. 4. Using i-*irasshai*, (select the guide book (index) and click on "thermometer – Fahrenheit vs. Celsius") have students do the activity.

Lesson 60

Adjective/Noun + -*mitai*	Seasonal Events
KEY GRAMMAR POINTS Internet Activity and Class Work	**CULTURE NOTES** **Online Resources** i-*irasshai* (online): maple tree Mini-Project and Discussion
Using the internet, have students find information on the weather in various cities around the world. They will write at least two sentences about today's weather and two about tomorrow or the weekend. Of each pair of sentences, one should be affirmative and one negative. When talking about future weather, they must use "adjective/noun + -*mitai desu.*" Have students report to the class and have the class ask him/her Q: [place]-*no kyoo-no tenki-wa doo desu-ka?* And after responding, classmates will ask Q: *Ashita /Shuumatsu-no* [place]-*no tenki-wa doo desu-ka?* S/he can respond, such as, *"Atatakai desu. Roku-juu-kyuu-do desu."* or *"Ii tenki ja nai-mitai desu. Samui-mitai desu."*	1. Have students use various search engines to find pictures illustrating seasonal events discussed in the Culture Notes. (Ex.) *hanami, ta-ue, tsuyu, taifuu,* harvest, *tsukimi,* snow festival, etc. Use those pictures on a horizontal annual time line chart or circular annual wheel, such as a large paper plate. Have them write the corresponding months in *kanji* and seasons in *hiragana*. (Ex.) *hanami*: はる、3月 4月 2. Have students visit other links to read about climate, weather and seasonal pastimes. They can also discuss why Japanese like cherry blossoms so much. 3. Using i-*irasshai*, have students read about maple trees and view photos (select the guide book (index) and click on "maple trees").

Writing *katakana* ナ〜ノ, ン Review of ア〜ド
OBJECTIVES Project
1. Have students use various search engines to look up *gairaigo* or "*katakana* (loan words)". 2. They can make their own list of words similar to those in #4 *Dekimasu-ka?*. 3. They can create writing practice word lists to switch with a partner, work in groups, or put individually on the board for other classmates to challenge.

Lesson 61

na-adjectives	
KEY GRAMMAR POINTS Class Work	
Brainstorming: Looking at the *na*-adjective list, have students review old vocabulary and come up with words that can go with the *na*-adjectives. (Ex.) *dame: kuruma, compuutaa, gakusei*, etc. Then, have them practice using these phrases in sentences, such as *"Toshokan-wa shizuka desu. / Shizuka-na toshokan desu."*	
Clothes	Traditional and Modern Clothing
EXPANDING YOUR VOCABULARY Games	**Online Resources** Discussion
1. Game 1: Make groups of 4-5 students each. The first person starts out with the statement *"Suutsukeesu-ni A-ga arimasu."* The next person repeats the sentence but also adds another item, saying *"A-to B-ga arimasu."* Each following person does the same, adding to the list. The game continues until someone cannot remember all items mentioned. Start a new game using new items and adding adjectives (*atarashii, ookii, aoi*, etc) where possible. 2. Game 2: (Preparation: The facilitator or students bring in items on the Clothing and Accessory list.) Lay out 15-20 items on a desk. Students have one minute to memorize the items. In groups of 4-5, each member states what was there. For example, if there was a red sweater, they can say, *"Akai seetaa-ga arimashita."* Team members alternate. Points go to the team that remembers the most items.	Have students use various search engines to research traditional Japanese clothing as well as trend-setting fashions, and discuss in class.

Lesson 62

Clothes	Writing *katakana* ハ〜ポ Review of *katakana* ア〜ノ、ン
OBJECTIVES: Comment further on clothing Class Work: Fashion Show	**OBJECTIVES** Project
Depending on the size and/or enthusiasm of your class, suggest staging a fashion show. 1. Each person will act as a model, dressing up as oddly or neatly as they choose. (Limits may need to be set.) They will bring in their items to show the others. 2. In pairs, they will write up a script with one person being the emcee for the other person's fashion show. They should try to use as many vocabulary words, phrases and expressions from Lessons 61 and 62 as possible. (Ex.) Kono XX-wa doo desu-ka? Kono XX-wa ii / kakkoii / kirei / etc. desu-ne. [color + item]-wa sugoi desu-ne. Mina-san, hoshii desu-ka? 3. Some kind of awards could be given at the end of the fashion show: *"ichi-ban hen"* award, *"ichi-ban omoshiroi"* award, *"ichi-ban kawaii"* award, etc.	1. Have students try various search engines for *gairaigo* or *katakana* loan words. 2. They should try to pick up words similar to those in #4 *Dekimasu-ka?* that also include *katakana* specific to this lesson (ハ〜ポ). 3. They can create writing practice word lists to switch with a partner, share in groups or put up individually on the board for other classmates to learn.

Lesson 63

Colors
KEY GRAMMAR POINTS   Game and Class Survey: *Nani-iro-ga ichiban suki desu-ka?*
1. Game: Materials needed per group: one white paper plate, nine plain wooden clothes pins, nine different colored markers. Preparation for each group: students make a color wheel using the paper plate, coloring each part of the "pie" in the colors learned (red, blue, black, white, yellow, brown, purple, pink, green). On the 9 clothes pins using black ink, they write out each color in *hiragana*. Their clothes pins are mixed in a bag. Groups compete against each other or the clock to see how quickly they can clip the correct clothes pin onto its matching color on the paper plate wheel.   2. Class Survey: Draw a <u>Class Survey Chart</u>* similar to the one below on the board. Student 1 asks Student 2 what color s/he likes best. After his/her answer, S1 puts a tally mark in that column. S2 then asks S3 the same question until all students have answered. The class then summarizes the numbers and favorite colors and reports as in the example, *"Aka-ga ichiban suki desu: 5-nin."*

	red	blue	white	black	green	pink	purple	yellow	brown
# of students									

Colors
VOCABULARY
Group Work: Game and Pair Work: Project
1. Game: Make groups of 3 or 4 students each. Use two sets of picture cards (created by students as homework) for each group. Shuffle the cards and distribute them. The game is played like the card game "Go Fish". Player 1 asks another player if they have an item of clothing: "~*ga arimasu-ka*?" If s/he does have it, s/he answers "*Hai, arimasu. Doozo.*" and gives it up. If not, s/he answers "*Iie, arimasen.*" Players lay down their pairs of clothing items. The winner has the most pairs.
2. Project: Students find a variety of pictures of people from magazines (fashion, etc.). In pairs, they write as many sentences they can about the clothing worn in the pictures. (Ex.) ~san-wa ~ga arimasu. [Adjective, such as color or other descriptor] desu. Pairs can either report to class orally or write a short paragraph and post it with the pictures on a wall or bulletin board.

Lesson 64

Japanese Money	Writing *katakana* マ〜モ Review of ア〜ポ	Counting from 100 through 9,999
CULTURE NOTES **Online Resources** **i-*irasshai* (online)**: banks, Buddhist offering box, coin box - *saisenbako*, money Discussion	**OBJECTIVES** Project (*Katakana* Writing Practice)	**OBJECTIVES**: Buzz Game
1. Have students use various search engines to view samples of bills and coins, read about tipping in Japan, check out prices of everyday items in Tokyo, etc. Then, discuss what they've learned. 2. Using i-*irasshai*, have students read about these money-related topics (select the guide book (index) and click on the topics listed above). Then, using any search engine, find further information on these topics and discuss their findings.	1. Have students try various search engines for *gairaigo* or *katakana* loan words. 2. They should try to pick up words similar to those in #4 *Dekimasu-ka*? that also include *katakana* specific to this lesson (マ〜モ). 3. They can create writing practice word lists to switch with a partner, share in groups, or put up individually on the board for other classmates to learn.	Students predetermine a number from 1~9 that is the "joker" number. This is a verbal counting game that can be played using numbers 100-900 or 1,000-9,000. In the former, students count by 10's. One student starts the count with 100. Each student that follows must continue the count but must say "buzz" when a number that includes the "joker" is reached. For example, if the "joker" is 7, the student(s) whose turn it is when the number reaches 170, 270, 370, etc. must NOT say that number but must say "buzz" instead. For the latter game, the counting is done by 100's, and the "buzzed" numbers in this case are 1,700, 2,700, etc. The game ends when 990 or 9900 is reached.

Lesson 65

Japanese Department Stores
CULTURE NOTES **Online Resources** Internet Activity and Discussion
1. Have students use various search engines to research Japanese department store websites. In pairs or small groups, have students look at one website (each group looking at a different store's site) and pick out 5-10 *katakana* words that are department store-related words and figure out the English equivalents. Teams trade off their lists and have other teams figure out the English meanings. They can also have discussions about illustrations or other discoveries from their particular department store's website. 2. Using three of the Japanese department store websites from above, have students form groups of three and investigate the cost of items at those stores. They can either print out the pictures or simply describe the items and report to the class the cost of their selected items.
Prices of Objects
OBJECTIVE: Comment on prices of objects "Price is Right" Game
Students use the items and prices from Activity #2 above. This game can be played in the same teams/groups. One team goes to the front of the room with pictures or descriptions of their items. Other teams must guess the price. After the first round of guesses, the team "up" will tell the guessing teams either "*Motto yasui desu.*" or "*Motto takai desu.*" After the third round of guesses, the team closest to the correct price wins. (In order to practice dollars and cents as well as yen, students can find comparable items from department stores in their area either from catalogs or internet websites to use in the game.)

Lesson 66

Counters	Review
KEY GRAMMAR POINTS	*Irasshai* **website:** for students - student notebook - Resources column - Choose Your Lesson - Japanese I <u>66</u> - Nan-to iimasu-ka? Part 1 and Part 2
Have students make number cards for 1~10 and place them face down on the table. In pairs or small groups, students flip one card and practice saying the numbers using various counters.	Students can review vocabulary words and sentence structures that they have studied so far by doing the activities.

Lesson 67

Stores	[place]-*de* [item]-*o kaimasu*	Convenience Store
VOCABULARY Pair Work	**KEY GRAMMAR POINTS** Class Work	**Online Resources** Discussion

Have your students create picture cards which represent stores, such as a shoe store, meat market, bakery, fish store, book store, vegetable store or stand, a park or movie theater. Students first review the above mentioned places in Japanese. Have them place the cards face down. One student picks one card. The other students guess what card this student has by asking questions in Japanese.
(Ex.) A: <u>Tomato</u>-ga arimasu-ka? (Do you have any tomatoes?)
       B: Hai, arimasu. (Yes, I do.)
       A: <u>Yao-ya</u> desu-ne. (It is a vegetable store, isn't it?)
	1. Have students write any items that they have learned so far on cards. (Ex.) *jisho, tokei, kutsu,* CD etc.
	2. Place the cards in a bag.
	3. One student chooses a card with the name of the item.
	4. The student tells the others where s/he buys this item.
	(Ex.) <u>*Hon-ya*</u>-*de jisho*-*o kaimasu.*
		Have students use various search engines to research and discuss how convenience stores are changing lifestyles in Japan.

25

Lesson 68

Japanese Signs	*Katakana*
CULTURE NOTE Some *kanji* commonly seen in a Japanese community **Online Resources** Discussion	*Irasshai* **website**: for students - student notebook - Exercises column - Matching *Katakana* Internet Activity: Game
Have students use various search engines to research more about Japanese signs.	Have students review *katakana* that they have learned.

Lesson 69

Spatial Relationships
KEY GRAMMAR POINTS Presentation and Pair Work
1. Presentation: Have students bring a group photograph of family members or friends. Have them prepare a short paragraph to describe who / where they are. (Ex.) [place]-*de* [activity]-*o* [verb]*mashita*. [person 1]-*to* [person 2]-*to* [person 3]-*ga imasu*. [person 1]-*wa* [person 2]-*no* [location word]-*ni imasu*. 2. Pair Work: Have each student prepare two sets of <u>template maps of a strip mall</u>* on separate sheets of paper like the examples on the next page. As in the example, have them decide two stores in the same locations on both maps. Student A has a blank map, and Student B adds the names of the other shops on the map without Student A seeing. Student A asks Student B where shops are located. (Ex.) The bookstore and meat shop are given. A: [name of the shop]-ga arimasu-ka? B: Hai, arimasu. / Iie, arimasen. A: (If Student B answers: "Hai,") Doko-ni arimasu-ka? B: Hon-ya/Niku-ya-no <u>migi/hidari</u>-ni arimasu. Student A listens and writes the name of the store. When all shops are filled in, Student A and Student B show their maps to each other to confirm the locations. Repeat the same activity by changing roles.

* example of template maps of a strip mall

Hon-ya			Niku-ya	

Hon-ya			Niku-ya	

Lesson 70

X-*no naka-ni*	Postal symbol and mailboxes; Japanese police
KEY GRAMMAR POINTS Pair Work and Discussion	**CULTURE NOTES** **i-*irasshai* (online):** mail carrier, mailbox, patrol officers, police bicycles, police officer (quiz), police stations – *kooban*, postal service (optional activity)
Have your students ask each other what they have in their bookbags. A: Kaban-no naka-ni nani-ga arimasu-ka? B: [item 1]-to [item 2]-to [item 3]-ga arimasu. Students make notes about who brings what kind of items to school. Have them discuss what the most common belongings in the class are.	Using i-*irasshai*, have students learn more about postal services and police in Japan (select the guide book (index) and click on the topics listed above).

Lesson 71

Particle: *-de* + motion verb	
KEY GRAMMAR POINTS Means of transportation-*de ikimasu* *Aruite ikimasu* Pair Work	
Have students create two kinds of cards: one with pictures of modes of transportation, such as a bus, car, train, taxi, subway, and a person walking. The other cards should have pictures of places, such as a supermarket, movie theater, department store, or restaurant. Place both stacks of cards facing down. Student A picks a place card asks Student B how s/he gets to a place. Student B picks a transportation card and answers. (Ex.) A: Nan-de <u>suupaa</u>-ni ikimasu-ka? B: <u>Basu</u>-de / Aruite ikimasu.	

Particle: *-de*	Means of Transportation
KEY GRAMMAR POINTS Discussion	**KEY GRAMMAR POINTS** **i-*irasshai* (online):** automobile, kiosk, public transportation, taxi, trains (boarding door, commuters, gift shops, special seating), transportation
Review all the functions of the particle *-de* learned previously.	Using i-*irasshai*, have students read more about the public transportation system in Japan (select the guide book (index) and click on the topics above).

Lesson 72

-pun / -fun	*Chikatetsu*
KEY GRAMMAR POINTS Class Work	**CULTURE NOTES** **Online Resources** Discussion
Have students bring in a ball or any small object that can be thrown. Students make a circle. One student says "*ip-pun,*" tosses the ball / object to the other student. The student who catches a ball then says "*ni-fun.*" Continue until they finish counting up to 10 (or 20) minutes. Apply this activity for practice using other counters that they have learned so far, such as for hours (*-jikan*) and miles (*-mairu*).	Have students use various search engines to research the Japanese public transportation system and discuss their findings in class.

Lesson 73

Review	*Katakana*
***Irasshai* website**: for students - student notebook - Resources column - Choose Your Lesson - Japanese I <u>73</u> - Nan-to iimasu-ka? Part 1 and Part 2 Game	***Irasshai* website**: for students - student notebook – Exercises column - Matching *Hiragana* with *Katakana* Game
Have students review the items that they have learned so far by doing this online activity.	Have your students review *katakana* that they have learned.

Volume 1
Workbook Answer Keys

Workbook Assignment Answer Keys
Particle Practice Answer Keys
Reading and Writing Practice Answer Keys

LESSON 1

PART 1
1. **Read all of the notes for Lesson 1.**
2. **Learn the new vocabulary for Lesson 1.**
3. **Complete a non-stop talking exercise.**

PART 2
1. **Reading practice** (English translation)
   It's orange juice. Here (please have some).
   Good afternoon, Mr./Ms. (teacher) Yokoyama.
   Good-bye, Mr./Ms. Kojima.
   It's tomato juice. Here (please have some).
2. **Reviewing vocabulary and culture notes**
   1. *Meishi* → Name cards or business cards that are exchanged in introductions. They provide valuable information which helps the recipient know what level of formality in language is appropriate to use.
   2. *Roomaji* → Literally, "Roman letters", they are the letters of the English alphabet.
   3. Japanese names
      a. How many names does a Japanese person have? → two (family name and given name)
      b. What is the order of the names? → family name first followed by given name
      c. Which name(s) do Japanese use in a self-introduction? → family name
   4. The meaning and use of the titles:
      -san →   used with girls' names as well as with the family names of adults.
      -kun →   used with boys' names by speakers who are the same age or older. Men sometimes use *-kun* in informal situations.
      -sensei → title suffix meaning literally "teacher"
3. **Preview the vocabulary and notes for Lesson 2.**

LESSON 2

PART 1
1. **Read all of the notes for Lesson 2.**
2. **Learn the new vocabulary.**
3. **Complete a non-stop talking exercise.**

PART 2
1. **Review all of the vocabulary and notes for Lessons 1 and 2.**
2. **Preview the vocabulary and notes for Lesson 3.**

LESSON 3
1. **Read all of the notes and learn the new vocabulary for Lesson 3.**
2. **Review Lessons 1 and 2.**
3. **Complete the Writing Practice.**
4. **Preview the vocabulary and notes for Lesson 4.**

WRITING PRACTICE
❶ **Study, trace and write.**
❷ **Read and copy the *hiragana*.**
   1. あ あ [aa] 2. あ い [ai] 3. あ う [au] 4. あ お [ao] 5. あ お い [aoi] 6. い い [ii] 7. い い え [iie]
   8. い え [ie] 9. う え [ue] 10. え え [ee] 11. お い [oi] 12. お お い [ooi]
❸ **Write the *hiragana*.**
   1. お い 2. あ う 3. え え 4. あ あ 5. あ お 6. い い え 7. う え 8. あ い 9. い い 10. お お い 11. い え
   12. あ お い
❹ **Dekimasu-ka? (Can you do it?)**
   1. i い 2. i い 3. i い i い e え 4. I い u う e え 5. U う e え 6. a あ o お i い 7. o お o お i い
   8. a あ a あ
❺ **More writing practice**

LESSON 4

PART 1
1. **Read all of the notes for Lesson 4.**
2. **Learn the new vocabulary.**

3. Writing practice あ、い、う、え、お (a, i, u, e, o)

PART 2

1. Reading practice

English translation

Interviewer: You're Mr./Ms. Satake, aren't you?

Ueno-san:　No, I am Ueno.

Interviewer: Oh, I'm sorry. You're Mr./Ms. Ueno.

Ueno-san:　Yes.

Interviewer: Are you a high school student?

Ueno-san:　No, I'm a junior high school student.

Interviewer: Are you a 9th grader?

Ueno-san:　No, I'm in the 8th grade.

1. (Is it Mr./Ms. Satake?) → Iie. (No)
2. (Is it Mr./Ms. Ueno?) → Hai. (Yes)
3. (Is he/she a college student?) → Iie. (No)
4. (Is he/she a high school student?) → Iie. (No)
5. (Is he/she an elementary school student?) → Iie. (No)
6. (Is he/she a junior high school student?) → Hai. (Yes)
7. (Is he/she a seventh grader?) → Iie. (No)
8. (Is he/she a ninth grader?) → Iie. (No)
9. (Is he/she an eighth grader?) → Hai. (Yes.)

2. Writing words with あ、い、う、え、お

1. ああ 2. あおい 3. うえ 4. あい 5. いい 6. ええ 7. あう 8. いいえ 9. おい 10. あお 11. いえ
12. おおい

3. Preview the vocabulary and notes for Lesson 5.

LESSON 5

1. Read all of the notes for Lesson 5.

2. Learn the new vocabulary.

3. Preview the vocabulary and notes for Lesson 6.

LESSON 6

PART 1

1. Read all of the notes for Lesson 6.

2. Learn the new vocabulary.

3. Complete the Writing Practice.

PART 2

1. Vocabulary review

1. is, am, are 2. Hello. 3. Good-bye. 4. yes 5. What's your name? 6. Excuse me; I'm sorry. 7. high school student 8. university, college 9. no 10. teacher 11. where 12. What grade (are you in)?

2. Complete a non-stop talking exercise.

3. Preview the vocabulary and notes for Lesson 7.

WRITING PRACTICE

❶ **Read and copy the** *hiragana.*

1. あか [aka] 2. かお [kao] 3. こえ [koe] 4. いけ [ike] 5. えき [eki] 6. かき [kaki] 7. こい [koi]
8. かう [kau] 9. ここ [koko] 10. きく [kiku] 11. いく [iku] 12. かい [kai]

❷ **Study, trace and write.**

❸ **Write the** *hiragana.*

1. きく 2. こえ 3. あか 4. こい 5. かき 6. ここ 7. いけ 8. かう 9. かい 10. いく 11. かお
12. えき

❹ **Dekimasu-ka?**

1. かぎ 2. うごく 3. げき 4. ごがく 5. がいこく 6. かいぎ 7. えいが 8. かげ 9. かがく

❺ **More writing practice**

LESSON 7

PART 1

1. Read all of the notes for Lesson 7.

2. Learn the new vocabulary.

3. *Hiragana* **reading practice**

PART 2

1. Writing practice あいうえお、かきくけこ、がぎぐげご

1. かぎ 2. うごく 3. げき 4. ごがく 5. がいこく 6. かいぎ 7. えいが 8. かげ 9. かがく
10. ごご 11. ぐあい 12. あおい

2. **Reading practice**
    1. (What grade is Mr./Ms. Ueda in?) → San-nen-sei desu. (He/she's a third year student.)
    2. (Is Mr./Ms. Ueda a junior high school student?) → Iie, kookoo-sei desu. (No, he/she's a high school student.)
    3. (How old is Mr./Ms. Ueda?) → Juu-has-sai desu. (He/she's 18 years old.)
    4. (Where is his/her school?/What school does he/she go to?) → Jefason-Kookoo desu. (Jefferson High School.)
    5. (Is Jefferson High School in Boston?) → Iie, Nyuu Yooku desu. (No, it's in New York.)
3. **Preview the vocabulary and notes for Lesson 8.**

LESSON 8

1. **Read all of the notes for Lesson 8.**
2. **Learn the new vocabulary.**
3. **Non-stop talking exercise**
4. **Preview the vocabulary and notes for Lesson 9.**

LESSON 9

PART 1
1. **Read all of the notes for Lesson 9.**
2. **Learn the new vocabulary.**
3. **Complete Writing Practice ❷ Study, trace and write.**
PART 2
1. **Complete the remainder of the Writing Practice.**
2. **Generating sentences**
    1. City Bank-**no** Sumisu-**san desu**. 2. Gakkoo-**wa** doko **desu**-ka? 3. Baabara-san-**wa nan-nen-**sei desu-**ka**? 4. Kore-**wa** nan **desu**-ka?
3. **Preview the vocabulary and notes for Lesson 10.**
WRITING PRACTICE
❶ **Read and copy the *hiragana*.**
    1. すし [sushi] 2. うさぎ [usagi] 3. せかい [sekai] 4. おそい [osoi] 5. おじ [oji] 6. すこし [sukoshi]
    7. ざしき [zashiki] 8. かぞく [kazoku] 9. すず [suzu] 10. かぜ [kaze] 11. うし [ushi]
    12. いそがしい [isogashii]
❷ **Study, trace and write.**
❸ **Write the *hiragana*.**
    1. うし 2. すし 3. ざしき 4. せかい 5. おじ 6. すず 7. おそい 8. かぜ 9. かぞく
    10. いそがしい 11. うさぎ 12. すこし
    1. こえ 2. うごく 3. げき 4. きじ 5. あさ 6. うえ 7. おさけ 8. がくせい 9. しずか 10. すぎ
    11. ぐあい 12. えき
❹ **More writing practice**

LESSON 10

PART 1
1. **Read all of the notes for Lesson 10.**
2. **Learn the new vocabulary.**
3. **Non-stop talking exercise**
PART 2
1. **Write it in Japanese!**
    1. Sore-wa nan desu-ka? 2. Kore-wa fakkusu desu. 3. Shitajiki-wa nan desu-ka? 4. Sore-wa eigo-de *pencil*-to iimasu. 5. Kore-wa eigo-de nan-to iimasu-ka? 6. Nan-to iimasu ka? 7. Shitajiki-to iimasu.
2. **Non-stop talking exercise**
3. **Preview the vocabulary and notes for Lesson 11.**

LESSON 11

1. **Read all of the notes for Lesson 11.**
2. **Learn the new vocabulary.**
3. ***Hiragana* reading practice**
4. **Preview the vocabulary and notes for Lesson 12.**

LESSON 12

PART 1

1. **Read all of the notes for Lesson 12.**
2. **Learn the new vocabulary.**
3. **Complete Writing Practice ❺ Study, trace and write.**

PART 2

1. **Matching questions and answers**

   _7_ Iie, chuugaku-sei desu.   _6_ Go-nen-sei desu.   _10_ *Computer*-to iimasu.
   _11_ Aa, chotto...   _4_ Iie, fakkusu ja nai desu. Denwa desu.   _2_ Kaban-to iimasu.
   _12_ Sumisu desu.   _5_ Yon-juu-go-sai desu.   _9_ Atoranta desu.
   _1_ Iie, jisho desu.   _8_ Hai, soo desu.   _3_ Are-wa shitajiki desu.

2. *Hiragana* **reading practice**
3. **Complete the remainder of the Writing Practice.**
4. **Preview the vocabulary and notes for Lesson 13.**

WRITING PRACTICE

❶ **Read and copy the *hiragana*.**

   1. です [desu] 2. だけ [dake] 3. ときどき [tokidoki] 4. てつだう [tetsudau] 5. うで [ude] 6. どこ [doko] 7. だいがく [daigaku] 8. でぐち [deguchi] 9. たこ [tako] 10. つぎ [tsugi] 11. かた [kata] 12. つくえ [tsukue]

❷ **Write the *hiragana*.**

   1. どこ 2. かた 3. でぐち 4. てつだう 5. です 6. だいがく 7. つくえ 8. ときどき 9. つぎ 10. だけ 11. たこ 12. うで

❸ **Dekimasu-ka?**

ま	て	あ	ど	は	の	ば	し	お	せ	む	す	じ	か	う	り	え	ぞ	ち	ん
	te	a	do				shi	o	se		su	ji	ka	u		e	zo	chi	
だ	そ	ぐ	き	ね	に	ろ	た	い	ぎ	み	ぬ	ら	ざ	こ	ぱ	ぜ	く	ゆ	つ
da	so	gu	ki				ta	i	gi				za	ko		ze	ku		tsu
げ	さ	わ	や	で	と	け	ぬ	づ	ず	ん	ち	ご	ひ	ぺ	が	る	を	ぬ	や
ge	sa			de	to	ke		zu	zu		ji	go			ga				

❹ **More writing practice**

❺ **Study, trace and write.**

LESSON 13

PART 1

1. **Read all of the notes for Lesson 13.**
2. **Learn the new vocabulary.**
3. **Non-stop talking exercise**
4. **Reading practice**
   isu (chair)
   akai isu (red chair)
   Akai isu desu. (It is a red chair.)
   Akai isu desu ka? (Is it a red chair?)
   Akai isu wa doko desu ka? (Where is the red chair?)
   Akai isu wa ii desu ka? (Is the red chair good?)

PART 2

1. **Write it in Japanese!**
   1. Enpitsu, (chotto) ii desu-ka? 2. Sumimasen. Denwa, ii desu-ka? 3. Nihongo-no hon desu. 4. Akai hon desu. 5. Eigo-no jisho-wa dore desu-ka?
2. **Preview the vocabulary and notes for Lesson 14.**

LESSON 14

1. **Read all of the notes for Lesson 14.**
2. **Learn the new vocabulary.**
3. **Complete the Writing Practice.**
4. **Preview the vocabulary and notes for Lesson 15.**

WRITING PRACTICE

❶ **Study, trace and write.**

❷ **Read and copy the *hiragana*.**

　1. がっこう [gakkoo]　2. きって [kitte]　3. こっき [kokki]　4. ざっし [zasshi]　5. いっさい [issai]

　6. けっか [kekka]　7. あさって [asatte]　8. きっと [kitto]　9. あった [atta]　10. けっこん [kekkon]

　11. しった [shitta]　12. いっかい [ikkai]

❸ **Write the *hiragana*.**

　1. けっか　2. あった　3. きっと　4. いっさい　5. ざっし　6. がっこう　7. こっき　8. しった

　9. けっこん　10. あさって　11. きって　12. いっかい

❹ **Dekimasu-ka?**

　1. ko こ ku く　2. a あ ka か i い　3. tsu つ ku く e え　4. i い su す　5. a あ o お i い　6. o お i い ku く tsu つ

　7. da だ i い ga が ku く se せ i い　8. o お ga が i い shi し su す　9. ta た chi ち

❺ **More writing practice**

LESSON 15

PART 1

1. **Read all of the notes for Lesson 15.**
2. **Learn the new vocabulary.**
3. **Prepare for an interactive activity.**
4. ***Hiragana* reading practice**

　1. なか [naka]　2. いぬ [inu]　3. なに [nani]　4. きのう [kinoo]　5. ながい [nagai]　6. さかな [sakana]

　7. きぬ [kinu]　8. にがつ [nigatsu]　9. のど [nodo]　10. にく [niku]　11. おなじ [onaji]　12. たのしい

　[tanoshii]　13. あに [ani]　14. いのち [inochi]　15. あなた [anata]　16. おねがい [onegai]　17. ぬう

　[nuu]　18. あね [ane]　19. おかね [okane]　20. ねこ [neko]

PART 2

1. ***Hiragana* reading practice**
2. **Prepare for an interactive activity.**
3. **Preview the vocabulary and notes for Lesson 16.**

LESSON 16

PART 1

1. **Read all of the notes for Lesson 16.**
2. **Learn the new vocabulary.**
3. **Prepare for an interactive activity.**
4. **Complete the Writing Practice.**

PART 2

1. **Reading practice**

ii (good)	akai (red)
ii tsukue (good desk)	akai isu (red chair)
Ii tsukue desu. (It's a good desk.)	Akai isu desu. (It's a red chair.)
Ii tsukue desu-ka? (Is it a good desk?)	Akai isu desu-ka? (Is it a red chair?)
Ii tsukue desu-ne. (It's a good desk, isn't it?)	Akai isu desu-ne? (It's a red chair, isn't it?)

　kazoku (family)
　go-kazoku (his/her family)
　Go-kazoku desu. (It is his/her family.)
　Daigakusei-no go-kazoku desu. (It is the college student's family.)
　Ano daigakusei-no go-kazoku desu. (It is that college student's family.)
　Ano daigakusei-no go-kazoku desu-ka? (Is it that college student's family?)

2. **Preview the vocabulary and notes for Lesson 17.**

WRITING PRACTICE

❶ **Read and copy the *hiragana*.**

　1. いぬ [inu]　2. なか [naka]　3. さん [-san]　4. きのう [kinoo]　5. さかな [sakana]　6. おねがい

　[onegai]　7. あに [ani]　8. ねこ [neko]　9. のど [nodo]　10. くん [-kun]　11. の [no]　12. あね [ane]

❷ **Write the *hiragana*.**

　1. いぬ　2. ねこ　3. なか　4. さん　5. あに　6. のど　7. おねがい　8. くん　9. きのう　10. さかな

　11. あね　12. の

❸ **Study, trace and write.**

❹ Dekimasu-ka?

あ き た す お け
さ い か せ て ぬ

❺ More writing practice

LESSON 17

1. **Read all of the notes for Lesson 17.**
2. **Learn the new vocabulary.**
3. *Hiragana* reading practice
   1. hanasu 2. hiku 3. heisei 4. futatsu 5. hatachi 6. higashi 7. fune 8. hoshii 9. heitai 10. hako
   11. hito 12. heijitsu 13. nihongo 14. haha 15. futsuka 16. hai
4. **Preview the vocabulary and notes for Lesson 18.**

LESSON 18

PART 1
1. **Read all of the notes for Lesson 18.**
2. **Learn the new vocabulary.**
3. **Reading practice**
   1. kabe 2. hebi 3. fubuki 4. betsu 5. suppai 6. kotoba 7. fudebako 8. sabishii 9. nabe 10. boku
   11. hibiku 12. hanabi 13. ippai 14. butaniku 15. pikapika 16. buubuu
PART 2
1. **Reading practice**
   1. pikapika 2. kabe 3. sabishii 4. fudebako 5. ippai 6. nabe 7. booshi 8. buubuu 9. suppai 10. hebi
   11. kotoba 12. hanabi 13. budoo 14. hibiki 15. bessoo 16. booeki 17. fubuki 18. boku 19. betsu
   20. butaniku
2. **Write it in Japanese!**
   1. Go-kazoku-wa nan-nin desu-ka? 2. Watashi-no kazoku-wa yo-nin desu. 3. Otooto-ga hitori imasu.
   4. Kore-mo ii desu.
3. **Preview the vocabulary and notes for Lesson 19.**

LESSON 19

PART 1
1. **Read all of the notes for Lesson 19.**
2. **Learn the new vocabulary.**
3. **Complete Writing Practice ❷ Study, trace and write.**
PART 2
1. **Complete the remainder of the Writing Practice.**
2. **Non-stop talking exercise**
3. **Vocabulary review**
   1. go-kazoku 2. chichi 3. haha 4. ane 5. kazoku 6. otoosan 7. okaasan 8. oneesan 9. otooto
   10. oniisan 11. otootosan 12. imootosan 13. imooto 14. ani
4. **Preview the vocabulary and notes for Lesson 20.**
WRITING PRACTICE
❶ **Read and copy the *hiragana*.**
   1. べつ [betsu] 2. へび [hebi] 3. ふでばこ [fudebako] 4. ぴかぴか [pikapika] 5. かべ [kabe]
   6. すっぱい [suppai] 7. ぼうし [booshi] 8. はなび [hanabi] 9. ひびき [hibiki] 10. ぶたにく
   [butaniku] 11. ぶどう [budoo] 12. さびしい [sabishii]
❷ **Study, trace and write.**
❸ **Write the *hiragana*.**
   1. ぶどう 2. すっぱい 3. はなび 4. かべ 5. ふでばこ 6. べつ 7. ぴかぴか 8. ぶたにく
   9. ひびき 10. ぼうし 11. へび 12. さびしい
❹ **Dekimasu-ka? [Can you find and circle all 15 words?]**
   あ ま ぬ ち で す ら り お す は い や ゆ こ う こ う せ い れ る だ い が く

34

みむか <s>ぞく</s> よりらあ<s>かい</s>もつ<s>く</s><s>え</s>わをわ<s>どこ</s>り<s>い</s><s>く</s><s>つ</s><s>え</s>あ
<s>は</s><s>は</s>うそぽ<s>は</s><s>た</s><s>ち</s><s>い</s><s>っ</s><s>さい</s>れるりえ<s>い</s><s>ご</s>す<s>ち</s><s>ち</s><s>ぼ</s><s>く</s>

です (is, am, are)　はい (yes)　こうこうせい (high school student)　だいがく (college)　かぞく
(family)　あかい (red)　つくえ (desk)　どこ (where)　いくつ (how old)　はは (my mother)　はたち
(20 years old)　いっさい (one year old)　えいご (English)　ちち (my father)　ぼく (I)

❺ More writing practice

LESSON 20

PART 1
1. **Read all of the notes for Lesson 20.**
2. **Learn the new vocabulary.**
3. **Write it in Japanese!**
   1. Enpitsu-ga arimasu-ka?　2. Hai, arimasu.　3. Akai enpitsu-wa arimasen.　4. Shitsumon-wa arimasen.
   5. Furui sutereo-ga arimasu.　6. Go-nin imasu.　7. Otootosan-ga imasu-ka?　8. Sensei-no kaban desu.
   9. Saitoo-san-no desu.　10. Watashi-no desu.

PART 2
1. **Review the notes and vocabulary for Lesson 20.**
2. **Reading practice**
   1. gakusei (student)
      ano gakusei (that student)
      ano gakusei-wa (that student)
      ano gakusei-wa nan-sai (that student, how old)
      Ano gakusei-wa nan-sai desu-ka? (How old is that student?)
   2. Fujimoto (Fujimoto)
      Fujimoto-san (Mr./Ms. Fujimoto)
      Fujimoto-san-no imooto-san (Mr./Ms. Fujimoto's younger sister)
      Fujimoto-san-no imooto-san-wa (Mr./Ms. Fujimoto's younger sister)
      Fujimoto-san-no imooto-san-wa nan-nen-sei　(Mr./Ms. Fujimoto's younger sister, what year)
      Fujimoto-san-no imooto-san-wa nan-nen-sei desu-ka? (What year is Mr./Ms. Fujimoto's younger sister in?)
   3. A: Otoosan desu-ka? (Is it your father?)
      B: Hai, soo desu. (Yes, it is.)
      A: Kono hito-wa oneesan desu-ka? (Is this person your older sister?)
      B: Iie, chigaimasu. Imooto desu. (No, it's not. It's my younger sister.)
      A: Otootosan-ga imasu-ka? (Do you have a younger brother?)
      B: Iie, imasen. (No, I don't.)
3. **Preview the vocabulary and notes for Lesson 21.**

LESSON 21

PART 1
1. **Read all of the notes for Lesson 21.**
2. **Learn the new vocabulary.**
3. **Reading practice**
4. **Complete Writing Practice ❷ Study, trace and write.**

PART 2
1. **Complete the remainder of the Writing Practice.**
2. **Write it in Japanese!**
   1. Denwa-wa doko desu-ka?　2. Asoko desu.　3. Eigo-no jisho-wa doko desu-ka?　4. Soko desu.
   5. Atarashii konpyuutaa-wa hayai desu.　6. Aa, soo desu-ka?
3. **Preview the vocabulary and notes for Lesson 22.**

WRITING PRACTICE
❶ **Read and copy the *hiragana*.**
   1. かみ [kami]　2. もしもし [Moshi-moshi.]　3. どうも [doomo]　4. いいます [iimasu]　5. めいし
   [meishi]　6. だめ [dame]　7. まあまあ [maa-maa]　8. すもう [sumoo]　9. いもうと [imooto]
   10. おなまえ [o-namae]　11. ちがいます [Chigaimasu.]　12. はじめまして [Hajimemashite.]
❷ **Study, trace and write.**

❸ **Write the *hiragana*.**

1. まあまあ (so-so) 2. どうも (Thanks.) 3. めいし (business card) 4. かみ (paper) 5. いもうと (younger sister) 6. ちがいます (That's not it.) 7. めいし (business card) 8. だめ (no good) 9. はじめまして (How do you do?) 10. もしもし (Hello?) 11. いいます (to say) 12. おなまえ (your name)

❹ **Dekimasu-ka?**

あ	い	う	え	お		た	ち	つ	て	と		は	ひ	ふ	へ	ほ
[a	i	u	e	o]		[ta	chi	tsu	te	to]		[ha	hi	hu	he	ho]
か	き	く	け	こ		な	に	ぬ	ね	の		ま	み	む	め	も
[ka	ki	ku	ke	ko]		[na	ni	nu	ne	no]		[ma	mi	mu	me	mo]
さ	し	す	せ	そ												
[sa	shi	su	se	so]												

❺ **More writing practice**

<h1 style="text-align:center">LESSON 22</h1>

1. **Read all of the notes for Lesson 22.**
2. **Learn the new vocabulary.**
3. **Reading practice**
   b. 1. watashi (I)
       watashi-no (my)
       watashi-no sensei (my teacher)
       watashi-no sensei-no (my teacher's)
       watashi-no sensei-no okaasan (my teacher's mother)
       watashi-no sensei-no okaasan-to (my teacher's mother and)
       watashi-no sensei-no okaasan-to otoosan (my teacher's mother and father)
       Watashi-no sensei-no okaasan-to otoosan desu. (They are my teacher's mother and father.)
     2. manga ("manga")
       manga-wa ("manga")
       manga-wa eigo ("manga" English)
       manga-wa eigo-de ("manga" in English)
       manga-wa eigo-de nan ("manga" in English, what)
       manga-wa eigo-de nan-to ("manga" in English, what)
       manga-wa eigo-de nan-to iimasu ("manga" in English, is called what)
       Manga-wa eigo-de nan-to iimasu-ka? (What is "manga" called in English?)
4. **Preview the vocabulary and notes for Lesson 23.**

<h1 style="text-align:center">LESSON 23</h1>

PART 1

1. **Read all of the notes for Lesson 23.**
2. **Learn the new vocabulary.**
3. ***Hiragana* reading practice** (English translation)
   1. Oh, I'm sorry. I've made a mistake. 2. What is Mr./Ms. Ishikawa's phone number? 3. This is Nishimoto. May I speak to Mr./Ms. Ueda?
4. **Complete the Writing Practice.**

PART 2

1. **Reading practice** (English translation)
   Watanabe: (He makes a phone call.)
   Yoneda: Hello?
   Watanabe: Is this Mr./Ms. Yamaguchi?
   Yoneda: No, it's not.
   Watanabe: Oh, I'm sorry. I have the wrong number.
2. **Preview the vocabulary and notes for Lesson 24.**
3. **Prepare for an interactive activity.**

WRITING PRACTICE

❶ **Read and copy the *hiragana*.**

1. わたし [watashi] 2. おはよう [Ohayoo.] 3. にちようび [nichi-yoobi] 4. ゆうめい [yuumei]
5. やすい [yasui] 6. ゆき [yuki] 7. ゆめ [yume] 8. でんわ [denwa] 9. を [o] 10. ようふく

[yoofuku] 11. ふゆ [fuyu] 12. よみます [yomimasu] 13. よこはま [Yokohama] 14. やくそく [yakusoku] 15. わふく [wafuku]

❷ **Write the *hiragana*.**

1. でんわ (telephone) 2. を 3. やくそく 4. ゆき 5. よみます 6. よこはま 7. ふゆ 8. やすい 9. にちようび 10. ゆめ 11. わふく 12. おはよう (Good morning.) 13. ゆうめい 14. わたし (I) 15. ようふく

❸ **Dekimasu-ka?**

あ	い	う	え	お		た	ち	つ	て	と		は	ひ	ふ	へ	ほ
[a	i	u	e	o]		[ta	chi	tsu	te	to]		[ha	hi	fu	he	ho]
か	き	く	け	こ		な	に	ぬ	ね	の		ま	み	む	め	も
[ka	ki	ku	ke	ko]		[na	ni	nu	ne	no]		[ma	mi	mu	me	mo]
さ	し	す	せ	そ
[sa	shi	su	se	so]

❹ **Study, trace and write.**

❺ **More writing practice**

LESSON 24

PART 1

1. **Read all of the notes for Lesson 24.**
2. **Learn the new vocabulary.**
3. ***Hiragana* reading practice**
4. **Prepare for an interactive activity.**

PART 2

1. **Complete the Writing Practice.**
2. **Write it in Japanese!**

1. Nan-ji desu-ka? 2. Shichi-ji desu. 3. Juu-ni-ji-han desu. 4. Go-ji desu-ka? 5. Miitingu-wa yo-ji desu. 6. Ima ni-ji-han desu.

3. **Preview the vocabulary and notes for Lesson 25.**

WRITING PRACTICE

❶ **Study, trace and write.**

❷ **Read and copy the *hiragana*.**

1. ちょっと [chotto] 2. じしょ [jisho] 3. きょうだい [kyoodai] 4. べんきょう [benkyoo] 5. じゅう [juu] 6. しゃしん [shashin] 7. おちゃ [ocha] 8. ちゅうがっこう [chuugakkoo] 9. しゅくだい [shukudai] 10. しょうがくせい [shoogakusei] 11. きょう [kyoo] 12. みょうじ [myooji] 13. びょうき [byooki] 14. とうきょう [Tookyoo] 15. ぎゅうにゅう [gyuunyuu] 16. じゃ、また。 [Ja, mata.] 17. ちゅうい [chuui] 18. ひゃく [hyaku]

❸ **Write the *hiragana*.**

1. おちゃ 2. ちょっと (a little) 3. じしょ (dictionary) 4. しゅくだい (homework) 5. しゃしん (photo) 6. きょうだい (siblings) 7. べんきょう (study) 8. じゅう (ten) 9. ちゅうがっこう (middle school) 10. しょうがくせい (elementary school student) 11. びょうき 12. きゅう (nine) 13. みょうじ 14. ひゃく 15. とうきょう (Tokyo) 16. じゃ、また。 (See you again.) 17. ぎゅうにゅう 18. ちゅうい

❹ **Dekimasu-ka?**

1. きょ 2. しゃ 3. ちゅ 4. ひょ 5. じょ 6. りゅ 7. じゃ 8. ちょ 9. しゅ 10. びょ 11. きゅ 12. しょ

❺ **More writing practice**

LESSON 25

1. **Read all of the notes for Lesson 25.**
2. **Learn the new vocabulary.**
3. **Reading practice**

1. furui 2. kuroi 3. dare 4. arigatoo 5. atarashii 6. sore 7. wakarimasu 8. sayoonara 9. yoroshiku 10. haru 11. are 12. irasshai

1. Ima juu-ji san-juu-rop-pun desu. (It's now 10:36.)   2. Roku-ji juu-go-fun desu. (It's 6:15.)   3. Ima nan-ji desu-ka? (What time is it now?)   4. Chigaimasu. Motto hayai desu. (No, that's not right. It's earlier.)   5. Chigaimasu. Motto osoi desu. (No, that's not right. It's later.)

4. Preview the vocabulary and notes for Lesson 26.

LESSON 26

PART 1

1. Read all of the notes for Lesson 26.

2. Learn the new vocabulary.

3. Reading practice (English translation)

1. That's from 6:06 to 6:30.   2. I have new comics.   3. What time is your job/work until?   4. What will you see/watch?   5. What time does your Japanese class begin and end?   6. Please do your homework.   7. Where is Mr./Ms. Nishimura's school?   8. Please read the phone number.   9. Please say this hiragana.

PART 2

1. Complete the Writing Practice.

2. Preview the vocabulary and notes for Lesson 27.

WRITING PRACTICE

❶ **Read and copy the *hiragana*.**

1. あります [arimasu] 2. がっこう [gakkoo] 3. を [o] 4. さようなら [sayoonara] 5. だれ [dare] 6. よろしく [yoroshiku] 7. ひとり [hitori] 8. ふたり [futari] 9. わかります [wakarimasu] 10. くろい [kuroi] 11. じゅぎょう [jugyoo] 12. いらっしゃい [irasshai] 13. なんじまで [nan-ji-made] 14. これ [kore] 15. ふるい [furui] 16. ばんごう [bangoo] 17. なんじから [nan-ji-kara] 18. ひらがな [hiragana]

❷ **Study, trace and write.**

❸ **Write the *hiragana*.**

1. さようなら (Good-bye.) 2. わかります (understand) 3. これ (this [thing])   4. ばんごう (number) 5. ひとり (one person) 6. じゅぎょう (class)   7. よろしく (Pleased to meet you.)   8. あります (exist, have) 9. を 10. くろい (black)   11. ふるい (old) 12. いらっしゃい (Welcome.) 13. ふたり (two people) 14. がっこう (school)   15. なんじまで (until what time)   16. だれ (who) 17. ひらがな (*hiragana*) 18. なんじから (from what time)

❹ **Dekimasu-ka?**

1. あります 2. ばんごう 3. くろい 4. わかります 5. ひとり 6. よろしく

❺ **More writing practice**

LESSON 27

PART 1

1. Read all of the notes for Lesson 27.

2. Learn the new vocabulary.

3. Reading practice (English translation)

1. What time do you get up in the morning?   2. Is it morning in Japan now?   3. I go to bed at 11:30.   4. It's not 7:30 in the morning.   5. What time does Mr./Ms. Yamamoto eat at night?   6. Does Mr. Suzuki go to bed at 8:00?

4. Writing practice

1. やまもとくんは あさ じゅういちじはんに おきますか。 (Does Mr. Yamamoto get up at 11:30 in the morning?)   2. にほんは いまは はちじ じゃ ない です。 (It is not 8:00 in Japan now.)   3. すずきさんは じゅういちじはんに ねますか。 (Does Mr./Ms. Suzuki go to bed at 11:30?)

PART 2

1. Write it in Japanese!

1. Asa nan-ji-ni okimasu-ka?   2. Asa go-ji-han-ni okimasu.   3. Nihon-wa ima asa desu-ka?   4. Itoo-san-wa go-ji-ni tabemasu.   5. Juu-ichi-ji-han-ni nemasu.   6. Asa-no shichi-ji-han ja nai desu.   7. Daigakusei-mo dorama-o mimasu.   8. Watashi-wa nyuusu-o mimasen.

2. Can you read it?

Yamamoto-san-wa yoru nan-ji-ni tabemasu-ka? (What time does Mr./Ms. Yamamoto eat in the evening?)

3. Preview the vocabulary and notes for Lesson 28.

LESSON 28

1. **Read the notes for Lesson 28.**
2. **Learn the new vocabulary.**
3. **Reading practice** (English translation)

1. What time is it in Japan now? 2. Where is this (here)? 3. It is not 10:30 in the morning now. 4. I get up at 6:30 a.m. 5. Please read this. 6. Is it early? Is it late? / Is it fast? Is it slow? 7. Are you going to look at that? 8. Work is from 7:00 until 4:00. 9. Oh, it's late, isn't it? 10. That person is busy.

4. **Preview the vocabulary and notes for Lesson 29.**

LESSON 29

PART 1

1. **Read all of the notes for Lesson 29.**
2. **Learn the new vocabulary.**
3. **Reading practice** (English translation)

1. What will you eat? 2. I'll eat fish and rice. 3. What will you drink? 4. I'll drink (green) tea. 5. Will you eat an egg? 6. No, I won't (eat one). 7. Will you drink water? 8. No, I won't (drink any).

4. **Review of small** や、ゆ、よ

1. じしょ (dictionary) 2. しゃしん (picture) 3. べんきょう (study) 4. ちょっと (a little) 5. じゅう (ten) 6. じゃ、また。(See you again.) 7. しゅくだい (homework) 8. きょうだい (siblings) 9. きゅう (nine) 10. きょう (today) 11. ちゅうがっこう (junior high school) 12. しょうがくせい (elementary school student)

PART 2

1. **Reading practice**

1. Professor Yamaguchi drinks water. 2. This fish is small, isn't it? 3. What is "gohan" called in English?

2. **Writing practice**

1. なにを のみますか。(What will you drink?) 2. この たまごは ちいさい ですね。(This egg is small, isn't it?) 3. さかなは えいごで fish と いいます。("Sakana" is called "fish" in English.) 4. おちゃを のみますか。(Do you drink green tea?) 5. いいえ、のみません。(No, I don't drink it.)

3. **Non-stop talking exercise**
4. **Preview the vocabulary and notes for Lesson 30.**

LESSON 30

PART 1

1. **Read all of the notes for Lesson 30.**
2. **Learn the new vocabulary.**
3. **Writing practice**

1. やまぐちせんせいは おみずを のみます。(Professor Yamaguchi drinks water.) 2. この さかなは ちいさい ですね。(This fish is small, isn't it?) 3. ごはんは えいごで なんと いいますか。(What is "gohan" called in English?)

PART 2

1. **Review all of the vocabulary from Lessons 28, 29, and 30.**
2. **Can you read them?**

1. Koko-wa ima asa no juu-ji-han ja nai desu. (It's not 10:30 in the morning here now.)
2. Watashi-wa asa roku-ji-han-ni okimasu. (I get up at 6:30 in the morning.)

LESSON 31

PART 1

1. **Read all of the notes for Lesson 31.**
2. **Learn the new vocabulary.**

PART 2

1. **Writing practice**

1. すこし だけ。(Only a little.) 2. けっこう です。(That's fine.) 3. いただきます。("I receive.") 4. ～は いかが ですか。(How about some ～?) 5. ごちそうさまでした。("It was a treat/feast.") 6. おはし (chopsticks)

2. **Reading practice** (English translation)

1. Please, come in/welcome. 2. It's new, isn't it? 3. Yes, it is. 4. That's small, but it's fast.

5. How about some (green) tea?   6. No, thank you.
3. **Preview the vocabulary and notes for Lesson 32.**

LESSON 32

PART 1
1. **Read all of the notes for Lesson 32.**
2. **Learn the new vocabulary.**
3. **Reading practice**
   1. Gochisoosama deshita. (It was a treat/feast./Thank you for the meal.)   2. Irasshaimase. (Welcome.)
   3. O-kimari desu-ka? (Have you decided on your order?)   4. Sumimasen. O-mizu, o-negai-shimasu. (Excuse me, could you please bring me some water?)   5. Jaa, nani-ni shimasu-ka? (Well, then, what would you like?)   6. Oshibori-to iimasu. (It's called an "oshibori.")   7. Watashi-wa yasai sandoitchi, o-negai shimasu. (Please give me a vegetable sandwich.)   8. Nan desu-ka? (What is it?)   9. Asoko-no teeburu-wa doo desu-ka? (How about that table over there?)   10. Nan-no sandoitchi-ga ii desu-ka? (What kind of sandwich would you like?)

PART 2
1. **Write it in Japanese!**
   1. Nani-ni shimasu-ka? なにに しますか。 2. Sakana-wa doo desu-ka? さかなは どう ですか。 3. Maa-maa desu. まあまあ です。 4. Eigo-no jugyoo-wa doo desu-ka? えいごの じゅぎょうは どう ですか。
   5. Sumimasen, o-mizu o-negai shimasu. すみません、 おみず おねがいします。 6. Iie, kekkoo/ii desu. いいえ、 けっこう／いい です。
2. **Preview the vocabulary and notes for Lesson 33.**

LESSON 33

1. **Read all of the notes for Lesson 33.**
2. **Learn the new vocabulary.**
3. **Reading practice**
4. **Writing practice**

na な	ki き	su す	tsu つ	mo も		n ん	e え	ni に	he へ	bi び
ho ほ	u う	no の	yo よ	ru る		a あ	ko こ	ha は	mu む	de で
i い	sa さ	ke け	fu ふ	o (wo) を		shi し	te て	ro ろ	ya や	ji じ/ち
so そ	ne ね	chi ち	re れ	gi ぎ		ku く	ri り	ma ま	wa わ	da だ
ka か	hi ひ	to と	mi み	ze ぜ		o お	ta た	yu ゆ	gu ぐ	zu ず/づ
me め	ra ら	se せ	nu ぬ	pa ぱ						

5. **Preview the vocabulary and notes for Lesson 34.**

LESSON 34

PART 1
1. **Read all of the notes for Lesson 34.**
2. **Learn the new vocabulary.**
3. **Reading practice**
PART 2
1. **Reading practice**
   1. Watashi-no tanjoobi-wa shi-gatsu juu-ni-nichi desu. (My birthday is April 12th.)   2. Kono hito-no o-tanjoobi-wa itsu desu-ka? (When is this person's birthday?)   3. Okaasan-no o-tanjoobi-wa nan-gatsu desu-ka? (What month is your mother's birthday?)   4. Minasan-ni o-tanjoobi-o kiite kudasai. (Please ask everyone when their birthday is.)   5. Boku-no tanjoobi-wa shichi-gatsu juu-hachi-nichi desu. (My birthday is July 18th.)
2. **Preview the vocabulary and notes for Lesson 35.**

LESSON 35

PART 1
1. **Read all of the notes for Lesson 35.**
2. **Learn the new vocabulary.**
3. **Reading practice**
   1. Kyoo-wa watashi-no tanjoobi desu. (Today is my birthday.)   2. Ashita-wa nan-nichi desu-ka? (What is

the date tomorrow?) 3. Roku-ji-ni okimasu. (I get up at 6:00.) 4. Tamago-o tabemasu. (I'll eat an egg.)
5. Goji-han-ni nyuusu-o mimasu. (I watch the news at 5:30.) 6. Ken-kun-wa ashita juu-hassai-ni narimasu.
(Ken will be 18 tomorrow.) 7. Moo sugu juu-gatsu-ni narimasu. (It will be October soon.) 8. O-tanjoobi-
wa itsu desu-ka? (When is your birthday?) 9. Sumimasen, kyoo-wa hachi-gatsu juu-yokka desu-ka?
(Excuse me, is today August 14th?)

PART 2

1. Write it in Japanese!

1. Roku-ji-ni okimasu. ろくじに おきます。 2. Ken-kun-wa ashita juu-hassai-ni narimasu. けんくんは
あした じゅうはっさいに なります。 3. Kyoo-wa watashi-no tanjoobi desu. きょうは わたしの たん
じょうび です。 4. Tamago-o tabemasu. たまごを たべます。 5. Sumimasen, kyoo-wa hachi-gatsu juu-
yokka desu-ka? すみません、きょうは はちがつ じゅうよっか ですか。 6. Ashita-wa nan-nichi desu-
ka? あしたは なんにち ですか。 7. Moo sugu juu-gatsu-ni narimasu. もう すぐ じゅうがつに なります

2. Preview the vocabulary and notes for Lesson 36.

LESSON 36

1. Read all of the notes for Lesson 36.

2. Reading practice (English translation)

1. It's now 3:06. 2. From what time until what time is your job? 3. What time do you get up in the
morning? 4. What will you drink? 5. I'll have some water, please. 6. Thank you for the meal. / It was
a treat/feast. 7. Will you be 16 years old tomorrow? 8. Today is my birthday. 9. I have / There is a new
phone. 10. Please read this again.

3. Writing practice

1. おみず、おねがいします。(I'll have some water, please.) 2. きょうは わたしの たんじょうび
です。(Today is my birthday.) 3. ごちそうさま でした。(Thank you for the meal. / It was a treat/feast.)
4. これを もう いちど よんで ください。(Please read this again.) 5. いま さんじ ろっぷん です。
(It's now 3:06.) 6. あさ なんじに おきますか。(What time do you get up in the morning?)
7. あたらしい でんわが ありますよ。(I have / there is a new phone.) 8. しごとは なんじから なんじ
まで ですか。(From what time until what time is your job?) 9. あした じゅうろくさいに なりますか
(Will you be 16 years old tomorrow?) 10. なにを のみますか。(What will you drink?)

4. Preview the vocabulary and notes for Lesson 37.

LESSON 37

PART 1

1. Read all of the notes for Lesson 37.

2. Learn the new vocabulary.

3. Reading practice (English translation)

1. It's break-time /vacation now. 2. Is it your lunch break? 3. When is your summer break until? 4. Class
is from 8:00 until 9:00. 5. Winter vacation is from December 21 until January 6. 6. How many holidays
are there in Japan? 7. The New Year holiday is coming soon, isn't it?

4. Writing practice

PART 2

1. Non-stop talking exercise

2. Reading and vocabulary practice

ひらがな	Roomaji	English	ひらがな	Roomaji	English
Ex. にく	niku	meat	10. のみもの	nomimono	drink
1. やさい	yasai	vegetable	11. とても	totemo	very
2. こうちゃ	koocha	(black) tea	12. みそしる	misoshiru	*miso* soup
3. おはし	ohashi	chopsticks	13. たんじょうび	tanjoobi	birthday
4. おいしい	oishii	delicious	14. いつ	itsu	when?
5. けっこう	kekkoo	fine	15. おめでとう	omedetoo	congratulations
6. すこしだけ	sukoshi dake	only a little	16. きょう	kyoo	today
7. たべもの	tabemono	food	17. あした	ashita	tomorrow
8. どう	doo	how?	18. なります	narimasu	become
9. まあまあ	maa-maa	so-so	19. もうすぐ	moo sugu	soon

3. Preview the vocabulary and notes for Lesson 38.

LESSON 38

PART 1
1. **Read all of the notes for Lesson 38.**
2. **Learn the new vocabulary.**
3. **Reading practice**
4. **Vocabulary and writing practice**

PART 2
1. **Write it in Japanese!**

1. Nani-ga hoshii desu-ka? なにが ほしい ですか。 2. Kuruma-ga hoshii desu. くるまが ほしいです。

3. Tanjoobi-ni nani-ga hoshii desu-ka? たんじょうびに なにが ほしい ですか。 4. Yoofuku-to kutsu-ga hoshii desu. ようふくと くつが ほしい です。 5. Dare-ga ichi-ban desu-ka? だれが いちばん ですか。

2. **Preview the vocabulary and notes for Lesson 39.**

LESSON 39

1. **Writing practice**

na な	ki き	su す	tsu つ	mo も		ん	e え	ni に	he へ	bi び
ho ほ	u う	no の	yo よ	ru る	a あ	ko こ	ha は	mu む	de で
i い	sa さ	ke け	fu ふ	o (wo) を	shi し	te て	ro ろ	ya や	ji じ/ぢ
so そ	ne ね	chi ち	re れ	gi ぎ	ku く	ri り	ma ま	wa わ	da だ
ka か	hi ひ	to と	mi み	ze ぜ	o お	ta た	yu ゆ	gu ぐ	zu ず/づ
me め	ra ら	se せ	nu ぬ	pa ぱ					

1. きょ 2. しゃ 3. ちゅ 4. ひょ 5. じょ 6. りゅ 7. じゃ 8. ちょ 9. しゅ 10. びょ
11. きゅ 12. しょ

2. **Preview the vocabulary and notes for Lesson 40.**

LESSON 40

PART 1
1. **Read all of the notes for Lesson 40.**
2. **Learn the new vocabulary.**
3. **Reading practice** (English translation)

1. What will you do? 2. I won't do that. 3. I will study during summer vacation. 4. I will go to school.
5. I won't go to the movies. 6. Where will Mr./Ms. Tanaka go during winter break? 7. Professor Itoh
will go to his relatives' house on his birthday.

4. **Writing practice**

PART 2
1. **Reading practice** (English translation)

1. Mr. Yamaguchi will go to Japan over spring break. 2. Professor Suzuki will go to her relatives' house
on her birthday. 3. Mr. Watanabe will work during summer vacation. 4. Mr. Miyamoto will have a party
during New Year's. 5. What do you want? 6. I want clothes and shoes. 7. Do you have money?
8. Please turn in your homework. 9. How old will you be?

2. **Writing practice**
3. **Preview the vocabulary and notes for Lesson 41.**

LESSON 41

PART 1
1. **Read all of the notes for Lesson 41.**
2. **Learn the new vocabulary.**
3. **Reading practice** (English translation)

1. Who will you eat lunch with? 2. Where are you going? 3. I get up at 6:00. 4. She is going to her
relatives' house with her younger sister.

4. **Write it in Japanese!**

1. Dare-to ikimasu-ka? だれと いきますか。 2. Tanaka-san-to ikimasu. たなかさんと いきます。

3. Tomodachi-to terebi-o mimasu. ともだちと terebiを みます。 4. Dare-to doko-ni ikimasu-ka? だれと どこに いきますか。 5. Dare-to tabemasu-ka? だれと たべますか。

PART 2

1. Writing practice

1. わたなべくんは なつやすみに しごとを します。(Mr. Watanabe will work during summer vacation.) 2. いとうせんせいは おたんじょうびに しんせきの うちに いきます。 (Professor Itoh will go to his relatives' house on his birthday.) 3. ろくじに おきます。 (I get up at 6:00.) 4. おひる だれと たべますか。 (Who will you eat lunch with?) 5. いもうとさんと しんせきの うちに いきます。 (She is going to her relatives' house with her younger sister.) 6. おかねが ありますか。 (Do you have money?) 7. ようふくと くつが ほしい です。(I want clothes and shoes.) 8. がっこうに いきます。 (I will go to school.) 9. なんさいに なりますか。 (How old will you be?) 10. しゅくだいを だして ください。 (Please turn in your homework.)

2. Preview the vocabulary and notes for Lesson 42.

LESSON 42

PART 1

1. Read all of the notes for Lesson 42.

2. Learn the new vocabulary.

3. Nihonjin-wa O-shoogatsu-ni nani-o shimasu-ka? [Sample answers]

1. おもちを たべます。O-mochi-o tabemasu. (They eat *mochi*.) 2. じんじゃに いきます。Jinja-ni ikimasu. (They go to shrines.) 3. しんせきの うちに いきます。Shinseki-no uchi-ni ikimasu. (They go to their relatives' house.) 4. Geemuを します。Geemu-o shimasu. (They play games.) 5. ねます。 Nemasu. (They sleep.)

PART 2

1. Vocabulary and grammar review

1. Sandoitchi-が ありますか。 Sandoitchi-ga arimasu-ka? 2. どう ですか。おいしい です。Doo desu-ka? Oishii desu. 3. おたんじょうびは いつ ですか。O-tanjoobi-wa itsu desu-ka? 4. おたんじょうび は なんがつ ですか。Otanjoobi-wa nan-gatsu desu-ka? 5. じゅうごさいに なります。Juu-go-sai-ni narimasu. 6. あしたは なんにち ですか。Ashita-wa nan-nichi desu-ka? 7. なつやすみは いつ まで ですか。Natsu-yasumi-wa itsu made desu-ka? 8. なにが ほしい ですか。Nani-ga hoshii desu-ka? 9. ようふくと くつが ほしい です。Yoofuku-to kutsu-ga hoshii desu. 10. うえださんは しんせきの うちに いきます。Ueda-san-wa shinseki-no uchi-ni ikimasu.

2. Can you read it?

Ashita watashi-wa shinseki-no uchi-ni ikimasu. (Tomorrow I am going to my relatives' house.)

3. Preview the vocabulary and notes for Lesson 43.

EXTRA

Writing practice

1. くつが ほしい です。 (I want shoes.) 2. ようふくが ありますか。(Do you have clothes?) 3. あした じゅうごさいに なります。(I will be 15 years old tomorrow.) 4. なつやすみは いつ まで ですか。(When will summer vacation end?) 5. おたんじょうびは なんがつ ですか。(What month is your birthday?)

LESSON 43

PART 1

1. Read all of the notes for Lesson 43.

2. Learn the new vocabulary.

3. Non-stop talking exercise

PART 2

1. Reading practice

1. Dore-ga hayai desu-ka? (Which one is fast?) 2. Nani-ga hoshii desu-ka? (What do you want?) 3. Dare-ga eiga-ni ikimasu-ka? (Who is going to the movies?) 4. Doko-ga ii desu-ka? (Which place is good?) 5. Dore-ga oishii desu-ka? (Which one is delicious?)

2. Preview the vocabulary and notes for Lesson 44.

LESSON 44

PART 1

1. Read all of the notes for Lesson 44.

2. **Learn the new vocabulary.**
3. **Non-stop talking exercise**
PART 2
1. **Grammar and vocabulary review**
   1. がっこうは どこ ですか。Gakkoo-wa doko desu-ka? 2. なんさい ですか。Nan-sai desu-ka?
   3. あさ なんじに おきますか。Asa nan-ji-ni okimasu-ka? 4. おたんじょうびは いつ ですか。
   O-tanjoobi-wa itsu desu-ka? 5. いま なんじ ですか。Ima nan-ji desu-ka? 6. えいごの じしょが
   ありますか。Eigo-no jisho-ga arimasu-ka?
2. **Can you read it?**
   Tanaka-san-no denwa-bangoo-wa nan-ban desu-ka? (What is Mr./Ms. Tanaka's telephone number?)
3. **Preview the vocabulary and notes for Lesson 45.**

LESSON 45

PART 1
1. **Read all of the notes for Lesson 45.**
2. **Reading practice**
3. **Non-stop talking exercise**
PART 2
1. **Yomimashoo!**
   Ikimashita. (I went.)
   Eiga-ni ikimashita. (I went to a movie.)
   Tomodachi-to eiga-ni ikimashita. (I went to a movie with friends.)
   Fuyu-yasumi-ni tomodachi-to eiga-ni ikimashita. (I went to a movie with friends during winter vacation.)
   Shimashita. (~ did.)
   Shigoto-o shimashita. (~ worked.)
   Roku-ji-made shigoto-o shimashita. (~ worked until 6:00.)
   Hachi-ji kara roku-ji-made shigoto-o shimashita. (~ worked from 8:00 to 6:00.)
   Yamamoto-san-wa hachi-ji-kara roku-ji-made shigoto-o shimashita. (Mr./Ms. Yamamoto worked from 8:00 to 6:00.)
2. **Nihongo-de kakimashoo! (Let's write in Japanese!)**
   1. えいがに いきました。Eiga-ni ikimashita. 2. だれと ゴルフを しましたか。Dare-to gorufu-o
   shimashita-ka? 3. その ひとは せんせい でした。Sono hito-wa sensei deshita. 4. いつから いつまで
   でしたか。Itsu-kara itsu-made deshita-ka? 5. パーティーは どう でしたか。Paatii-wa doo deshita-ka?
   6. なんじに おきましたか。Nan-ji-ni okimashita-ka? 7. ついたちに デートを しました。Tsuitachi-ni
   deeto-o shimashita.
3. **Preview the vocabulary and notes for Lesson 46.**

LESSON 46

PART 1
1. **Read all of the notes for Lesson 46.**
2. **Learn the new vocabulary.**
3. **Writing questions** [Sample questions]
   1. Paatii を しますか。 Paatii-o shimasu-ka? (Will you have a party?)
   2. Nyuusu／えいがを みますか。Nyuusu/Eiga-o mimasu-ka? (Do you watch news/movies?)
   3. あさ ろくじ／しちじに おきますか。Asa roku-ji/shichi-ji-ni okimasu-ka? (Do you wake up at
   6:00/7:00 in the morning?)
   4. なんじに がっこうに いきますか。Nan-ji-ni gakkoo-ni ikimasu-ka? (What time do you go to school?)
   5. *(name of food)*を たべますか。*(name of food)*-o tabemasu-ka? (Do you eat *name of food*?)
   6. Rajio を ききますか。Rajio-o kikimasu-ka? (Do you listen to the radio?)
PART 2
1. **Nihongo de kakimashoo!**
   1. Tanjoobi-ni eiga-ni ikimashita. たんじょうびに えいがに いきました。2. O-shoogatsu-ni jinja-ni
   ikimashita. おしょうがつに じんじゃに いきました。3. Yasumi-ni gakkoo-ni ikimasen. やすみに

がっこうに いきません。 4. Kinoo Tookyoo-ni ikimashita-ka? Iie, ikimasen deshita. きのう とうきょう に いきましたか。 いいえ、 いきません でした。 5. Shooji-kun-wa imashita-ka? しょうじくんは いま したか。

2. It doesn't belong because...

1. おみず Not a food 2. ふたり Not a date 3. こくばん Not an ordinal number 4. どこ Not a place

5. おにいさん Not a humble family term 6. し Not a particle

3. Preview the vocabulary and notes for Lesson 47.

LESSON 47

PART 1

1. Read all of the notes for Lesson 47.

2. Learn the new vocabulary.

3. Kakimashoo!

1. Doko-de tabemasu-ka? どこで たべますか。 2. Uchi-de zasshi-o yomimasu. うちで ざっしを よみ ます。 3. Nan-ji-ni uchi-ni kaerimasu-ka? なんじに うちに かえりますか。 4. Doko-de kaimono-o shimasu-ka? どこで かいものを しますか。 5. Doko-de benkyoo-o shimasu-ka? どこで べんきょうを しますか。 6. Doko-kara kimashita-ka? どこから きましたか。 7. Kinoo resutoran-de tabemashita. きのう resutoran で たべました。

PART 2

1. Yomimashoo!

1. Doko-kara kimashita-ka? (Where did you come from?) 2. Uchi-de shigoto-o shimasu. (She works at home.) 3. Takeda-san-wa doko-ni imasu-ka? (Where is Mr./Ms. Takeda?) 4. Doko-de benkyoo-o shimasu ka? (Where do you study?) 5. Doko-de tabemasu-ka? (Where does she eat?) 6. Doko-de hon-o yomimasu-ka? (Where do you read books?) 7. Tanaka-sensei-no okaasan-ga kimashita. (Mr./Ms. Tanaka's mother is here/came.) 8. Nan-ji-ni uchi-ni kaerimasu-ka? (What time are you returning home?) 9. Jugyoo-de ongaku-o kikimashita. (I listened to music in class.) 10. Uchi-de zasshi-o yomimasu. (He reads magazines at home.) 11. Doko-de kaimono-o shimasu-ka? (Where do you shop?) 12. Kinoo resutoran-de tabemashita. (Yesterday we ate in a restaurant.)

Answer to the question: restaurant

2. Can you read it?

Kinoo watashi-wa Yamamoto-san-no uchi-de Yamamoto-san-no okaasan-to oishii koocha-o nomimashita. (Yesterday, I had delicious tea with Mr./Ms. Yamamoto's mother at their house.)

3. Preview the vocabulary and notes for Lesson 48.

LESSON 48

PART 1

1. Read all of the notes for Lesson 48.

2. Learn the new vocabulary.

3. Can you read these?

1. Kyoo-wa nan-yoobi desu-ka? (What day is it today?) 2. Yamamoto-san-to Tanaka-san-wa mokuyoobi-ni Tookyoo-ni ikimasu. (On Thursday, Mr./Ms. Yamamoto and Mr./Ms. Tanaka will go to Tokyo.)

PART 2

1. Kakimashoo!

1. Nan-yoobi-ni tenisu-o shimasu-ka? なんようびに tenisu を しますか。 2. Kin-yoobi-ni nani-o shimasu-ka? きんようびに なにを しますか。 3. Boku-/Watashi-wa mainichi shukudai-o shimasu. ぼく ／わたしは まいにち しゅくだいを します。 4. Getsu-yoobi-ni arubaito-o shimasu. げつようびに arubaito を します。 5. Nichi-yoobi-mo doraibu-ni ikimashita. にちようびも doraibu に いきました。

2. Unscramble the days of the week.

1. にちようび (Sunday) 2. どようび (Saturday) 3. すいようび (Wednesday) 4. もくようび (Thursday) 5. げつようび (Monday) 6. きんようび (Friday) 7. かようび (Tuesday)

3. Preview the vocabulary and notes for Lesson 49.

LESSON 49

PART 1

1. Read all of the notes for Lesson 49.

2. Learn the new vocabulary.

3. Reading practice (English translation)

1. Please look at this kanji. 2. Please read this kanji. 3. Please read that kanji once more. 4. You did very well. 5. What is the date today? 6. I went to Tokyo yesterday. 7. What do you do on weekends? 8. Are your weekends fun? 9. Excuse me, but what day was yesterday?

PART 2

Reading and vocabulary practice

1. tsumaranai (boring) 2. omochi (rice cake) 3. Gomen kudasai. ("Excuse me." *announcing that you are at the entrance of someone's home*) 4. Ojama shimasu. ("Excuse me." *when interrupting someone at work or at home*) 5. deshita (was, were) 6. kikimasu (listen, ask) 7. yomimasu (read) 8. ongaku (music) 9. zasshi (magazine) 10. shinbun (newspaper) 11. kinoo (yesterday) 12. kimasu (come) 13. kaerimasu (return) 14. mainichi (every day) 15. nan-yoobi (what day of the week) 16. shuumatsu (weekend)

REVIEW LESSON 1

PART 1

1. Read all of the notes for Review Lesson 1.

2. Review the vocabulary.

Colors: あかい　あおい　くろい

School related words: せんせい　ちゅうがっこう　こうこうせい　しょうがっこう　だいがく

Classroom objects: こくばん　かみ　いす　つくえ　かばん　えいご　ほん　じしょ

Family related terms: [humble form] ちち　おとうと　いもうと　きょうだい　あね

[honorific form] おねえさん　おにいさん　ごかぞく

3. Writing practice - What would you say?

1. だれ です か。 2. さようなら。 3. (それは) だめ です。 4. いいえ、ちがいます。 5. ああ、そう です か。 6. めいし です。 どうぞ。 7. (すみません。)～いい です か。 8. ～は にほんごで なんと いいますか。

REVIEW LESSON 2

PART 1

1. Read all of the notes for Review Lesson 2.

2. Review the vocabulary.

3. Reading and writing practice

1. Nan-ji-ni okimasu-ka? (What time does he get up?) → 6 じにおきます。 Roku-ji-ni okimasu. (He gets up at 6:00.) 2. Shigoto-wa nan-ji-kara nan-ji-made desu-ka? (From what time to what time does he work?) → 9 じから 5 じはんまでです。 Ku-ji-kara go-ji han-made desu. (He works from 9:00 to 5:30.) 3. Juu-ji han-kara juu-ichi-ji han-made nani-ga arimasu-ka? (What does he have from 10:30 to 11:30?) → Miitingu があります。 Miitingu-ga arimasu. (He has a meeting.) 4. Hiru, nan-ji-ni tabemasu-ka? (What time does he eat lunch?) → 12 じ 40 ぷんにたべます。 12-ji 40-pun-ni tabemasu. (He eats at 12:40.) 5. Nihongo-no jugyoo-wa nan-ji-kara nan-ji-made desu-ka? (From what time to what time is his Japanese class?) → 6 じ から 7 じまでです。 6-ji kara 7-ji-made desu. (It is from 6:00 to 7:00.) 6. Yoru, hachi-ji-kara ku-ji han-made nani-ga arimasu-ka? (What does he have from 8:00 to 9:30 in the evening?) → Deeto があります。 Deeto-ga arimasu. (He has a date.) 7. Nan-ji-ni nemasu-ka? (What time does he go to bed?) → 11 じはん に ねます。 11-ji han-ni nemasu. (He goes to bed at 11:30.)

PART 2

Reading and writing practice

1. Watashi/Boku-wa asa [time]-ni okimasu. わたし／ぼくはあさ [time] におきます。

2. Nihongo-no jugyoo-wa [time]-kara [time]-made desu. にほんごのじゅぎょうは [time] から [time] までです。

3. Hiru, [time]-ni tabemasu. ひる、[time] にたべます。

4. Gakkoo-wa [time]-made desu. がっこうは [time] までです。

5. Shukudai-wa [time]-kara [time]-made desu. しゅくだいは [time] から [time] までです。

6. Yoru, [time]-ni nemasu. よる、[time] にねます。

REVIEW LESSON 3

PART 1

1. Read all of the notes for Review Lesson 3.

2. **Review the vocabulary.**

3. **Writing practice - What would you say?**

1. おねがいします。 Onegai shimasu. 2. ごちそうさuntil でした。 Gochisoosama deshita. 3. けっこうです。 Kekkoo desu. 4. すこしだけ。 Sukoshi dake. 5. いただきます。 Itadakimasu. 6. おたんじょうびは いつ ですか。 Otanjoobi-wa itsu desu-ka? 7. なにが ほしい ですか。 Nani-ga hoshii desu-ka? 8. どこに いきますか。 Doko-ni ikimasu-ka? 9. あした、なにを しますか。 Ashita, nani-o shimasu-ka? 10. だれと いきますか。 Dare-to ikimasu-ka?

PART 2

1. **Reading and writing practice - Question & Answer**

1. じゅうがつ はつか　にじゅうごにち　2. ごかぞく　3. を みます／に いきます　4. かいもの　5. おねえさん　6. しんせき に いきます　7. にじゅうよっか に　8. おとうさん

2. **Writing practice: Fall break**

わたしの あきやすみはじゅうがつ はつか から にじゅうごにち まで です。かぞくと Nyuu Yooku に いきます。にじゅういちにちに myuujikaruを みます／に いきます。にじゅうににちに あねと かいものに いきます。にじゅうさんにちに かぞくと しんせきの うちに いきます。にじゅうよっかにちちの たんじょうび paatiiを します。

(*Roomaji* version)

Watashi-no aki yasumi-wa juu-gatsu hatsu-ka-kara ni-juu-go nichi-made desu. Kazoku-to Nyuu Yooku-ni ikimasu. Ni-juu-ichi nichi-ni myuujikaru-o mimasu/-ni ikimasu. Ni-juu-ni nichi-ni ane-to kaimono-ni ikimasu. Ni-juu san nichi-ni kazoku-to shinseki-no uchi-ni ikimasu. Ni-juu yokka-ni chichi-no tanjoobi paatii-o shimasu.

(English translation)

My fall break is from October 20th to the 25th. I am going to New York with my family. We are going to see a musical on the 21st. On the 22nd, I am going shopping with my older sister. On the 23rd, I will visit my relatives' house with my family. On the 24th, we will have a birthday party for my father.

REVIEW LESSON 4

PART 1

1. **Read all of the notes for Review Lesson 4.**

2. **Review the vocabulary.**

3. **Writing practice - What would you say?**

1. あけまして おめでとうございます。 ことしも どうぞ よろしく おねがいします。 Akemashite omedetoo gozaimasu. Kotoshi-mo doozo yoroshiku o-negai-shimasu. 2. ごめん ください。 Gomen kudasai. 3. おじゃまします。 O-jama shimasu. 4. そろそろ しつれいします。 Soro soro shitsurei shimasu. 5. おじゃましました。 O-jama shimashita. 6. きょうは なんようび ですか。 Kyoo-wa nan-yoobi desu-ka? 7. 2じに (わたしのうちに)きて ください。 2-ji-ni (watashi-no uchi-ni) kite kudasai. 8. どれの／どの keeki が いいですか。 Dore-no/dono keeki-ga ii desu-ka?

PART 2

1. **Reading and writing practice - Question & Answer**

1. すい　2. くがつ　みっか　3. ごかぞく　おてら　4. がっこう　5. しました　6. おねえさんのうち　7. ともだち　8. きん　9. ど　じゅう

2. **Writing practice: This week**

3. **Dialogue**

1. She is going to a party. 2. She is going there with Mamoru. 3. She is planning to come home at 9:00. 4. He is going to read magazines at home.

4. **Preview the vocabulary and notes for Lesson 50.**

LESSON 50

PART 1

1. **Read all of the notes for Lesson 50.**

2. **Learn the new vocabulary.**

3. **Non-stop talking exercise**

PART 2

1. *Katakana* recognition

カ　ミ　ト　マ　ン　ア　ス　キ　イ　ウ　ヲ　エ　レ　オ　ク　フ　ロ　メ　ズ　コ

2. **Watashi-no sukejuuru** [Sample answers]

   1. Suugaku-wa nan-yoobi desu-ka? (What days do you have math?) → げつ/か/すい/もく/きんようびと げつ/か/すい/もく/きんようびです。／まいにちです。 Getsu/ka/sui/moku/kin-yoobi-to getsu/ka/sui/moku/kin-yoobi desu.／Mainichi desu. (It is on Monday/Tuesday/Wednesday/ Thursday/Friday and Monday/Tuesday/Wednesday/Thursday/Friday.／It's every day.)

   2. Eigo-no jugyoo-ga arimasu-ka? (Do you have English class?) → はい、あります。／いいえ、 ありません。 Hai, arimasu. / Iie, arimasen. (Yes, I do./No, I don't.)

   3. Nihongo-no jugyoo-wa nan-ji-kara desu-ka? (What time does Japanese class start?) → はち/く/じゅう/ じゅういち/じゅうに/いち/に/さん/よじ から です。 Hachi/ku/juu/juu-ichi/juu-ni/ichi/ni/san/yo-ji kara desu. (It's from eight/nine/ten/eleven/twelve/one/two/three/four o'clock.)

   4. Eigo-no-jugyoo-wa nan-ji-made desu-ka? (What time does English class end?) → はち/く/じゅう/ じゅういち/じゅうに/いち/に/さん/よじ まで です。 Hachi/ku/juu/juu-ichi/juu-ni/ichi/ni/san/yo-ji made desu. (It's until eight/nine/ten/eleven/twelve/one/two/three/four o'clock.)

   5. Rekishi-wa nan-yoobi desu-ka? (What days do you have history?) → げつ/か/すい/もく/きんようびと げつ/か/すい/もく/きんようびです。／まいにちです。 Getsu/ka/sui/moku/kin-yoobi-to getsu/ka/sui/moku/kin-yoobi desu.／Mainichi desu. (It is on Monday/Tuesday/Wednesday/Thursday/ Friday and Monday/Tuesday/Wednesday/Thursday/Friday.／It's every day.)

3. **Nihongo-de kaite kudasai.**

   1. えいごは すいようびと きんようび です。 Eigo-wa sui-yoobi-to kin-yoobi desu. 2. れきしは なんようび ですか。 Rekishi-wa nan-yoobi desu-ka? 3. ちりの べんきょうを します。 Chiri-no benkyoo-o shimasu. 4. スミスさんと たなかさんは フランスごの べんきょうを します。 Sumisu-san-to Tanaka-san-wa furansu-go-no benkyoo-o shimasu.

4. **Preview the vocabulary and notes for Lesson 51.**

LESSON 51

PART 1
1. **Read all of the notes for Lesson 51.**
2. **Learn the new vocabulary.**
3. **Non-stop talking exercise**

PART 2
1. **Nihongo-de kakimashoo!**

   1. すうがくは かんたん ですか。 Suugaku-wa kantan desu-ka? 2. にほんごの じゅぎょうは おもしろい ですか。 Nihongo-no jugyoo-wa omoshiroi desu-ka? 3. かんたん ですか。むずかしい ですか。 Kantan desu-ka? Muzukashii desu-ka? 4. きょうは えいごが ありますか。 Kyoo-wa eigo-ga arimasu-ka? 5. れきしは なんようび ですか。 Rekishi-wa nan-yoobi desu-ka?

2. **Preview the vocabulary and notes for Lesson 52.**

LESSON 52

PART 1
1. **Read all of the notes for Lesson 52.**
2. **Learn the new vocabulary.**
3. **Complete Writing Practice ❷ Study, trace and write.**

PART 2
1. **Complete the remainder of the Writing Practice.**
2. **Can you read them?**

   1. Anmari suki ja nai desu. (I don't like it very much.) 2. Suugaku-to bijutsu-to rekishi-ga daisuki desu. (I really like math, art, and history.) 3. Nani-ga suki desu-ka? (What do you like?) 4. Furui Nihon-no eiga-wa anmari suki ja nai desu. (I don't like old Japanese movies very much.)

3. **Preview the vocabulary and notes for Lesson 53.**

EXTRA

Nihongo-de kakimashoo!

   1. Nishioka-san-wa ongaku-ga daisuki desu. にしおかさんは おんがくが だいすき です。 2. Nani-ga suki desu-ka? なにが すき ですか。 3. Anmari suki ja nai desu. あんまり すき じゃない です。 4. Dare-ga suki desu-ka? だれが すき ですか。 5. Kore-ga suki desu. これが すき です。

WRITING PRACTICE

❶ **Read and copy the *katakana*.**

1. ウ [u] 2. オ [o] 3. ア [a] 4. イ [i] 5. エ [e] 6. ウー [uu] 7. アー [aa] 8. オー [oo]

❷ **Study, trace and write.**

❸ **Identify the *katakana*.**

1. A ア 2. I イ i イ 3. O オ i イ o オ 4. A ア i イ o オ 5. i イ 6. A ア i イ 7. Aa アー
8. O オ 9. A ア

❹ **Dekimasu-ka?**

1. ド<u>イ</u>ツ 2. <u>ウ</u>ガンダ 3. スペ<u>イ</u>ン 4. <u>ア</u>ルバニ<u>ア</u> 5. <u>ウ</u>クラ<u>イ</u>ナ 6. <u>エ</u>スト二<u>ア</u>
7. <u>イ</u>タリ<u>ア</u> 8. <u>エ</u>チ<u>オ</u>ピ<u>ア</u> 9. <u>オ</u>ランダ 10. <u>イ</u>ンドネシ<u>ア</u> 11. サ<u>ウ</u>ジ<u>ア</u>ラビ<u>ア</u>
12. <u>オー</u>ストリ<u>ア</u>

❺ **More writing practice**

LESSON 53

PART 1

1. **Read all of the notes for Lesson 53.**
2. **Learn the new vocabulary.**
3. **Yomimashoo!** (*Roomaji* reading and English translation)

1. Tabemono-wa nani-ga ichiban suki desu-ka? (Among all foods, what do you like best?) 2. Dare-ga ichiban suki desu-ka? (Who(m) do you like best?) 3. Yakyuu-to suiei-ga suki desu. (I like baseball and swimming.) 4. Suugaku-no sensei-ga ichiban suki desu-ne. (I like the math teacher the best.) 5. Kenji-kun-wa rekishi-ga daisuki desu. (Kenji likes history very much.) 6. Watanabe-san-no okaasan-wa keeki-wa suki ja nai desu. (Mr./Ms. Watanabe's mother does not like cake.) 7. Chichi-to haha-wa kono hon-ga suki desu. (My father and mother like this book.) 8. Sore-wa anmari suki ja nai desu. (I don't really like that.) 9. Kukkii-ga suki desu-ka? (Do you like cookies?) 10. Nomimono-wa nani-ga suki desu-ka? (What drinks do you like?)

PART 2

1. **Katakana-o yomimashoo!**
2. **Kakimashoo!**

1. けんじくんは れきしが だいすき です。 Kenji-kun-wa rekishi-ga daisuki desu. 2. ちちと ははは このほんが すき です。 Chichi-to haha-wa kono hon-ga suki desu. 3. のみものは なにが すき ですか。 Nomimono-wa nani-ga suki desu-ka? 4. やきゅうと すいえいが すき です。 Yakyuu-to suiei-ga suki desu. 5. だれが いちばん すき ですか。 Dare-ga ichiban suki desu-ka? 6. それは あんまり すき じゃ ない です。 Sore-wa anmari suki ja nai desu.

3. **Preview the vocabulary and notes for Lesson 54.**

LESSON 54

PART 1

1. **Read all of the notes for Lesson 54.**
2. **Learn the new vocabulary.**
3. **Can you read these?**

1. たべものは なにが すき ですか。 Tabemono-wa nani-ga suki desu-ka? (What foods do you like?)
2. わたしも テニスを しますよ。 Watashi-mo tenisu-o shimasu-yo. (I play tennis, too.)
3. おんがくが だいすき です。 Ongaku-ga daisuki desu. (I like music a lot/very much.)

PART 2

1. **Complete the Writing Practice.**
2. **Preview the vocabulary and notes for Lesson 55.**

WRITING PRACTICE

❶ **Read and copy the *katakana*.**

1. キ [ki] 2. コ [ko] 3. ケ [ke] 4. カ [ka] 5. イ [i] 6. ク [ku] 7. ゴ [go] 8. ア [a] 9. ギ [gi]
10. ガ [ga] 11. グ [gu] 12. ゲ [ge]

❷ **Identify the *katakana*.**

1. ka カ go ゴ 2. A ア ka カ 3. Ka カ i イ 4. ko コ ku ク 5. Ki キ e エ 6. Gu グ goo ゴー

❸ **Study, trace and write.**

❹ **Dekimasu-ka?**

1. イ ラ ク 2. ウ ガ ン ダ 3. エ ク ア ド ル 4. ニ カ ラ グ ワ 5. ウ ク ラ イ ナ 6. ギ ア ナ
7. コ ス タ リ カ 8. エ チ オ ピ ア 9. ガ ー ナ 10. グ ア テ マ ラ 11. メ キ シ コ 12. ケ ニ ア

❺ **More writing practice**

LESSON 55

PART 1

1. **Read all of the notes for Lesson 55.**
2. **Learn the new vocabulary.**
3. **Katakana-o yomimashoo!**

   1. sa 2. ko 3. zu 4. ke 5. shi 6. ze 7. ku 8. ji 9. su 10. ki 11. za 12. se 13. zo 14. ka 15. so

PART 2

1. **Kakimashoo!**

   1. Bareebooru-ga sukoshi dekimasu. バレーボールが すこし できます。 2. Sumoo-ga dekimasu-ka?
   すもうが できますか。 3. Nihongo-wa anmari dekimasen. にほんごは あんまり できません。
   4. Juudoo-wa dekimasen. じゅうどうは できません。 5. Nihongo-wa zenzen wakarimasen. にほんごは
   ぜんぜん わかりません。 6. Koohii-wa zenzen nomimasen. Koohii は ぜんぜん のみません。

2. **Preview the vocabulary and notes for Lesson 56.**

LESSON 56

PART 1

1. **Read all of the notes for Lesson 56.**
2. **Learn the new vocabulary.**
3. **Can you read these?**

   1. Gakki-wa nani-ga dekimasu-ka? (What musical instruments can you play?) 2. Tokidoki uta-o utaimasu-
   ka? (Do you sing sometimes?) 3. Yakyuu-ga suki desu-kedo anmari joozu ja nai desu. (I like baseball,
   but I'm not very good at it.)

PART 2

1. **Complete the Writing Practice.**
2. **Preview the vocabulary and notes for Lesson 57.**

WRITING PRACTICE

❶ **Study, trace and write.**
❷ **Read and copy the *katakana*.**

   1. シ [shi] 2. ソ [so] 3. セ [se] 4. サ [sa] 5. イ [i] 6. ス [su] 7. ゾ [zo] 8. ア [a] 9. ジ [ji] 10. ザ [za]
   11. ズ [zu] 12. ゼ [ze]

❸ **Kakimashoo!**

   1. シカゴ 2. ソーセージ 3. スキー 4. アイス 5. ガス 6. コース 7. ソース 8. サイズ

❹ **Dekimasu-ka?**

   1. サ モ ア 2. シ リ ア 3. ス ペ イ ン 4. セ ネ ガ ル 5. ソ マ リ ア 6. エ ス ト ニ ア
   7. コ ス タ リ カ 8. エ チ オ ピ ア 9. ス イ ス 10. イ ス ラ エ ル 11. メ キ シ コ 12. イ ギ リ ス

❺ **More writing practice**

LESSON 57

PART 1

1. **Read all of the notes for Lesson 57.**
2. **Learn the new vocabulary.**
3. **Katakana-o yomimashoo!**

PART 2

1. **Kakimashoo!**

   1. Kantan-na shitsumon desu. かんたんな しつもん です。 2. Tokidoki uta-o utaimasu-ka?
   ときどき うたを うたいますか。 3. Ongaku-wa nani-ga ichiban suki desu-ka? おんがくは なにが
   いちばん すき ですか。 4. Gakki-wa nani-ga dekimasu-ka? がっきは なにが できますか。

2. **Can you read it?**

   Ongaku-wa nani-ga ichiban suki desu-ka? (What kind of music do you like best?) Kurashikku-ga
   ichiban suki desu. (I like classical music the best.)

3. **Preview the vocabulary and notes for Lesson 58.**

LESSON 58

PART 1
1. **Read all of the notes for Lesson 58.**
2. **Learn the new vocabulary.**
3. **Complete Writing Practice ❸ Study, trace and write.**

PART 2
1. **Complete the remainder of the Writing Practice.**
2. **Dekimasu-ka?**
   horizontal (left to right)
   なります (become)　たのしい (pleasant)　ゆき (snow)　しつもん (question)　はち (eight)　しごと (work)　はじめまして (How do you do?)　みず (water)　きんようび (Friday)　まいにち (every day)　かんたん (easy)　えいが (movie)　きます (come)　かみ (paper)　むずかしい (difficult)　おもしろい (interesting)　うた (song)　すいようび (Wednesday)　どこ (where)

   vertical (left to right)
   なつ (summer)　よみます (read)　なまえ (name)　はは (mother)　じしょ (dictionary)　あした (tomorrow)　すこし (a little)　うち (house)　ちがいます (be different)　いま (now)　すうがく (math)　しんせき (relative)　しんぶん (newspaper)　かようび (Tuesday)　れきし (history)　けど (but)　いい (good)
3. **Preview the vocabulary and notes for Lesson 59.**

WRITING PRACTICE
❶ **Read and copy the *katakana*.**
   1. ト [to]　2. ダ [da]　3. ツ [tsu]　4. タ [ta]　5. チ [chi]　6. ズ [zu]　7. テ [te]　8. ジ [ji]　9. デ [de]　10. ド [do]　11. サッカー [sakkaa]　12. クッキー [kukkii]

❷ **Kakimashoo!**
   1. ドア　2. テスト　3. デザート　4. ギター　5. スケート　6. データ　7. スーツ　8. カセット　9. ソーダ　10. チーズ　11. デート　12. ツアーガイド

❸ **Study, trace and write.**

❹ **Dekimasu-ka?**
   1. ウガンダ　2. シリア　3. エストニア　4. ケニア　5. コスタリカ　6. エチオピア　7. ドイツ　8. パキスタン

❺ **More writing practice**

LESSON 59

PART 1
1. **Read all of the notes for Lesson 59.**
2. **Learn the new vocabulary.**
3. **Affirmative to negative**
   1. おいしくない　2. むずかしくない　3. つまらなくない　4. おおきくない　5. いそがしくない

PART 2
1. **Yomimashoo!**
   A: Shikago-no tenki-wa doo desu-ka? (How's the weather in Chicago?)
   B: Yuki desu. (It's snowy.)
   A: Aa, yuki desu-ka. Nan-do desu-ka? (Oh, it's snowy? What's the temperature?)
   B: Ni-juu-go-do desu. Samui desu. Bosuton-wa? (It's 25 degrees. It's cold. How about Boston?)
   A: Samuku-nai desu. Go-juu-san-do desu. (It's not cold. It's 53 degrees.)
   B: Aa, soo desu-ka. Hare desu-ka? (Oh, really? Is it sunny?)
   A: Iie, hare ja nai desu. Kumori desu. (No, it's not sunny. It's cloudy.)
2. **Dekimasu-ka?**
   1. Tookyoo-no tenki-wa doo desu-ka? (How is the weather in Tokyo?)　2. Chotto samui desu-ne. (It's a little cold, isn't it?)　3. Sono atarashii hon-wa omoshirokunai desu. (That new book is not interesting.)
3. **Preview the vocabulary and notes for Lesson 60.**

LESSON 60

PART 1
1. **Read all of the notes for Lesson 60.**
2. **Learn the new vocabulary.**
3. **Complete Writing Practice ❷ Study, trace and write.**

PART 2
1. **Complete the remainder of the Writing Practice.**
2. **Preview the vocabulary and notes for Lesson 61.**
3. **Prepare for an interactive activity.**

WRITING PRACTICE

❶ **Read and copy the** *katakana.*

   1. ニ [ni] 2. ネ [ne] 3. ナ [na] 4. ノ [no] 5. ヌ [nu] 6. ン [n] 7. ナ [na] 8. ネ [ne] 9. ニ [ni]
   10. ン [n] 11. ヌ [nu] 12. ノ [no]

❷ **Study, trace and write.**

❸ **Kakimashoo!**

   1. ノート 2. ネクタイ 3. アンテナ 4. テニス 5. カヌー 6. センター 7. コンサート
   8. アクセント

❹ **Dekimasu-ka?**

   1. <u>アイスランド</u> 2. <u>インドネシア</u> 3. <u>ウガンダ</u> 4. <u>エストニア</u> 5. <u>ニカラグワ</u>
   6. <u>アフガニスタン</u> 7. <u>パナマ</u> 8. <u>セネガル</u> 9. <u>ケニア</u> 10. レバノン 11. モナコ
   12. <u>スーダン</u>

❺ **More writing practice**

LESSON 61

PART 1
1. **Read all of the notes for Lesson 61.**
2. **Learn the new vocabulary.**
3. **Prepare for an interactive activity.**

PART 2
1. **Yomimashoo!** (*Roomaji* reading and English translation)
   1. Kono nekutai-ga hoshii desu-ka? (Do you want this necktie?) 2. Sono seetaa-ga suki desu-ka? (Do you like that sweater?) 3. Sukaato-wa kirei desu-ne. (The skirt is pretty, isn't it?) 4. Kono jiinzu-wa doo desu-ka? (How about these jeans?) 5. Ano hito-wa buutsu-ga takusan arimasu. (That person has a lot of boots.)
2. **Preview the vocabulary and notes for Lesson 62.**

LESSON 62

PART 1
1. **Read all of the notes for Lesson 62.**
2. **Learn the new vocabulary.**
3. **Complete Writing Practice ❸ Study, trace and write.**
4. **Prepare for an interactive activity.**

PART 2
1. **Complete the remainder of the Writing Practice.**
2. **Preview the vocabulary and notes for Lesson 63.**

WRITING PRACTICE

❶ **Read and copy the** *katakana.*

   1. ヒ [hi] 2. バ [ba] 3. ヘ [he] 4. ブ [bu] 5. ベ [be] 6. ボ [bo] 7. フ [fu] 8. ホ [ho] 9. ハ [ha]
   10. ビ [bi] 11. パ [pa] 12. ペ [pe]

❷ **Kakimashoo!**

   1. ピアノ (piano) 2. コーヒー 3. ナイフ 4. ハンバーガー (hamburger) 5. ペン (pen) 6. スポーツ
   (sport(s)) 7. バス 8. ベンチ 9. ベッド 10. ジーパン 11. ボート 12. スープ 13. ホッケー
   14. ヘアピン 15. パスポート 16. ステーキ

❸ **Study, trace and write.**

❹ **Dekimasu-ka?**

   1. <u>ハイチ</u> 2. <u>ポーランド</u> 3. <u>スペイン</u> 4. <u>カンボジア</u> 5. <u>コロンビア</u> 6. <u>ハンガリー</u>
   7. <u>パキスタン</u> 8. <u>エチオピア</u> 9. <u>フランス</u> 10. <u>ブラジル</u> 11. <u>ベルギー</u> 12. <u>ホンジュラス</u>

❺ **More writing practice**

LESSON 63

PART 1
1. **Read all of the notes for Lesson 63.**

2. Learn the new vocabulary.

3. Matching *hiragana* **and** *katakana*

_4_ む	_12_ あ	_15_ み	_17_ は	_16_ て
_6_ う	_14_ し	_8_ お	_7_ も	_10_ に
_1_ ま	_13_ え	_2_ い	_20_ ん	_5_ の
_9_ ふ	_3_ な	_11_ め	_19_ せ	_18_ き

PART 2

1. Kakimashoo!

1. Murasaki-ga suki desu. むらさきが すき です。 2. Midori-no kooto-ga hoshii desu. みどりの コート が ほしい です。 3. Kimu-san-no seetaa-wa nani-iro desu-ka? キムさんの セーターは なにいろ です か。 4. Chairoi/Chairo-no zubon-ga hoshii desu-ka? ちゃいろい／ちゃいろの ズボンが ほしい です か。 5. O-genki desu-ka? おげんき ですか。

2. Preview the vocabulary and notes for Lesson 64.

LESSON 64

PART 1

1. Read all of the notes for Lesson 64.

2. Learn the new vocabulary.

3. Complete Writing Practice ❷ Study, trace and write.

PART 2

1. Complete the remainder of the Writing Practice.

2. Preview the vocabulary and notes for Lesson 65.

WRITING PRACTICE

❶ **Read and copy the** *katakana*.

1. マ [ma] 2. ヒ [hi] 3. サ [sa] 4. ミ [mi] 5. ム [mu] 6. ハ [ha] 7. ヘ [he] 8. モ [mo] 9. セ [se]
10. ス [su] 11. メ [me] 12. フ [fu]

❷ **Study, trace and write.**

❸ **Kakimashoo!**

1. ゲーム 2. ミス 3. パーマ 4. メモ 5. ハム 6. ミシン 7. ママ 8. モーター 9. デモ
10. トマト 11. マイク 12. ハーモニカ 13. メカニズム 14. バドミントン 15. ペンネーム

❹ **Dekimasu-ka?**

1. アムステルダム 2. ストックホルム 3. ミネアポリス 4. モントリオール 5. メルボルン
6. ローマ 7. ミラノ 8. マニラ 9. マドリッド 10. モスクワ

❺ **More writing practice**

LESSON 65

PART 1

1. Read all of the notes for Lesson 65.

2. Learn the new vocabulary.

PART 2

1. Reading practice

1. キャ [kya] 2. シュ [shu] 3. ミュ [myu] 4. チョ [cho] 5. ニュ [nyu] 6. キョ [kyo] 7. チャ [cha]
8. ジュ [ju] 9. シャ [sha] 10. チュ [chu] 11. ジャ [ja] 12. キュ [kyu] 13. リャ [rya] 14. ヒュ [hyu]
15. ショ [sho] 16. ピュ [pyu]

2. Preview the vocabulary and notes for Lesson 66.

LESSON 66

PART 1

1. Read all of the notes for Lesson 66.

2. Learn the new vocabulary.

3. Complete Writing Practice ❸ Study, trace and write.

PART 2

1. Complete the remainder of the Writing Practice.

2. Preview the vocabulary and notes for Lesson 67.

❶ **Read and copy the** *katakana.*

1. ヤ [ya] 2. ミ [mi] 3. ピ [pi] 4. モ [mo] 5. ユ [yu] 6. メ [me] 7. ニュ [nyu] 8. マ [ma]
9. ジャ [ja] 10. ヨ [yo] 11. ショ [sho] 12. ム [mu]

❷ **Kakimashoo!**

1. ヨガ 2. ユーターン 3. ユーモア 4. ヨット 5. ヤンキー 6. ヨーヨー 7. ユタ 8. タイヤ
9. ユネスコ 10. ヨセミテ 11. ユーコン 12. ユニーク

❸ **Study, trace and write.**

❹ **Kakimashoo!**

1. シャツ (shirt) 2. ジュース (juice) 3. パジャマ (pajama) 4. ニュース (news) 5. バーベキュー
(barbecue) 6. ジャケット (jacket) 7. キャンプ 8. チャーミング 9. シャンプー
10. コンピューター (computer) 11. ビュイック 12. シチュー

❺ **More writing practice**

LESSON 67

PART 1

1. **Read all of the notes for Lesson 67.**
2. **Learn the new vocabulary.**

PART 2

1. **Yomimashoo!** [English translation]

   1. Where will you buy the fish? 2. I bought this interesting magazine at that bookstore. 3. What time does the shoe store open and close? 4. Where is your school? 5. I bought a tomato and lettuce there yesterday. 6. Whose souvenir is it?

2. **Preview the vocabulary and notes for Lesson 68.**

LESSON 68

PART 1

1. **Read all of the notes for Lesson 68.**
2. **Learn the new vocabulary.**
3. **Complete Writing Practice ❸ Study, trace and write.**

PART 2

1. **Complete the remainder of the Writing Practice.**
2. **Preview the vocabulary and notes for Lesson 69.**

WRITING PRACTICE

❶ **Read and copy the** *katakana.*

1. ラ [ra] 2. レ [re] 3. リ [ri] 4. ロ [ro] 5. ラ [ra] 6. ル [ru] 7. レ [re] 8. ロ [ro] 9. ル [ru]
10. リ [ri] 11. レ [re] 12. ラ [ra]

❷ **Kakimashoo!**

1. ホテル (hotel) 2. ゴルフ (golf) 3. レモン (lemon) 4. ラジオ (radio) 5. レストラン (restaurant)
6. カメラ (camera) 7. テレビ (TV) 8. プレゼント (present) 9. アルバイト (part-time job)
10. ミルク (milk) 11. サラダ (salad) 12. オレンジ (orange) 13. スリッパ (slippers) 14. ステレオ
(stereo) 15. ベルト (belt) 16. トイレ (toilet)

❸ **Study, trace and write.**

❹ **Dekimasu-ka?**

1. アイルランド 2. イスラエル 3. レバノン 4. リベリア 5. コロンビア
6. ウクライナ 7. モロッコ 8. イタリア 9. ラオス 10. ペルー 11. フランス
12. マレーシア

❺ **More writing practice**

LESSON 69

PART 1

1. **Read all of the notes for Lesson 69.**
2. **Learn the new vocabulary.**
3. **Yomimashoo!**

   1. Hawai (Hawaii) 2. tawaa (tower) 3. wain (wine) 4. Aiowa (Iowa) 5. waffuru (waffle) 6. Otawa (Ottowa) 7. waishatsu (dress shirt) 8. wanpiisu (dress) 9. Washinton (Washington) 10. waipaa (wiper)

11. wakkusu (wax)   12. Waiomingu (Wyoming)

PART 2

1. **Shitsumon** [sample questions and answers]

    Q. さかなや／やおや／ふくや／パンやは どこに ありますか。

      Sakana-ya/yao-ya/fuku-ya/pan-ya-wa doko-ni arimasu-ka?

      (Where is the fish shop/vegetable shop/clothes store/bakery?)

    A. デパート／えき／スーパー／だいがくの まえ／みぎ／ひだりに あります。

      Depaato/eki/suupaa/daigaku no mae/migi/hidari-ni arimasu.

      (It's in front of/to the right of/to the left of the department store/station/super market/university.)

2. **Preview the vocabulary and notes for Lesson 70.**

LESSON 70

PART 1

1. **Read all of the notes for Lesson 70.**
2. **Learn the new vocabulary.**
3. **Kakimashoo!**

PART 2

1. **Kakimashoo!** [sample answers]

    としょかん／ぎんこう／こうばん／ゆうびんきょくは パンや／だいがく／デパート／こうえんの
まえ／みぎ／ひだりに あります。

    Toshokan/ginkoo/kooban/yuubinkyoku-wa pan-ya/daigaku/depaato /kooen-no mae/migi/hidari-ni arimasu.

    (The library/bank/police box/post office is in front of /right of/left of the bakery/college/department store/park.)

2. **Preview the vocabulary and notes for Lesson 71.**

LESSON 71

PART 1

1. **Read all of the notes for Lesson 71.**
2. **Learn the new vocabulary.**
3. **Can you read it?**

    Moku-yoobi-ni kuruma-de toshokan-ni ikimashita. (On Thursday I went to the library by car.)

PART 2

1. **Yomimashoo!**

Wisukonshin (Wisconsin)	weetaa (waiter)	wookaa (walker)
mirukusheeki (milk shake)	chesu (chess)	aisutii (iced tea)
fasshon (fashion)	firumu (film)	ferii (ferry)
fooku (fork)	Jeshika (Jessica)	kyandii (candy)

2. **Preview the vocabulary and notes for Lesson 72.**

LESSON 72

PART 1

1. **Read all of the notes for Lesson 72.**
2. **Learn the new vocabulary.**
3. **What's wrong?**

    1. がっこうから しんせきの うちを あるいて ごふんぐらい です。 → まで

      Gakkoo-kara shinseki-no uchi-made aruite go-fun gurai desu.

      (From school to my relatives' house, it takes about 5 minutes on foot.)

    2. アトランタから ワシントンまで くるまと なんじかんぐらい ですか。 → で

      Atoranta-kara Washinton-made kuruma-de nan-jikan gurai desu-ka.

      (About how many hours is it from Atlanta to Washington by car?)

    3. えきまで なんマイル です＿。 → か Eki-made nan-mairu desu-ka. (How many miles is it to the station?)

4. **Dekimasu-ka?** (sample answer)

    きのうせんせいとわたしのともだちがえきから くつしたまであるいていきました。 → ぎんこう

    Kinoo sensei-to watashi-no tomodachi-ga eki-kara ginkoo-made aruite ikimashita.

    (Yesterday, the teacher and my friend walked from the station to the bank.)

PART 2
Complete the Vocabulary section of Lesson 73.
DAYS OF THE WEEK
Monday: 月ようび getsu-yoobi, Tuesday: 火ようび ka-yoobi, Wednesday: 水ようび sui-yoobi, Thursday: 木ようび moku-yoobi, Friday: 金ようび kin-yoobi, Saturday: 土ようび do-yoobi, Sunday: 日ようび nichi-yoobi

SCHOOL SUBJECTS
history: れきし rekishi, art: びじゅつ bijutsu, math: すうがく suugaku, Japanese: にほんご nihongo, geography: ちり chiri, P.E.: たいいく taiiku, English: えいご eigo, French: フランスご furansugo, German: ドイツご doitsugo, Spanish: スペインご supeingo

SPORTS
swimming: すいえい suiei, baseball: やきゅう yakyuu, tennis: テニス tenisu, soccer: サッカー sakkaa, sumo: すもう sumoo, judo: じゅうどう juudoo, karate: からて karate, golf : ゴルフ gorufu, ski: スキー sukii, basketball: バスケットボール basukettobooru, football: フットボール futtobooru, volleyball: バレーボール bareebooru

WEATHER
weather: てんき tenki, rain: あめ ame, sunny: はれ hare, snow: ゆき yuki, cloudy: くもり kumori, hot: あつい atsui, cold: さむい samui, warm: あたたかい atatakai, cool: すずしい suzushii, #degrees: #ど #do

MUSIC
music: おんがく ongaku, musical instrument: がっき gakki, piano: ピアノ piano, violin: バイオリン baiorin, guitar: ギター gitaa, drum: ドラム doramu, song: うた uta, sing: うたいます utaimasu

CLOTHING
clothes: ふく fuku, socks: くつした kutsushita, jeans: ジーンズ jiinzu, pants/slacks: ズボン zubon, necktie: ネクタイ nekutai, hat/cap: ぼうし booshi, shirt: シャツ shatsu, sweater: セーター seetaa, pretty: きれい kirei, strange: へん hen, cute: かわいい kawaii, cool/neat: かっこいい kakkoii

COMMUNITY PLACES
store/shop: (お)みせ (o)mise, shoe store: くつや kutsu-ya, meat shop: にくや niku-ya, bakery: パンや pan-ya, fish store: さかなや sakana-ya, bookstore: ほんや hon-ya, vegetable store: やおや yao-ya, park: こうえん kooen, movie theater: えいがかん eigakan, hotel: ホテル hoteru, station: えき eki, school: がっこう gakkoo, department store: デパート depaato, restaurant: レストラン resutoran, bus stop: バスてい basu-tei

COLORS
color: いろ iro, black: くろ(い) kuro(i), brown: ちゃいろ(い) chairo(i), blue: あお(い) ao(i), green: みどり midori, purple: むらさき murasaki, red: あか(い) akai, white: しろ(い) shiro(i), yellow: きいろ(い) kiiro(i)

OTHER WORDS
1. どこ doko 2. わたし watashi 3. わたしの watashi-no 4. どれ dore 5. これ kore 6. ちょっと chotto 7. ここ koko 8. ひと hito 9. だれ dare 10. この kono 11. その sono 12. しつもん shitsumon 13. だれの dare-no 14. いま ima 15. しごと shigoto 16. どう doo 17. でも demo /けど kedo 18. とても totemo 19. いつ itsu 20. きょう kyoo 21. あした ashita 22. はる haru 23. なつ natsu 24. ふゆ fuyu 25. あき aki 26. ともだち tomodachi 27. きのう kinoo 28. まいにち mainichi 29. しゅうまつ shuumatsu 30. いちばん ichi-ban 31. ときどき tokidoki 32. だいじょうぶ daijoobu 33. ぜんぜん zenzen 34. いっしょに issho-ni 35. みたい mitai 36. おとこのひと otoko-no-hito 37. おんなのひと onna-no-hito 38. いくら ikura 39. たくさん takusan 40. いくつ ikutsu 41. まち machi 42. ぐらい gurai

Volume 1 Particle Practice Answer Keys

Particle Practice 1 - (L. 1-8)

2. a) **ne** b) **no** c) **ka** d) **wa, ka**

3. a)   A: Mari-san desu-(**ne**)? [confirmation]
       B: Hai, Mari desu.
       A: Daigaku-sei desu-(**ka**)? [question]
       B: Iie, kookoo-sei desu.

   b)   A: Hajimemashite. Kita-Kookoo-(**no**) Mari desu.
       B: Hajimemashite. Nishi-Chuugakkoo-(**no**) Kenji desu.
         Kita-Kookoo-(**wa**) doko desu-(**ka**)?
       A: Nagoya desu. Kenji-kun-(**wa**) nan-sai desu-(**ka**)?
       B: 14-sai desu.

Particle Practice 2 - (L. 9-19)

2. a) **de, to** b) **mo** c) **to** d) **ga** e) **no** f) **yo** g) **no**

3. a) A: Kono eigo-(**no**) jisho-wa dare-(**no**) desu-(**ka**)?
     B: Chika-san-(**no**) desu-(**yo**). [It is Chika's!]
     A: Aa, soo desu-ka.
  b) A: *Stapler*-wa nihongo-(**de**) nan-(**to**) iimasu-(**ka**)?
     B: Hotchikisu-(**to**) iimasu.
  c) A: Gokyoodai-(**ga**) imasu-ka?
     B: Hai, ani-(**to**) ane-(**ga**) imasu.
     A: Aa, soo desu-ka. Watashi-(**mo**) ani-(**to**) ane-(**ga**) imasu.

Particle Practice 3 - (L. 20-30)

2. a) **no, no** b) **kara, made** c) **ni** d) **no** e) **o** f) **ni**

3. a) A: Asa nan-ji-(**ni**) okimasu-(**ka**)?
     B: 6-ji-(**ni**) okimasu.
  b) A: Kore-wa Taka-kun-(**no**) nooto desu-(**ka**)?
     B: Iie, Toshi-kun-(**no**) desu.
  c) A: Kyoo, arubaito-(**ga**) arimasu.
     B: Aa, soo desu-ka. Nan-ji-(**kara**) desu-ka?
     A: 4-ji-(**kara**) desu.
     B: Nan-ji-(**made**) desu-ka?
     A: 6-ji-(**made**) desu.
  d) A: Sumimasen. Gakkoo-(**no**) denwa bangoo-(**wa**) nan-ban desu-(**ka**)?
     B: Ichi ni san-(**no**) yon go roku nana desu.
  e) A: Nyuusu-(**o**) mimasu-ka?
     B: Iie, anime-(**o**) mimasu.

Particle Practice 4 - (L. 31-41)

2. a) **ni** b) **ni, ni** c) **to, ni** d) **ni, ga** e) **ni** f) **ni** g) **ni**

3. a) A: Moo sugu o-tanjoobi desu-ne.
     B: Hai. 17-sai-(**ni**) narimasu.
     A: Aa, soo desu-ka. O-tanjoobi-(**ni**) nani-(**ga**) hoshii desu-ka?
     B: Eeto, nihongo-no jisho-(**ga**) hoshii desu.
  b) A: Amanda-san, ashita nani-(**o**) shimasu-ka?
     B: Tomodachi-(**to**) kaimono-(**ni**) ikimasu.
     A: Aa, soo desu-ka. Watashi-wa chichi-(**to**) eiga-(**ni**) ikimasu.
     B: Ii desu-ne.
  c) [At a restaurant, two people are deciding what to order.]
     A: Kazuya-kun, nani-(**ni**) shimasu-ka?
     B: Boku-wa yakitori-(**ni**) shimasu.
     A: Jaa, watashi-wa tenpura-(**ni**) shimasu.

Particle Practice 5 - (L. 42-49)

2. a) **ga** b) **ni, o** c) **ni, ni** d) **de, o**
3. a)   A: Mari-san-wa haru-yasumi-(**ni**) nani-(**o**) shimasu-ka?
        B: Sukii-(**ni**) ikimasu.
        A: Hee, ii desu-ne. Doko-(**ni**) ikimasu-ka?
        B: Nagano-(**ni**) ikimasu. Kenji-kun-wa?
        A: Boku-wa arubaito-(**o**) shimasu.
        B: Doko-(**de**) arubaito-(**o**) shimasu-ka?
        A: Resutoran-(**de**) shimasu.
   b)   A: O-tanjoobi-ni nani-(**ga**) hoshii desu-ka?
        B: Sutereo-(**ga**) hoshii desu.
        [Persons A and B are at the stereo section of a department store.]
        A: Dore-(**ga**) ii desu-ka?
        B: Kono chiisai sutereo-(**ga**) ii desu.
   c)   A: Kinoo-(**no**) yoru nani-(**o**) shimashita-ka?
        B: Tomodachi-(**to**) kaimono-(**ni**) ikimashita.
        A: Sorekara, doko-(**ni**) ikimashita-ka?
        B: Resutoran-(**ni**) ikimashita.
        A: Soo desu-ka? Sono resutoran-wa nani-(**ga**) oishii desu-ka?
        B: Tenpura-(**ga**) oishii desu-yo.

Particle Practice 6 - (L. 50-57)

2. a) **wa, to, ga** b) **wa** c) **wa, ga** d) **ga**
3. a)   A: Ashita, konsaato-(**ni**) ikimasen-ka?
        B: Ii desu-ne.
        A: Ongaku-(**wa**) nani-(**ga**) suki desu-ka?
        B: Rokku-(**to**) jazu-(**ga**) suki desu.
        A: Soo desu-ka. Jaa, jazu-(**no**) konsaato-(**ni**) ikimashoo!
        B: Ee, ii desu-ne.
   b)   A: Piano-(**ga**) joozu desu-ne.
        B: Iie, mada heta desu-yo. A-san-(**mo/wa**) piano-(**ga**) dekimasu-ka?
        A: Iie, piano-(**wa**) zenzen dekimasen.
        B: Soo desu-ka. Jaa, gakki-(**wa**) nani-(**ga**) dekimasu-ka?
        A: Gitaa-(**ga**) sukoshi dekimasu.

Particle Practice 7 - (L. 58-66)

2. a) **no, ga** b) **no** c) **ga** d) **o**
3. a)   A: Irasshaimase.
        B: Hanbaagaa-(**o**) 2-tsu-(**to**) sarada-(**o**) 1-tsu kudasai.
        A: Hai. O-nomimono-wa?
        B: Eeto, koora-(**o**) 2-tsu kudasai.
   b)   [Customer B is looking at skirts on display. Clerk A is approaching B.]
        A: Irasshaimase.
        B: Anoo, pinku-(**no**) sukaato-(**ga**) arimasu-ka?
        A: Sumimasen. Arimasen-kedo.
        B: Soo desu-ka. Jaa, midori-(**no**) sukaato-(**ga**) arimasu-ka?
        A: Hai, arimasu.
        B: Jaa, sore-(**o**) kudasai.
   c)   A: Irasshaimase.
        B: Eeto, murasaki-(**no**) saifu-(**ga**) arimasu-ka?
        A: Hai, arimasu
        B: Sore-(**wa**) ikura desu-ka?
        A: 3,000-en desu.
        B: Soo desu-ka. Chotto takai desu-ne.
        A: Kono saifu-(**wa**) doo desu-ka? 1,500-yen desu-yo.
        B: Soo desu-ne. Jaa, kore-(**o**) kudasai.

Particle Practice 8 - (L. 67-73)

2. a) **de, o** b) **wa, wa, ni** c) **ni, ga** d) **ni, no, ni** e) **no, ni, ga** f) **de**

3. a)   A: A, sono shatsu-wa atarashii desu-ne.

        B: Hai, do-yoobi-(**ni**) kaimashita.

        A: Soo desu-ka. Doko-(**de**) kaimashita-ka?

        B: Depaato-(**de**) kaimashita.

   b)   A: Sumimasen. Kono machi-(**ni**) kooen-(**ga**) arimasu-ka?

        B: Hai, arimasu.

        A: Doko-(**ni**) arimasu-ka?

        B: Kita-Chuugakkoo-(**no**) mae-(**ni**) arimasu.

        A: Koko-(**kara**) kooen-(**made**) tooi desu-ka? Chikai desu-ka?

        B: Chotto tooi desu. Basu-(**de**) ikimasu-ka?

        A: Hai. Basu-(**de**) nan-pun gurai desu-ka?

        B: 20-pun gurai desu.

        A: Soo desu-ka. Doomo.

   c)   [Looking at B's family photo]

        A: Kono hito-(**wa**) dare desu-ka?

        B: Haha desu.

        A: Okaasan-(**no**) migi-(**ni**) dare-(**ga**) imasu-ka?

        B: Ani-(**ga**) imasu.

Volume 1 Reading and Writing Practice Answer Keys

Topic: がっこう (School) **Reading and Writing Practice 1 (~ L. 26)**
Hiragana Review (all)
A. Read the following words and put them in order from the lowest grade to the highest grade.
  (c) → (b) → (a) → (d)
B. Write the appropriate word in *hiragana* in the spaces provided.
  1. がっこう、から、まで   2. えいご、じ、から、じ、まで
C. Answer the question below by filling in the blanks in Japanese. Write in *hiragana*.
  1. <u>ちゅうがく</u> 3 <u>ねんせい</u>   2. <u>こうこう</u> 1 <u>ねんせい</u>
D. Read the following passage and answer the questions in English.
  1. Jefferson High School   3. It begins at 8:00 and ends at 3:00.
  2. It is in Washington.   4. He is in the 11th grade (2nd year in high school).
E. Write a similar passage based on your own information. (sample passage)
  Watashi-no gakkoo-wa <u>Sentoraru</u> Kookoo desu.
              (name of your school)
  <u>Sentoraru</u> Kookoo-wa   <u>Atoranta</u> desu.
  (name of your school)   (town/city name)
  Gakkoo-wa <u>8-ji han</u>-kara <u>3-ji 45-fun</u>-made desu.
         (starting time)   (ending time)
  Watashi -wa ima <u>kookoo 1-nen-sei</u> desu.
              (school grade)

> English translation:
> My school is Central High School.
> Central High School is in Atlanta. My school begins at 8:30 and ends at 3:45. I am in the 10th grade.

F. Now write it in *hiragana*. Write loan words in *roomaji*. (sample passage)
  わたしのがっこうは Sentoraru こうこうです。 Sentoraru こうこうは Atoranta です。 がっこうは 8 じはんから 3 じ 45 ふんまでです。 わたしはいまこうこう 1 ねんせいです。

Topic: かぞく (Family) **Reading and Writing Practice 2 (~ L. 26)**
Hiragana Review (all)
A. Find the humble equivalent from the box below and write its letter in the parentheses.
  1. おねえさん   (d)   4. おかあさん (c)
  2. おとうとさん   (f)   5. おにいさん (a)
  3. いもうとさん   (e)   6. おとうさん (b)
B. Write the appropriate word in *hiragana* in the spaces provided.
  ごかぞく、にん、おかあさん、おとうとさん
C. Answer the following questions by filling in the blanks in Japanese. Write in *hiragana*.
  1. いもうとさん   2. めぐみさん   3. しょうがく、ねんせい
D. Read the following passage and answer the questions in English.
  1. five people   3. 19 years old   5. Kenji
  2. Yuka   4. college   6. Kita High School
E. Write a similar passage based on your own information. (sample passage)
  Boku-no kazoku-wa <u>5</u>-nin desu.
         (number of family members)
  <u>Chichi-to haha-to ani-to imooto</u>-ga imasu.
  (List all of your family members using "-to" to connect family terms.)
  <u>Ani</u>-no namae-wa   <u>Maikeru</u> desu.
  (a family member) (name of the family member)
  <u>Ani</u>-wa   <u>19</u>-sai desu.
  (the same family member) (age)
  <u>Daigaku 2-nen-sei desu.</u>
  (some additional information about that family member)

> English translation:
> There are five people in my family. I have a father, mother, older brother, and younger sister. My brother's name is Michael. He is 19 years old. He is in his 2nd year of college.

F. Now write it in *hiragana*. Write loan words in *roomaji*. (sample passage)
  ぼくのかぞくは 5 にんです。 ちちとははとあにといもうとがいます。 あにのなまえは Maikeru です。 あには 19 さいです。 だいがく 2 ねんせいです。

Topic: もちもの **(Possessions)**　　　　　　　　**Reading and Writing Practice 3 (~L. 26)**

Hiragana **Review (all)**

A. What do you find in the following places? Choose the items from the box below and write the letters in the parentheses.

　　1. in a pencil case: (b)(e)(g)

　　2. in a book bag: (a)(c)(d)(f)(h)

B. なにがありますか。You are taking inventory of the office supplies. You found the following items. Complete this list for your Japanese teacher. Fill in the blanks with the appropriate word in *hiragana*.

　　<u>あかい</u> pen　　　　　　<u>くろい</u> <u>えんぴつ</u>　　　　<u>おおきい</u> nooto　　　　<u>あおい</u> hotchikisu

C. Read the following dialogue and answer the questions in English.

　　1. two (or more)　　　　　　　　3. Kaori (person B's) younger brother

　　2. Person B　　　　　　　　　　4. a) It's new. b) It's fast.

D. Write whom the following things belong to. Write the sentence in *roomaji*. Then fill in the blanks with appropriate words in *hiragana*. (Use *roomaji* for the item in #5.)

　　1. Mr. Tanaka's (big): Kono ookii enpitsu-wa Tanaka-san-no desu.

　　　　この <u>おおきい</u> <u>えんぴつ</u>は <u>たなかさんの</u>です。

　　2. Kenji-kun's (blue): Kono aoi kaban-wa Kenji-kun-no desu.

　　　　この <u>あおい</u> <u>かばん</u>は <u>けんじくんの</u>です。

　　3. Akira-kun's (English): Kono eigo-no hon-wa Akira-kun-no desu.

　　　　この <u>えいごの</u> <u>ほん</u>は <u>あきらくんの</u>です。

　　4. Sachiko-san's (old): Kono furui fudebako-wa Sachiko-san-no desu.

　　　　この <u>ふるい</u> <u>ふでばこ</u>は <u>さちこさんの</u>です。

　　5. Mariko-san's (red): Kono akai nooto-wa Mariko-san-no desu.

　　　　この <u>あかい</u> <u>nooto</u> は <u>まりこさんの</u>です。

Topic: スケジュール **（Schedules）**　　　　　　**Reading and Writing Practice 4 (~ L. 40)**

Hiragana **Review (all)**

A. Choose the appropriate English verb from the box below and write its letter in the parentheses.

　　1. おきます (c)　　　　3. たべます (b)　　　　5. します (d)

　　2. ねます　 (e)　　　　4. のみます (a)　　　　6. みます (f)

B. Write the appropriate word in *hiragana* in the spaces provided.

　　1. あさ、に おきます

　　2. から、まで、べんきょう、します

　　3. ひる、に たべます、ごはん、にく、たべます

C. Read the following passage and answer the questions in English.

　　1. at 6:30　　　　　　　　3. rice, fish and eggs　　　　　5. watches TV

　　2. begins at 9:00 and ends at 10:00　　4. works part-time　　　　6. at 11:30

D. Write a similar passage based on your own schedule. (sample passage)

　　Boku-wa asa <u>7-ji</u>-ni <u>okimasu</u>. Nihongo-no jugyoo-wa <u>9-ji 45-fun</u>-kara <u>10-ji 50-pun</u>-made desu.

　　　　　(time)　　(get up)　　　　　　　　　　　(time)　　　　　(time)

　　Hiru, <u>yasai-to niku-to gohan</u>-o <u>tabemasu</u>.

　　　　　(list food items)　　　　　(eat)

　　[If you have a part-time job.]

　　Boku-wa arubaito-ga arimasu. Arubaito-wa <u>4-ji</u>-kara <u>6-ji</u>-made desu.

　　　　　　　　　　　　　　　　　　(time)　　(time)

　　[Write an activity you do in the evening.]

　　Boku-wa yoru <u>9-ji</u>-ni <u>denwa-o shimasu</u>. <u>12-ji han</u>-ni nemasu.

　　　　　(time)　　(activity) + (verb)　　(time)

E. Now write it in *hiragana*. Write loan words in *roomaji*. (sample passage)

ぼくはあさ7じにおきます。にほんごの
じゅぎょうは9じ45ふんから10じ50ぷん
までです。ひる、やさいとにくとごはん
をたべます。ぼくは arubaito があります。
Arubaito は4じから6じまでです。ぼくは
よる9じにでんわをします。12じはんに
ねます。

> English translation:
> I get up at 7:00 in the morning. Japanese class begins at 9:45 and ends at 10:50. For lunch, I eat vegetables, meat and rice. I have a part-time job. I work from 4:00 to 6:00. I make phone calls at 9:00 at night. I go to bed at 12:30.

Topic: たべものとのみもの (Food and Drinks)　　　　**Reading and Writing Practice 5 (~ L. 41)**

Hiragana **Review (all)**

A. Write "T " (*tabemono*) if it is a food and "N " (*nomimono*) if it is a drink.
   1. すきやき (T)　　　　3. すし (T)　　　　5. みず (N)
   2. おちゃ (N)　　　　4. suteeki (T)　　　6. juusu (N)
B. Write the appropriate word in *hiragana* in the spaces provided.
   1. きょう、じ、たべます　　ごはん、さかな、たべます
   2. じ、をのみます、おいしい
C. Complete the following dialogues by filling in the blanks with an appropriate word in *hiragana*.
   1. A: なににしますか　　　B: こうちゃ、にします　　A: にします
   2. B: すこしだけ　　　　　B: けっこうです
D. Read the following passage and answer the questions in English.
   1. bread and egg(s)　　　　3. a vegetable sandwich
   2. orange juice　　　　　　4. go to Pizza House (with his family at 8:00)
E. Write a similar passage based on your own information. (sample passage)
   Watashi-wa asa <u>6-ji 45-fun</u>-ni <u>tabemasu</u>.
   　　　　　　　(time)　　　　　(eat)
   <u>Tamago-to beekon-to bisuketto</u>-o <u>tabemasu</u>.
   　　　(list of foods)　　　　　　(eat)
   <u>Koohii</u>-mo　　<u>nomimasu</u>. Hiru <u>12-ji han</u>-ni <u>supagetii</u>-o <u>tabemasu</u>.
   (name of a drink) (drink)　　　　(time)　　(name of a dish) (will eat)
   Kyoo-no yoru, <u>7-ji</u>-ni <u>tomodachi</u>-to <u>Besuto Tekisasu</u>-ni ikimasu.
   　　　　　　(time)　　(person)　　(name of a restaurant)
   <u>Besuto Tekisasu</u>-no　　<u>buritoo</u>-wa oishii desu.
   (name of a restaurant)　(food item)

> English translation:
> I eat breakfast at 6:45. I eat eggs, bacon and a biscuit. I also drink coffee. I will eat spaghetti at 12:30 for lunch. Tonight I will go to Best Texas at 7:00 with my friends. The burritos at Best Texas are delicious.

F. Now write it in *hiragana*. Write loan words in *roomaji*. (sample passage)

わたしは あさ 6じ 45ふん に たべます。たまごと beekon と bisuketto を たべます。Koohii
も のみます。ひる 12じはんに supagetii を たべます。きょうのよる、7じに ともだちと
Besuto Tekisasu に いきます。Besuto Tekisasu の buritoo は おいしいです。

Topic: たんじょうび (Birthdays)　　　　　　　**Reading and Writing Practice 6 (~ L. 41)**

Hiragana **Review (all)**

A. Read the following dates and put them in order from the earliest date to the latest date.
   (b) → (a) → (d) → (c) → (e)
B. Crossword puzzle: Complete the puzzle in *hiragana* based on the following clues.
   ACROSS　　　　　　　　　　　　　　　DOWN
   1. the 5th (of the month) いつか　　　　a. February にがつ
   2. the 23rd (of the month) にじゅうさんにち　b. "Happy Birthday!" おたんじょうびおめでとう
   3. 20 years old はたち　　　　　　　　c. the 1st (of the month) ついたち
   4. the 24th (of the month) にじゅうよっか　　d. the 20th (of the month) はつか
   5. the 10th (of the month) とおか　　　　e. July しちがつ

C. Answer the question. Write in *hiragana*.

(Answers will vary depending on each student's birthday.)

D. Read the following passage and answer the questions in English.

1. September 5th
2. 13 yrs. old
3. a red bag
4. older brother; 20 yrs. old
5. tomorrow; author's family

E. Write a similar passage based on your information. (sample passage)

Watashi-no tanjoobi-wa <u>shi</u>-gatsu <u>juuyokka</u> desu.
                  (month)   (day)

<u>Juu-go</u>-sai-ni narimasu. Tanjoobi-ni <u>MP3 pureeyaa [MP3 player]</u>-ga hoshii desu.
 (age)   (item)

<u>Otooto</u>-no tanjoobi-wa   <u>roku</u>-gatsu <u>sanjuu-nichi</u> desu. <u>Juu-is</u>-sai-ni narimasu.
(family member: chichi/haha/ani, etc.) (month)   (day)   (age)

F. Now write it in *hiragana*. Write loan words in *roomaji*. (sample passage)

わたしのたんじょうびは しがつ じゅうよっか
です。じゅうごさいになります。たんじょうびに
MP3 pureeyaa が ほしいです。おとうとのたんじょう
びは ろくがつさんじゅうにちです。じゅういっさい
になります。

English translation:
My birthday is April 14th. I will be 15 years old. I want an MP3 player for my birthday. My younger brother's birthday is June 30th. He will be 11 years old.

Topic: やすみの日 **(Leisure Time Activities)**   **Reading and Writing Practice 7 (~ L. 48)**

Hiragana **Review (all)**

A. Choose the appropriate verb from the box below and write its letter on the line.

1. おんがくを <u>f</u>
2. えいがに <u>g</u>
3. ざっしを <u>h</u>
4. かいものを <u>b</u>
5. terebi を <u>c</u>
6. resutoran で <u>a</u>

B. Write the appropriate time word in the boxes in *hiragana*.

あさ		ひる		よる
dawn		noon		sunset

C. Answer the following questions by filling in blanks with an appropriate word in *hiragana*.

1. しんせきのうち
2. えいが、 みます
3. ともだち
4. 5/ごじ

D. Read the following passage and answer the questions in English.

1. Saturday
2. read a magazine
3. to her friend's house
4. listen to music
5. go to bed

E. Write a similar passage based on your own schedule. (sample passge)

Ashita-wa doyoobi desu. Boku-wa asa <u>9-ji han</u>-ni okimasu.
                                       (time)

<u>10-ji</u>-kara <u>11-ji</u>-made <u>uchi</u>-de <u>anime-o mimasu</u>.
(time)   (time)   (place)   (activity) + (verb)

Hiru <u>2-ji</u>-ni <u>gakkoo</u>-ni ikimasu.
   (time)   (place)

Sorekara, <u>tomodachi-to tenisu-o shimasu</u>.
        (activity) + (verb)

Yoru-wa <u>shinseki-no uchi</u>-de <u>paatii-o shimasu</u>.
       (place)   (activity) + (verb)

<u>12-ji han</u>-ni nemasu.
 (time)

English translation:
Tomorrow is Saturday. I will get up at 9:30 in the morning. I will watch anime from 10:00 to 11:00 at home. I will go to school at 2:00 in the afternoon. Then, I will play tennis with a friend. In the evening, we will have a party at my relative's house. I will go to bed at 12:30.

F. Now write it in *hiragana*. Write loan words in *roomaji*. (sample passage)

あしたは どようびです。ぼくは あさ 9じはんに おきます。10じ から 11じ まで うち
で animeを みます。ひる 2じに がっこうに いきます。それから、ともだちと tenisu を
します。よるは しんせきの うちで paatii を します。12じはんに ねます。

Hiragana **Review (all)**

A. Read the following days of the week put them in order by numbering them #1 ~ #7.

　<u>#3</u> 火よう日　　　　<u>#7</u> 土よう日　　　　　<u>#6</u> 金よう日　　　　　<u>#1</u> 日よう日

　<u>#4</u> 水よう日　　　　<u>#2</u> 月よう日　　　　　<u>#5</u> 木よう日

B. Below is your family tree. Using the words in the box on the right, label your family members.

　(a) ちち　　　(b) はは　　　(c) あに　　　(d) あね　　　(e) おとうと　　　(f) いもうと

C. Answer the question below by filling in the blanks with an appropriate word in *hiragana*.

　1. いきました　　　　　3. かいもの、しました　　　5. しました

　2. えいが、みました　　4. よみました

D. Read the following passage and answer the questions in English.

　1. his family

　2. went fishing in the river (with his younger brother)

　3. went hiking in the mountains (with his father and older sister)

　4. on Friday

　5. very fun

　6. to go camping again (with his friends)

E. Write a similar passage based on your own information. (sample passage)

　Yasumi-ni <u>tomodachi</u>-to　　　<u>Maiami</u>-ni ikimashita. <u>Suiyoobi</u>-ni

　　(family member/person)　　(some place)　　　(day of the week)

　<u>biichi</u>-ni ikimashita.　<u>Kinyoobi</u>-ni <u>kii raimu pai [key lime pie]</u>-o tabemashita.

　(activity) + (verb)　(another day of the week)　(another activity) + (verb)

　<u>Doyoobi</u>-ni　　<u>Maiami Dorufinzu [Miami Dolphins]</u>-no geemu-o mimashita.

　(another day of the week)　　　(another activity) + (verb)

F. Now write it in *hiragana*. Write loan words in *roomaji*. (sample passage)

　やすみにともだちと Maiami にいきました。

　すいようびに biichi にいきました。

　きんようびに kii raimu pai を たべました。

　どようびに Maiami Dorufinzu の geemu を みました。

> English translation:
> For vacation, I went to Miami with my friends. On Wednesday, we went to the beach. On Friday, we ate key lime pie. On Saturday, we went to a Miami Dolphins game.

Katakana **Review (~ ゾ *zo*)**

A. Write the corresponding *katakana* on the line.

　1. か <u>カ</u>　　　　2. ご <u>ゴ</u>　　　　3. う <u>ウ</u>　　　　4. き <u>キ</u>

B. Read the following *katakana* words and choose their English equivalents from the box below.

　1. (h)　2. (c)　3. (f)　4. (d)　5. (i)　6. (e)　7. (b)　8. (j)　9. (a)　10. (g)

C. Complete the following sentences by writing the corresponding *katakana* above the *roomaji* and the appropriate word in *hiragana* on the additional lines.

　1. サッカー、(だい)すき　　　　　　3. サイクリング、しました

　2. スキー、じょうず　　　　　　　　4. ホッケー、できません

D. Read the following passage and answer the questions in English.

　1. soccer　　　　　　3. not at all　　　　　5. at school

　2. not really　　　　4. for 2 hours　　　　6. a friend/friends

E. Write a similar passage about yourself. (sample passage)

　Supootsu-wa <u>tenisu</u>-ga ichiban suki desu.

　　　(favorite sport)

　<u>Bareebooru</u>-mo shimasu.

　(another sport you play)

　<u>Yakyuu</u>-wa zenzen dekimasen-kedo, mimasu.

　(another sport you don't play but watch)

　<u>Kinyoobi</u>-ni, <u>uchi</u>-de <u>basukettobooru</u>-o shimashita.

　(time word)　(place)　(a sport you played)

> English translation:
> As for sports, I like tennis the best. I also play volleyball. I cannot play baseball at all, but I watch it. On Friday, I played basketball at home.

F. Now write it in *hiragana*. Write loan words in *roomaji*. (sample passage)

Supootsu は tenisu が いちばん すき です。Bareebooru も します。やきゅうは ぜんぜん できません けど、みます。きんようびに うちで basukettobooru を しました。

Topic: たべものとのみもの (Food and Drinks)   Reading and Writing Practice 10 (~ L. 60)

Katakana Review (~ ノ no、 ン n)

A. Choose the corresponding picture for each word below, and write its letter in the parentheses.
   1. (b) 2. (f) 3. (h) 4. (c) 5. (a) 6. (e) 7. (d) 8. (g) 9. (i)

B. Complete the following sentences by writing the corresponding *katakana* above the *roomaji* and the appropriate word in *hiragana* on the additional lines.
   1. おいしい、クッキー   3. ココア、おきまり、ココア、コーヒー、ケーキ
   2. サンドイッチ

C. Read the following passage and complete the chart below in English. Masako is trying to watch what she eats. She is talking about her daily diet with her nutritionist.
   Based on the passage, complete this chart with the food and drinks she usually has.

Breakfast	Lunch	Dinner
toast	spaghetti	chicken salad
egg(s)	cheese cake	tacos
tomato juice	iced coffee	ice cream

D. Write a similar passage about yourself. (sample passage)
   <u>Hiru,</u>   <u>chiizu-</u>to   <u>pasuta</u>-o tabemasu.
   (time of day) (name of a food) (name of a food)
   Sorekara, <u>sooda</u>-o nomimasu. Dezaato-ni, <u>kukkii</u>-o tabemasu.
       (name of a drink)   (name of a dessert)

English translation: At noon, I eat cheese and pasta. And I drink soda. For dessert, I eat cookies.

E. Now write it in *hiragana*. Write in *katakana* where appropriate. (sample passage)
   ひる、チーズとパ(pa)スタを たべます。それから、ソーダを のみます。デザートに クッキーを たべます。

Topic: ふく (Clothing)   Reading and Writing Practice 11 (~ L. 64)

Katakana Review (~ モ mo)

A. Match these accessories and clothing items with their corresponding pictures and *katakana* from the box below. Write the letter and the number in the parentheses.
   ❶ (c, 5)   ❷ (d, 1)   ❸ (e, 2)   ❹ (a, 4)   ❺ (b, 3)

B. Crossword Puzzle: Complete the puzzle in *katakana* based on the following clues.

Across
   1. earring イヤリング
   2. necklace ネックレス
   3. sneakers スニーカー
   4. skirt スカート
   5. hiking boots ハイキングブーツ

Down
   a. necktie ネクタイ
   b. one piece ワンピース
   c. suit スーツ
   d. vest ベスト
   e. cardigan カーディガン

C. Read the following passage and answer the questions in English.
   1. Jeff's mom's   3. a) Jeff: cute pajamas   4. Mom's birthday party
   2. went shopping   b) Dad: an expensive handbag   5. chocolate chip ice cream cake
                             c) sister: pretty accessories

D. Write a similar passage about your own shopping spree. (sample passage)
   <u>Ka-yoobi</u>-ni <u>An-san</u>-to kaimono-ni ikimashita.
   (day of the week) (person)
   <u>Depaato</u>-ni ikimashita. <u>An-san</u>-wa <u>aoi</u> <u>zubon</u>-o
    (place)   (person) (adjective) (item of clothing)
   kaimashita. Watashi-wa <u>midori-no</u> <u>sukaato</u>-o kaimashita.
               (adjective) (item of clothing)

English translation:
On Tuesday I went shopping with Ann. We went to the department store. Ann bought a pair of blue pants. I bought a green skirt.

E. Now write it in *hiragana*. Write in *katakana* where appropriate. (sample passage)

かようびにアンさんとかいものにいきました。デパートにいきました。アンさんは
あおいズボンをかいました。わたしはみどりのスカートをかいました。

Topic: まち (Community)   **Reading and Writing Practice 12 (~ L. 68)**

Katakana Review (~ ロ ro)

A. Read the lists of things to buy and choose a store to go to from the box below.

  1. c   2. a   3. h   4. f

B. Read the following statements and guess the location of where each activity takes place. Choose the answer from the box below and write it in *katakana* on the line.

  1. スケートリンク   2. テニスコート   3. パンや   4. スイミングプール

C. Complete the following sentences by writing the corresponding *katakana* above the *roomaji* and the appropriate word in *hiragana* on the additional lines.

  1. ホテル 、 あります   2. レストラン、 たべます   3. バス、 ちかい

D. Read the following passage and answer the questions in English.

  1. small   3. a bakery   5. blueberry muffins

  2. one   4. yes

E. Write a similar passage about your own town. (sample passage)

Watashi-no machi-wa <u>shizuka</u> desu.
          (adjective to describe your town)
<u>Eigakan</u>-ga   <u>futatsu</u> arimasu.   <u>Kooen</u>-mo arimasu.
(store/building #1) (number)   (store/building #2)
<u>Kooen</u>-wa   <u>gakkoo</u>-kara chikai desu.
(store/building #2)   (a place such as your house, school, etc.)
Yoku, sono <u>kooen</u>-ni ikimasu.
        (store/building #2)
Soko-de, <u>tomodachi-to sakkaa-o shimasu.</u>
         (an activity you do there)

> English translation:
> My town is quiet. There are two movie theaters. There is also a park. The park is near my school. I often go to that park. I play soccer with my friends there.

F. Now write it in *hiragana*. Write in *katakana* where appropriate. (sample passage)

わたしの まちは しずか です。えいがかんが ふたつ あります。こうえんも あります。
こうえんは がっこう から ちかい です。よく、その こうえんに いきます。そこで、
ともだちと サッカーを します。

Topic: りょこう (Travel)   **Reading and Writing Practice 13 (~ L. 71)**

Katakana Review (all)

A. Match the following names of the countries to their location on the map. Choose from (a) through (h), and write the letter in the parentheses.

  1. (g) 2. (d) 3. (f) 4. (h) 5. (e) 6. (c) 7. (b) 8. (a)

B. Write the following names of the cities in *katakana*.

  1. ホノルル   3. ニューヨーク   5. シアトル   7. ワシントン, D.C.

  2. アトランタ   4. オーランド   6. ラスベガス   8. サンフランシスコ

C. Complete the following sentences by writing the corresponding *katakana* above the *roomaji* and the appropriate word in *hiragana* on the additional lines.

  1. ねん、 トロント、 フランスご   3. なつ、 シンガポール、 ペンパル、 います

  2. はるやすみ、 ごかぞく、 フロリダ

D. Read the following passage and answer the questions in English.

  1. Thanksgiving   4. 22   7. skate and eat Chicago pizza

  2. Detroit   5. Chicago

  3. her family   6. her older sister and her family

E. Write a similar passage about yourself. (sample passage)
Boku-wa <u>fuyu-yasumi</u>-ni <u>tomodachi</u>-to <u>Nyuu Yooku</u>-ni
    (event/special occasion) (person)   (name of the place)
ikimashita. <u>Basu</u>-de ikimashita.
    (transportation)
<u>Nyuu Yooku</u>-de <u>kaimono</u>-o shimashita. <u>Nyuu Yooku</u>-wa
  (the place)   (an activity you did there)   (the place)
<u>totemo samui</u> desu. Tsugi-wa <u>Tekisasu</u>-ni ikimasu.
(adjective to describe the place)(another place)
<u>Ookii suteeki</u>-o tabemasu.
(an activity you will do there)

English translation:
I went to New York with my friends during winter break. We went by bus. In New York, we shopped. New York is very cold. Next time, I will go to Texas. I will eat a big steak.

.F. Now write it in *hiragana*. Write in *katakana* where appropriate. (sample passage)
ぼくは ふゆやすみに ともだちと ニューヨークに いきました。バスで いきました。ニューヨークで かいものを しました。ニューヨークは とても さむい です。つぎは テキサスに いきます。おおきい ステーキを たべます。

Topic: おんがく (Music)   **Reading and Writing Practice 14 (~ L. 71)**

Katakana Review (all)
A. Match the person with the instrument s/he can play. Write the letter in the parentheses.
1. (e) 2. (d) 3. (a) 4. (b) 5. (c)
B. Crossword Puzzle: Complete the puzzle in *katakana* based on the following clues.

Across
1. heavy metal ヘビーメタル
2. salsa サルサ
3. French horn フレンチホルン
4. country カントリー
5. rock-n-roll ロックンロール

Down
a. soundtrack サウンドトラック
b. cymbals シンバル
c. big band ビッグバンド
d. flute フルート
e. tambourine タンバリン

C. Read the following passage and answer the questions in English.
1. big drum, new piano, old bass guitar, clarinet
2. a bass guitar
3. heavy metal
4. the clarinet
5. classical music

D. Write a similar passage about yourself. (sample passage)
Boku-wa yoku ongaku-o kikimasu.
Ongaku-wa <u>jazu</u>-ga ichiban suki desu. <u>Rokku</u>-mo suki desu.
    (music genre)   (another music genre)
[If you go to concerts] <u>Jazu</u>-no konsaato-ni ikimasu.
          (music genre)
[If you play some musical instrument] Gakki-wa <u>gitaa</u>-ga dekimasu-kedo, anmari joozu ja nai desu.
                        (instrument)

English translation:
I often listen to music. I like jazz the best. I also like rock. I go to jazz concerts. I can play the guitar, but I'm not very good at it.

E. Now write it in *hiragana*. Write in *katakana* where appropriate. (sample passage)
ぼくは よく おんがくを ききます。おんがくは ジャズが いちばん すき です。ロックも すき です。ジャズの コンサートに いきます。がっきは ギターが できますけど、あんまり じょうず じゃない です。

Culture Matrix - Volume 1 (L. 1~73)

L.	Topics Covered in Lesson	Culture Notes in Lesson	*Irasshai* Website www.gpb.org/irasshai - for students Student Notebook (SN) Online Resources (OR) Use various search engines to look up the following topics	i-*irasshai* Culture Topics and Activities Look under "Guidebook (Index)" and click on the following key words
1	Introductions and Greetings	- Japanese names - *Meishi*	(SN) Choose Your Lesson: Activities (OR) Japanese names Japanese name cards	- English – Japanese dictionary - etiquette – greetings - nameplate - *hyoosatsu* - welcome
2	Greetings; Asking for and Confirming Names	- *Sensei* - *Ohayoo ~ ohayoo gozaimasu.*	(SN) Choose Your Lesson: Activities (OR) Japanese greetings	- etiquette – greetings - greetings (activity) - school greetings
3	Apologizing	- Bowing - Body contact - Pointing to oneself	(SN) Writing Practice Sheet: *hiragana a-o* Choose Your Lesson: Activities (OR) Japanese bowing Japanese body language	- etiquette – greetings
4	Specify Grade in School; Numbers 1-10	- School levels in Japan	(SN) Choose Your Lesson: Activities (OR) Education in Japan Japanese numbers	- education – overview - school - school offices - textbook – how to open one and read it
5	Asking / Stating School Affiliation and Grade		(SN) Choose Your Lesson: Activities	
6	Expressing (Lack of) Understanding	- Seniority within organizations - Japanese way of counting	(SN) Choose Your Lesson: Activities Writing Practice Sheet: *hiragana* ka-ko ga-go (OR) Seniority in Japan Japanese way of counting	
7	Asking about and Stating Age; Numbers 1-99	- *Shichi-Go-San* - *Seijin-shiki*	(SN) Choose Your Lesson: Activities (OR) *Shichi-go-san* *Seijin-shiki* Japanese holidays	
8	Stating School or Work Affiliation	- Affiliations	(SN) Choose Your Lesson: Activities (OR) Japanese affiliations and social hierarchy	
9	Asking about and Identifying Objects	- Japanese writing supplies - English loan words in modern Japanese	(SN) Choose Your Lesson: Activities Writing Practice Sheet: *hiragana* sa-so za-zo (OR) Japanese school / office supplies Japanese loan words	- *gairaigo* (activity)

L.	Topics Covered in Lesson	Culture Notes in Lesson	Irasshai Website / Online Resources	i-irasshai
10	Asking / Telling Object Names in Japanese/English		(SN) Choose Your Lesson: Activities	- cat - *manekineko* - cow -*akabeko* - monk doll – *daruma* - paper folding – *origami* - stamp - *hanko*
11	Asking Permission to Use Objects; Appreciation	- Granting a request - Refusing a request	(SN) Choose Your Lesson: Activities (OR) *Doomo arigatoo gozaimasu*	
12	Asking about / Identifying Objects (Colors)		(SN) Choose Your Lesson: Activities Writing Practice Sheet: *hiragana* ta-to da-do (OR) Colors in Japanese	
13	Expressing Approval / Disapproval	- Discipline in Japanese schools - School uniforms - Popularity of comics (*manga*)	(SN) Choose Your Lesson: Activities (OR) Japanese school discipline Japanese school uniforms Japanese *manga*	- comic books – *manga* - duckboard - locker (quiz) - school shoes – changing (activity) - uniforms (activity)
14	Asking a Favor; Taking Leave (Informal)		(SN) Choose Your Lesson: Activities What would you say? Writing Practice Sheet: *hiragana* small tsu	
15	Identifying Family Members	- Honorific and humble forms - Family relationship terms	(SN) Choose Your Lesson: Activities (OR) Japanese honorifics Japanese family titles	
16	Identifying Family Members	- Family relationship terms - Remember that when you are talking about ~, use the honorific / humble form	(SN) Choose Your Lesson: Activities Writing Practice Sheets: *hiragana* na-no (OR) Japanese honorifics Japanese family titles	
17	Identifying Family Members (by Name); Review		(SN) Choose Your Lesson: Activities	
18	Asking about / Stating Number of Family Members		(SN) Choose Your Lesson: Activities	
19	Addressing Family Members; Review	- Addressing older and younger siblings - *Mama* and *papa*	(SN) Choose Your Lesson: Activities Writing Practice Sheet: *hiragana* ha-ho ba-bo pa-po (OR) Addressing Japanese siblings Japanese *mama* and *papa*	
20	Asking about and Expressing Possession	- *Katei kyooshi* (tutor)	(SN) Choose Your Lesson: Activities	

L.	Topics Covered in Lesson	Culture Notes in Lesson	Irasshai Website / Online Resources	i-irasshai
21	Asking about / Telling the Location and Size of Objects		(SN) Choose Your Lesson: Activities Writing Practice Sheet: *hiragana* ma-mo	
22	Understanding Teachers' Basic Commands; Review	- Polite responses when one does not have what is asked for - *Juku* ("cram schools")	(SN) Choose Your Lesson: Activities (OR) *Juku* Cram schools	- after school activities and field day - volleyball
23	Using the Telephone	- Telephones and *keitai denwa* (cellular phones) - Telephone etiquette	(SN) Choose Your Lesson: Activities What would you say? Writing Practice Sheet: *hiragana* ya, yu, yo wa, wo (OR) Japanese telephones *Keitai denwa* Japanese telephone etiquette	- telephone (activity) - telephone directories - telephone numbers (activity)
24	Asking and Telling Time (Hours and Half Hours)		(SN) Choose Your Lesson: Activities Writing Practice Sheet: *hiragana* small ya, yu, yo	- time zones (activity)
25	Telling Time; Review	- The importance of being on time	(SN) Choose Your Lesson: Activities (OR) Being on time in Japan	etiquette - time
26	Telling What Time Activities Begin and End		(SN) Choose Your Lesson: Acti... Writing Practice ...	
27	Telling What Time Activities Take Place		(SN) Choose Your Lesson: Activities	- greetings (activity)
28	Commenting on Schedules; Review		(SN) Choose Your Lesson: Activities	
29	Telling the Foods and Beverages One Consumes	- The Japanese diet	(SN) Choose Your Lesson: Activities (OR) Japanese diet Japanese food	- bakery (5) - fish market (7) - coffee (4) - tea (8)
30	Identifying Japanese Foods	- *Kissaten* - Japanese breakfast - Japanese dishes	(SN) Choose Your Lesson: Activities (OR) *Kissaten* Japanese breakfast Japanese dishes	- bakery (5) - fish market (7) - coffee (4) - tea (8) - etiquette – sushi - fruit (2) - grocery shopping - noodles (3) - rice cooker - soy sauce - sushi (3) - tempura - toaster and breakfast - *udon* - vegetables (3)

L.	Topics Covered in Lesson	Culture Notes in Lesson	Irasshai Website / Online Resources	i-irasshai
31	Following Proper Mealtime Etiquette	- Politely refusing food and drink offers - *Itadakimasu.* - *Gochisoosama deshita.* - Chopsticks - Holding chopsticks	(SN) Choose Your Lesson: Activities (OR) *Itadakimasu* *Gochisoosama deshita* Japanese chopsticks How to hold Japanese chopsticks	- chopsticks (2) - etiquette – cleaning up after meals
32	Ordering Food in a Restaurant	- Tipping - No refills on coffee - *Oshibori* - Refusal gesture	(SN) Choose Your Lesson: Activities (OR) Tipping in Japan Coffee refills in Japan *Oshibori* Japanese refusal hand gesture	- appetizer ordering (activity) - curtains – *noren* (restaurant) - moist towel (quiz) - noodle restaurant – menu item - pay cashier (activity) - restaurant phrases (activity) - sushi ordering (activity) - tipping (quiz) - wait staff - welcome
33	Rules of Etiquette for Using Chopsticks; Review	- Chopsticks etiquette - Importance of food preparation and presentation - Use of many small plates and bowls - Plastic food samples	(SN) Choose Your Lesson: Activities What would you say? (OR) Japanese chopstick etiquette Japanese food preparation Japanese dinner Japanese plastic food samples	- chopsticks (2) - food (2) - sashimi – how to eat (video)
34	Stating the Date; Asking / Telling When Birthdays Are		(SN) Choose Your Lesson: Activities (OR) Japanese birthdays	
35	Asking for and Stating the Date		(SN) Choose Your Lesson: Activities (OR) Japanese calendar / dates	
36	Understanding the Origin and Use of *Kanji*	- Blood type and personality - An observation on culture	(SN) Choose Your Lesson: Activities (OR) Japanese blood types Japanese *kanji* history / origin	- population, crowds and blood types
37	Asking / Telling about When Holidays / Events Occur	- *Kurisumasu* (Christmas) - *O-shoogatsu* (New Year's) - *Setsubun* - *Hina-matsuri* (Doll Festival) - *Kodomo-no-hi* (Children's Day) - *Tanabata* (the Star Festival) - *O-bon* (the Festival of Souls) - Japanese national holidays	(SN) Choose Your Lesson: Activities (OR) Japanese Christmas *Kurisumasu* Japanese New Year *Setsubun* *Hinamatsuri* *Kodomonohi* *Tanabata* *Obon* *Taiku no hi* / Japanese Sports Day Japanese national holidays	- Children's Day – *kabuto* decoration - Doll Festival (*hina matsuri*) and Children's Day - dolls (quiz) - pond

L.	Topics Covered in Lesson	Culture Notes in Lesson	Irasshai Website / Online Resources	i-irasshai
38	Asking about / Expressing Wants		(SN) Choose Your Lesson: Activities	
39	Review		(SN) Choose Your Lesson: Activities	
40	Asking about / Stating Holiday / Leisure-Time Activities		(SN) Choose Your Lesson: Activities (OR) Japanese leisure time	
41	Review		(SN) Choose Your Lesson: Activities What would you say?	
42	Japanese New Year's	- O-shoogatsu (Japanese New Year's) - Greetings - Nengajoo (New Year's cards) - O-sechi ryoori (New Year's cuisine) - O-mochi (rice cakes) - Activities	(SN) Nengajoo Project Gallery (OR) Japanese New Year Japanese New Year greetings Osechi Omochi	- big bell (video) - New Year celebration – oshoogatsu - shimenawa
43	Visiting a Japanese Home	- Slippers - Sitting on the floor - Giving the host a gift - Calling the host from genkan	(OR) Japanese slippers Sitting on the floor in Japan Gift giving in Japan Gomen kudasai	When Visiting Japanese Homes: - etiquette – gift - etiquette – sitting - etiquette – time - gift (quiz) - house – removing shoes (activity) - sitting (activity) - Western-style room (quiz) Traditional Japanese Rooms: - alcove (2) - Buddhist altar - chair – zaisu - curtains – noren (house) - cushion – zabuton - fusuma doors - scrolls – kakejiku - table (2) - tatami (5) - wood carving - ranma Parts of a Japanese House - doors (3) - gate - mon - heating and air conditioning - house tiles – kawara - house walls – kabe - housing (2) - solar power – hot water

L.	Topics Covered in Lesson	Culture Notes in Lesson	Irasshai Website / Online Resources	i-irasshai
44	Visiting a Japanese Home	- Japanese bathing etiquette - Restroom etiquette - Being a guest in a Japanese home	(OR) Japanese bathing etiquette Japanese bathroom etiquette Visiting a Japanese house	Japanese Bathrooms: - baths (6) - etiquette – bathtub - hair care - hot springs (2) - toilets - wash bowl Japanese Bedrooms: - bed (2) - hanger - pillow Japanese Kitchens / Cleaning: - gas stove - house cleaning - kitchen - laundry - microwave – *denshi renji* and *oobun renji* - oven - recycling items - refrigerator - rice cooker - sink - thermos – *dendoo jaa potto* - tissue box (quiz) - toaster and breakfast - washing machine
45	Talking about Past Activities			
46	Talking about Daily Activities		(OR) Japanese daily activities Japanese music Japanese television Japanese free time and hobbies Japanese newspapers	- e-mail (activity) - library - magazines (quiz) - movies - music – *hoogaku* and *yoogaku* - newspapers - novels - *pachinko* - radio / stereo - television - *terebi* - VCR

L.	Topics Covered in Lesson	Culture Notes in Lesson	Irasshai Website / Online Resources	i-irasshai
47	Telling Where Actions Occur			
48	Days of the Week			
49	Review Days and Dates		(OR) Japanese days of the week (SN) Choose Your Lesson: Activities What would you say?	
50	School Subjects		(SN) *Hiragana* Chart *Katakana* Chart (OR) Japanese school subjects	- art class - biology lab - chemistry class - education – overview - English class (2) - geology classroom - gymnasium - home economics class - music class - school - school schedule - teachers
51	Talking about School Subjects		(SN) Choose Your Lesson: Activities (OR) Japanese school life	- after school activities and field day – *undookai* - blackboard - broadcasting room - calligraphy - computer lab - duckboard - etiquette room - etiquette - greetings - field trip - school - graduating class gifts - infirmary - language lab - library - locker (quiz) - school cleaning (video) - school greetings - school lunch (video) - school offices - school seating (quiz) - school shoes – changing (activity) - school sink - school transportation - shoe cabinet

L.	Topics Covered in Lesson	Culture Notes in Lesson	*Irasshai* Website / Online Resources	*i-irasshai*
52	Asking about and Expressing Likes and Dislikes	- Japanese adults not expressing their dislikes	(SN) Choose Your Lesson: Activities Writing Practice Sheet: *katakana* a-o	
53	Asking about and Stating What One Likes Best	- *Yakyuu* (baseball)	(SN) Choose Your Lesson: Activities (OR) Japanese baseball Japanese high school baseball	
54	Invitations and Preferences	- Declining an invitation	(SN) Choose Your Lesson: Activities Writing Practice Sheet: *katakana* ka-ko ga-go	
55	Asking about and Stating Ability	- Japanese traditional sports *Juudoo* *Karate* *Kendoo* *Sumoo*	(SN) Choose Your Lesson: Activities (OR) Japanese traditional sports Judo Karate Kendo Sumo	- sword fighting - *kendo*
56	Compliments	- Compliments - Karaoke	(SN) Choose Your Lesson: Activities Writing Practice Sheet: *katakana* sa-so (OR) Japanese compliments Japanese karaoke	- karaoke machine
57	Commenting on Music	- Japanese traditional musical instruments *Koto* *Shamisen* *Shakuhachi* *Taiko*	(SN) Choose Your Lesson: Activities What would you say? (OR) Japanese traditional musical instruments *Koto* *Shamisen* *Shakuhachi* *Taiko*	
58	Weather	- Weather comments as greetings	(SN) Choose Your Lesson: Activities Writing Practice Sheet: *katakana* ta-to (OR) Climate in Japan Japanese weather as greeting	
59	Temperature	- Celsius ~ Fahrenheit - Conversion between Celsius and Fahrenheit	(SN) Choose Your Lesson: Activities (OR) Climate in Japan Converting temperature in Japan	- thermometer – Fahrenheit vs. Celsius (activity)
				- special education - swimming - textbook – how to open one and read it (activity) - uniforms (activity) - volleyball

L.	Topics Covered in Lesson	Culture Notes in Lesson	Irasshai Website / Online Resources	i-irasshai

60	Weather	- Seasonal events
		  hanami
		  tsuyu
		  taifuu
		  tsukimi
			(SN) Choose Your Lesson: Activities
			Writing Practice Sheets: *katakana* na-no
			(OR) Japanese seasonal events
			Japanese cherry blossoms
			Hanami
			Japanese rainy season
			Japanese *taifuu*
			Tsukimi
				- bamboo curtains – wind bells
				- flowers
				- kimono – *yukata*
				- maple tree

61	Clothing		(SN) Choose Your Lesson: Activities (OR) Japanese clothing Traditional Japanese clothing	- kimono - kimono – *yukata* - uniforms (activity)
62	Clothing		(SN) Choose Your Lesson: Activities Writing Practice Sheet: *katakana* ha-ho (OR) Japanese fashion	- *mino and zoori* (quiz)
63	Describing Objects	- *O-genki desu-ka?* - *Irasshaimase.*	(SN) Choose Your Lesson: Activities (OR) Japanese color adjectives *O-genki desu-ka* *Irasshaimase*	
64	Prices	- Japanese money	(SN) Choose Your Lesson: Activities Writing Practice Sheet: *katakana* ma-mo (OR) Japanese money Japanese prices	- bullet train – buy tickets (activity) - commuter train – buy tickets (activity) - fish market – buy shrimp (activity) - fruit stand – buy fruit (activity) - money - pay cashier (activity) - stamp vending machine (activity) - vegetable market – buy bamboo shoots (activity)
65	Commenting on Prices	- Japanese department stores	(SN) Choose Your Lesson: Activities (OR) Japanese department stores	
66	Asking for and Stating Quantities		(SN) Choose Your Lesson: Activities What would you say? Writing Practice Sheet: *katakana* ya, yu, yo wa, wo	
67	Community	- Specialty shops - *O-miyage* (souvenir gifts)	(SN) Choose Your Lesson: Activities (OR) Japanese *o-miyage* / souvenirs	- fish market – buy shrimp (activity) - fruit stand – buy fruit (activity) - vegetable market – buy bamboo shoots (activity)

L.	Topics Covered in Lesson	Culture Notes in Lesson	Irasshai Website / Online Resources	i-Irasshai
68	Community	- Getting around in Japan - Some *kanji* commonly seen in a Japanese community	(SN) Choose Your Lesson: Activities Writing Practice Sheet: *katakana* ra-ro (OR) Getting around in Japan Japanese station *kanji*	- public transportation - transportation
69	Spatial Relationships	- Animal sounds	(SN) Choose Your Lesson: Activities (OR) Japanese animal sounds	
70	More Places and Spatial Relationships	- Postal symbol and mailboxes - Japanese police	(SN) Choose Your Lesson: Activities Writing Practice Sheet: *katakana wa, wo* (OR) Japanese mailboxes / post boxes Japanese postal symbol Japanese police boxes	- airmail (quiz) - crime - mail (3) - mailbox - patrol officers - police (3) - postal service
71	Transportation		(SN) Choose Your Lesson: Activities (OR) Transportation in Japan Japanese trains Japanese train stations Buses in Japan Japanese bicycles Japanese taxis	- automobile - bicycles - bullet train - *shinkansen* - kiosk - public transportation - taxi - timetable - trains (5) - transportation
72	How Long it Takes to Get to a Place	- *Chikatetsu*	(SN) Choose Your Lesson: Activities (OR) Japanese subways	
73	Review		(SN) Choose Your Lesson: Activities What would you say?	

Volume 2
Suggested Activities

General Suggested Activities
Additional Suggested Classroom Activities

General Suggested Activities

A. When beginning a new lesson:

1. Make sure that your students know the topic and objectives for the lesson. They are listed at the beginning of each lesson.

    Ex.)   SEMESTER 1
           TOPIC: Introductions and greetings

    ## LESSON 1

    ### OBJECTIVES

    At the end of this lesson you will be able to:
    - ☑ Introduce yourself
    - ☑ Greet someone for the first time
    - ☑ Address people by name
    - ☑ Pronounce common Japanese names

2. Have your students make vocabulary/expression cards for the lesson – Write the lesson number in a corner so that they will know in which lesson it appears. On one side, write the vocabulary word, its part of speech, and its usage in a sentence. On the other side, write the English equivalents, as in the example below. Students can use the cards at any time they want to review the vocabulary words. They can also use them to test each other in pairs or in small groups.

    Ex.)   **Front**   **Back**

L1 **desu** (verb) (Ex.) Ken desu.	L1 **am, are, is** (verb) (Ex.) I am Ken.

3. Distribute the **video checksheet** for the lesson to your students before you show the video lesson. Allow them to stop the video or watch it again as necessary. Have your students go over the answers to the video checksheets in class.

4. Make sure that your students read all the notes such as **VOCABULARY NOTES, KEY GRAMMAR POINTS,** and **CULTURE NOTES**.

5. Make sure that your students do the ***INTERACTIVE ACTIVITIES***, one of the most valuable parts of the lesson.

6. Check or have your students check answers to workbook assignments with the **Workbook Assignment Answer Keys**, included in this guide.

7. Prior to the **A.I. (Audio Interaction)** session for the lesson, have your students preview the **A.I. pages**. The A.I. session should give them a chance to show what they have learned in the lesson.

B. When reviewing:

1. *Hiragana / Katakana / Kanji*:
    a. **Flashcard templates** are available in this guide and on our website: www.gpb.org/irasshai - **"for students" - student notebook - R+W Support column - Flashcard Templates**. Have your students cut out the card for each individual character. They can be used for learning and reviewing the characters individually as well as for review by a group of students. Lay out the cards on a large flat surface. One student will read out one of the cards, and other students can race to find the card. If it is the correct card, the student can keep it. At the end, count the number of the cards each student has.

b. For those who want to go over **how to read the basic *hiragana* and *katakana***, reference charts are available in both the textbooks and workbooks. Interactive charts are available online at www.gpb.org/irasshai - **"for students" - student notebook - R+W Support column - *Hiragana* Chart / *Katakana* Chart**. If you click on a character, you will hear its pronunciation.

c. **Writing Practice Sheets** for *hiragana*, *katakana* and *kanji* are available in the workbooks as well as online at www.gpb.org/irasshai - **"for students" - student notebook - R+W Support column - Writing Practice Sheets**. Click on the lesson number to find the practice sheet of *hiragana*, *katakana* or *kanji* that you want to review.

2. Vocabulary:
For review, use the vocabulary cards that your students have made so far. They can work in pairs or groups. If they want to work in groups, divide the class into two groups or more. Choose a student from one group to act as the questioner. The questioner will say a word/expression in English and the other group will have a representative write the Japanese equivalent on the board. After giving 10 questions to the group, other students of the first group will check the answers. After that, switch the groups to do another set of 10 questions.

3. Particles:
Use the **Particle Practice Sheets** to review the particles that your students have learned so far. Each practice sheet covers the corresponding group of lessons covered on each test. They are best used right before the test. It might be helpful to re-read all the notes regarding the particles from the lessons in the textbook before they start the practice sheet.

4. Before the test: **Practice Test**
The practice test should play an important role in students' preparation for a test. A day or two before the scheduled Practice Test day, make a copy of the test **checklist** and **practice test** for each student to take home and complete as homework. On the Practice Test day, have students switch their practice tests with a partner and go over the answers together in class. When done, return the practice tests and go over the items on the checklist. Ask the class to review the items that they do not understand. Have them write down what they need to review and focus on these items at home.

C. When exploring general cultural topics regarding Japan:
Please refer to the **Culture Matrices** in this guide or online at www.gpb.org/irasshai
- **"for facilitators" - culture matrix 1 / culture matrix 2**
- **"for students" - student notebook - Resources column - Culture Matrices**
You will find suggested topics for online research as well as topics and activities which can be found within **i-*irasshai***, www.gpb.org/irasshai - **"for students" - i-*irasshai***. Look for the provided key words under "Guidebook (Index)."

Additional Suggested Classroom Activities

Preliminary Lesson 1

Dialogue at a Party	Counters
KEY GRAMMAR POINTS Pair Work and Presentation	*INTERACTIVE ACTIVITIES* Part 1 *Nan-sai desu-ka? Juu-is-sai desu.* Pair Work
Imagine that you are meeting Japanese people at a party. Create a dialogue in which you introduce yourself to a person and try to get to know the person by asking questions. Find out the following things: age, birthday, grade, school, family, city, likes, abilities, etc. 　[age]　　Nan-sai desu-ka? 　[birthday] O-tanjoobi-wa itsu desu-ka? 　[grade]　　Nan-nen-sei desu-ka? 　[school]　Gakkoo-wa doko desu-ka? 　[family]　Go-kazoku-wa nan-nin desu-ka? 　　　　　Go-kyoodai-ga imasu-ka? 　[city]　　~-san / -kun-no machi-wa doko desu-ka? Doko-kara chikai desu-ka? 　[likes]　　(category)-wa nani-ga suki desu-ka? 　[abilities] (category)-wa nani-ga dekimasu-ka? After practicing the dialogue with a partner, perform it in front of the class.	Make two sets of cards, one with numbers 1 ~ 20 and the other with counters. Person A picks up one counter card and asks a question using the counter. Person B picks up one number card and answers the question using that number.

Guessing Game (~-*ga hoshii desu*)
KEY GRAMMAR POINTS Pair Work
Using a clothing mail-order catalog, Student A asks Student B what s/he likes best among the items on various pages by saying "*Dore-ga ichiban suki desu-ka*?" (Which one do you like best?). After Student A learns Student B's taste by going through some pages, Student A will guess which item Student B wants among the items of another page by saying, "*Kore-ga hoshii desu-ka*?" (Do you want this one?). If Student A can finally guess right, they will stop there, switch roles and repeat the activity until Student B can guess Student A's taste correctly.

Preliminary Lesson 2

Self-Introduction	Interview
KEY GRAMMAR POINTS Presentation	**KEY GRAMMAR POINTS** Pair Work
Have each student create his / her own script to tell the rest of the class about his / her abilities. They can choose any kind of sport, musical instrument, or something else they are good at. After memorizing the script, have each of them give a presentation to the class. (Ex.) Konnichi-wa. Ongaku-wa (genre)-ga ichiban suki desu. Ichiban suki-na aatisuto-wa (artist) desu. Gakki-wa (music instrument)-ga dekimasu. Getsu-yoobi-to sui-yoobi-ni (music instrument)-no ressun-ni ikimasu. (music instrument)-wa muzukashii desu-kedo, tanoshii desu. [Hello. I like (genre) among music. My favorite artist is (artist). I can play the (musical instrument). I go to my (music instrument) lesson(s) on Mondays and Wednesdays. The (musical instrument) is difficult, but fun.]	Have students interview each other regarding memorable summer event(s) using <u>the interview sheet</u>* below. After the interviews, the pair will decide which person's story they will tell the rest of the class.

*Interview Sheet:

Summer Event: _____	
When: _____	Where: _____
With whom: _____	Weather: _____
Activities: _____	
Comment: _____	

Price-Guessing Game
KEY GRAMMAR POINTS Pair Work
Have the students bring a mail-order catalog to class. Student A will hold the catalog closely and show an item to Student B without showing its price. Student B will guess how much it is by saying "~*doru desu-ka*?" If it costs more than the price Student B said, Student A says, "*Motto takai desu.*" If it costs less than the price Student B said, student A says, "*Motto yasui desu.*" When the price comes close (within one dollar), Student A's turn is over, and they will switch roles.

Lesson 1

Blind Date	Vocabulary Review
KEY GRAMMAR POINTS Pair Work	*Irasshai* **website**: for students - student notebook – Exercises column - Matching *Roomaji* with English Game
Make pairs, boy / girl if possible. Have the students decide on any imaginary person they want to be. Have them ask questions (name, age, grade, favorite subjects, food and drinks, and skills in music, sports, and foreign languages) to each other and decide if they will be a good match.	Have students work on this game to review the vocabulary they have learned so far.

Lesson 2

Holiday Presentation	Favorite TV Shows
KEY GRAMMAR POINTS Group Work	**KEY GRAMMAR POINTS** Pair Work
Divide the class into a few small groups. Have students review the Japanese national holidays listed in Volume 1, Lesson 37. Each group decides which holiday they want to give a presentation on. 1. Have students try various search engines and research information on their chosen holiday or festival. 2. Print out photos or draw pictures and make posters. 3. Write a script to explain what the holiday is about and give a presentation to the class. (Ex.) 5-gatsu 5-ka-wa kodomo-no hi desu. Kodomo-no hi-wa eigo-de "Children's Day"-to iimasu. Kodomo-no hi-ni kashiwa mochi-o tabemasu. Otoko-no-ko-no uchi-dewa kabuto-to koinobori-o kazarimasu. [May 5th is *kodomo-no hi*. *Kodomo-no hi* is called "Children's Day" in English. On *kodomo-no hi*, people eat *kashiwa mochi* (rice cake with sweet beans). Boys' families display *kabuto* (helmets) and *koinobori* (carp streamers).]	Have each student find a partner to work with. They will interview each other to find out what their favorite show on TV is using the interview sheet* below. After the interview, bring all the pairs together to report the results. Have a student take a poll and write the responses on the blackboard to see what the most popular TV shows among the class are.
Katakana Review	
Irasshai **website**: for students - student notebook - Exercises column - Matching *Katakana* Game	
Have students work on this game to review *katakana* characters. Make sure that they pronounce the *katakana* character they see on the screen.	

* Interview Sheet:

My Favorite TV Show: _____
Program Type (ex. comedy, drama, etc.): _____
    Day of the Week: _____
    Time: from _____ to _____
    My Favorite Character: _____

Lesson 3

Watashi-no Machi
INTERACTIVE ACTIVITIES Class Work

Have students make a brochure to advertise the town where their school is. Have them do research if needed. Divide the class into a few groups to work on different information regarding the town: (1) places to stay, (2) things to do and (3) restaurants of interest. After gathering sufficient information, have them create a brochure with maps, photos, pictures and descriptions.
 	
(Sample Description)
Town: [school name]-wa [town name]-ni arimasu.
Map: [town name]-wa [state name]-ni arimasu.
Location: [major city]-kara #-mairu gurai desu.
          [town name]-wa [describing adjective] desu.
Places to stay: Kono machi-ni hoteru-ga #-tsu arimasu.
          [hotel 1]–wa ichiban [describing adj.] desu.
          [hotel 2]-wa ichiban [describing adj.] desu.
          [hotel 3]-wa ichiban [describing adj.] desu.
Things to do: Kono machi-ni [place 1]-to [place 2]-to [place 3]-ga arimasu.
          [place 1]-de [activity](-o) ~masu.
          [place 2]-de [activity](-o) ~masu.
          [place 3]-de [activity](-o) ~masu.
Where / what to eat: Kono machi-ni resutoran-ga #-tsu arimasu.
          [restaurant 1]-no [food]-wa oishii desu.
          [restaurant 2]-wa yasui desu. [restaurant 3]-wa takai desu.

~wa doo desu-ka?	*Hiragana* and *Katakana* Review
KEY GRAMMAR POINTS **INTERACTIVE ACTIVITIES** Pair Work	***Irasshai* website:** for students - student notebook - Exercises column - Matching *Hiragana* with *Katakana* Game
Have students bring a mail-order clothing catalog to class. Have them ask each other's opinions on some clothes. They should make sure that they know the adjectives they can use to describe clothing before this activity.	Have students work on this game to review *hiragana* and *katakana* characters. Make sure that they pronounce the characters they see on the screen.

Lesson 4

Kazoku	*Hiragana* and *Katakana* Review
INTERACTIVE ACTIVITIES Guessing Game	*Shiritori* Game
Divide the class into three groups. Each group decides on describing a family from either a cartoon or drama. Each group writes three hints for other groups to guess whose family they are describing. After each hint is given, allow other groups to guess. When they figure out who the family it is, another group takes a turn to give hints. [sample hints] 1. Kono hito-no go-kazoku-wa 4-nin desu. 2. Kono kazoku-wa inu-o katteimasu. 3. Oneesan-no o-namae-wa Lisa-san desu. → [answer] Bart Simpson	Divide the class into two groups. Draw a vertical line to divide the blackboard space into two and write the *hiragana* あ. One student from each group comes to the front of the class to write any word which starts with あ in *hiragana*. The next student from each group comes to the front and writes any word which starts with the last letter of the previous word. They can use either a *hiragana* word or a *katakana* word. (Remember to write loan words in *katakana*.) Do not write any word which ends with ん because there is no word which starts with ん. Give them a time limit of 5 ~ 10 minutes to do this activity. After the time is over, count the words each group came up with and decide the winner. (Ex.) あき - きらい - いす - すこし - しずか - カメラ - ラジオ - おはよう

Lesson 5

Times / Activities

KEY GRAMMAR POINTS; *INTERACTIVE ACTIVITIES*
Pair Work

Have each student write down what they did from the time they got up in the morning to the time they went to bed the previous day. Have each student find a partner and get as much information as s/he can get from the partner by asking questions. They also need to ask what time they did each activity. After 2 minutes, have them change roles. Whichever student gets more information wins this game.
[example activities]

got up	ate lunch	played sports	went to a friend's house
ate breakfast	went to a meeting	watched TV	went to the movies
went to school	worked part-time	did homework	ate dinner
went to ___ class	went shopping	studied ___	went to bed

Plain Forms	Grammar and Vocabulary Review
KEY GRAMMAR POINTS *INTERACTIVE ACTIVITIES*	*Irasshai* **website**: for students - student notebook - Resources column - Choose Your Lesson - Japanese II <u>5</u> - *Nan-to iimasu-ka?* Part 1 and 2 Game
Have students make a set of verb cards to practice with. One side should have the plain form and its usage example(s) with both plain form and *-masu* form, and the other side should have the English translation as <u>the example</u>* below. From this lesson, students should make all of the verb entries in the plain form and also clarify if the verb is a *u*-verb, *ru*-verb or irregular verb. Refer to the Verb section in the textbook appendices.	Have students work on this game to review some of the vocabulary and grammar they have learned so far.

*(Ex.)   Front   Back

L5 わかる (*u*-verb) (Ex.) これがわかる？ これがわかりますか。	L5 to understand (Ex.) Do you understand this?

Lesson 6

Doko-no kuni desu-ka? *~de-wa nani-go-o hanashimasu-ka?*	The Origin and Use of *Kanji*
VOCABULARY **KEY GRAMMAR POINTS** Game	**CULTURE NOTES** **Online Resources** Discussion
Have students make a series of index cards with the name of a country and its language on each. One student picks a card from the stack and writes on the board 3-4 words related specifically to that country. (Ex.) pizza, spaghetti, Rome. He then asks the class "*Doko-no kuni desu-ka?*" and students must give the answer (*Itaria* / Italy). After they give the correct answer, the student asks "*~de-wa nani-go-o hanashimasu-ka?*" The class must answer correctly.	Have students use various search engines to research *kanji*, its origin, types, usage, etc. and discuss any new information they learn.

Lesson 7

Dochira-kara desu-ka?	Place-*no* + Cardinal Direction
KEY GRAMMAR POINTS Game	**KEY GRAMMAR POINTS** Group Work
Have each student think up five world famous or historical people and write each person's name on a card. (They must know where each person is from.) In pairs, one student picks a card from his partner's	1. Print out some world maps. Have students make questions and answers about where various countries are located. (Ex.) Q: *~-wa doko-ni arimasu-ka?*

93

stack. S/he role-plays that person. The partner asks "*O-namae-wa?*" The other student reads the name. The partner then asks "*Dochira-kara desu-ka?*" If he knows where that famous person was born, he keeps the card. The winner has the most cards. (Ex.) Picasso: Spain, Gandhi: India, Mozart: Austria, Socrates: Greece, Einstein: Germany. (Students should try to pick people from places that they know how to say in Japanese.)	A: *~-wa ~-no kita / minami / nishi / higashi-ni arimasu.* 2. Have students form groups of 3-4. Each group draws a map with their school in the middle and other buildings such as a supermarket, post office, etc. to the north, south, east and west of it. Each group then presents their map to the class using the following pattern: [name of the building]-*wa gakkoo-no* [cardinal direction]-*ni arimasu.*

Reading *Kanji*

KANJI NOTES
Class Work

Have students use their imagination. Have them draw pictures from the *kanji* 日 and 月 and come up with sentences or stories that will help them remember the meaning and /or pronunciation(s). (Sometimes the more bizarre, the better!) (Ex.) 人 This <u>person</u>'s name is JEAN [*jin*]. (Ex.) 月 → It GETS [*getsu*] bright when the <u>moon</u> is full. Students can vote on the best drawings or stories.

Lesson 8

shima, yama, kawa, mizuumi, umi	Reading *Kanji*: 木 本 人 山 川
VOCABULARY **Online Resources** **i-*irasshai* (online)**: gardens, mountains – tectonics Discussion	**KANJI NOTES** Class Work
1. Have students use various search engines to find photos and read more on Mount Fuji and Lake Biwa. 2. Using i-*irasshai*, have students learn of the importance of gardens in daily life in Japan (select the guide book (index) and click on the topics listed above). 3. Using i-*irasshai*, have students learn why Japan is mostly mountainous, and has so many earthquakes and volcanoes (select the guide book (index) and click on the topics listed above).	Repeat the same activity as in Lesson 7's *kanji* section using the new *kanji*.

Lesson 9

Ichiban + adjective, Place / category-*de ichiban* + adjective + noun *desu.*	Reading *Kanji*: 大 小
KEY GRAMMAR POINTS Game	**KANJI NOTES** Class Work
Have students come up with multiple choice questions in Japanese and write them on cards. Some may be factual questions (Ex.) *Amerika-de ichiban furui daigaku-wa nan desu-ka?* (What is the oldest university in the US?), and some may be opinion questions (Ex.) *~kookoo-de ichiban omoshiroi sensei-wa dare desu-ka?* (Who is the most interesting teacher at this school?) All questions must use the *ichiban* + adjective pattern, and answers to all factual questions must be known by the writer of the question. All cards are mixed up and combined in a pile. One student at a time picks a card, reads the question and tallies the number of responses for each answer. Results will show how many students know the answers to the fact questions as well as what students' opinions are.	Repeat the same activity as in Lesson 7's *kanji* section using the new *kanji*.

Lesson 10

Dore-gurai; Giving and Receiving Compliments Appropriately	Writing *Kanji*: 月 日
KEY GRAMMAR POINTS; CULTURE NOTES Group Work	**WRITING PRACTICE** Class Work
Divide the class into small groups of 3-4 students. Students recite a short dialog, which begins by Student A complimenting Student B on something. Sample dialog: A: <u>Tenisu</u>-ga joozu desu-ne. (You're good at tennis, aren't you?)	[This activity only works if you have a chalkboard in your room.] Bring in paint-by-number or

B: Iie, mada heta desu-yo. (No, I'm still pretty bad at it.) A: Iie, joozu desu-yo. (No, you are good.) Dore-gurai <u>tenisu-o</u> shimashita-ka? (How long have you played?) B: <u>Ichi-nen-kan</u> gurai shimashita. (About a year.) A: Aa, soo desu-ka. (Oh, really. Is that so?) Student B goes on to compliment Student C, and they recite the dialog changing the underlined parts. Student C compliments Student D, and the cycle continues until all students can recite similar dialogs from memory.	watercolor paint brushes and little paper cups of water. Send several students to the board to practice writing *kanji* in the correct stroke order using brushes and water.

Lesson 11

-te form	Writing *Kanji*: 木 本 人 Review: 月 日
KEY GRAMMAR POINTS *Irasshai* **website**: for students - student notebook - Resources column - Grammar Helpdesk - Volume 2: Verbs Project and Group Work	**WRITING PRACTICE** Class Work
1. Go to the *Irasshai* website (path listed above) to see all verbs learned so far in their *-te* forms and the various usages of the *-te* form of verbs. 2. Students can make flashcards with the verb in the plain form on one side and the *-te* form on the back. They can practice with them in pairs or individually. They should challenge themselves to give the *-te* form of verbs on all their cards as quickly as possible. 3. Similar to the Interactive Activity, Part 1, #2, have students work in small groups with one group competing against the others. Have students create cue cards of what someone is doing now. (Ex.) He's watching a movie / speaking Japanese / buying a shirt. One person picks a cue card, shows it to one member from the other groups, and each <u>draws</u> an illustration to illicit what someone is doing now. (Ex.) *Terebi-o mite-imasu. Koohii-o nonde-imasu.* The group that guesses the cue the fastest earns a point.	Repeat the same activity as in Lesson 10's *kanji* section using the new *kanji*.

Lesson 12

Using the *-te* form + *imashita* to Express Past Continuous Actions	Vocabulary Review
KEY GRAMMAR POINTS Game	**INTERACTIVE ACTIVITIES** Class Work
Have students think of all the names of places they have learned. (Ex.) *daigaku* (college), *uchi* (home), *toshokan* (library), *eigakan* (movie theater). Each word is written on a card and all cards are combined. Split the class into two teams. One student picks a card and makes the question [place]-*de nani-o shite-imashita-ka*? (What were you doing at [the place]?) Each team tries to come up with as many possible answers using as many possible verbs that would make sense. (Ex.) at the library: I was sleeping / reading a book / talking with friends / studying / looking at dictionaries, etc. The answers must be logical activities for that particular place. The team with the most activities wins that round.	Have students review all words and phrases in the Vocabulary review. Then, write English translations of each one on a card. Combine the cards into one stack. Someone writes the longest phrase / sentence from the left column on the board in *kana*. (カナダは アメリカの きたに あります。) This will be the base of a crossword puzzle. Divide students into two teams. One member picks a card and gets 1 point if s/he can give the Japanese equivalent. S/he gets another point if s/he can write that word sharing any one letter of it with one from the base of the puzzle. The next person does the same. If s/he cannot find a "shared letter" off of which to write his / her word, the card goes back to the bottom of the stack and only 1 point is earned. The game continues with each team earning 0-2 points and no more words can be written based off those already written on the board.

Writing *Kanji*: 大 小 (review: 月 日 木 本 人)
WRITING PRACTICE Class Work
Repeat the same activity as in Lesson 10's *kanji* section using the new *kanji*.

Lesson 13

#-jikan-me	School cleaning /Education
KEY GRAMMAR POINTS Group Work	**CULTURE NOTES** **i-*irasshai* (online):** school sink (quiz), school cleaning (video), school transportation
1. Have your students make a class schedule chart showing what time each period begins and ends. The chart can be similar to the ones in the textbook. See the <u>example chart</u> below*. 2. One student tells the others what time one of her / his class begins or ends. For example, "*Nihongo-no jugyoo-wa 8-ji 5-fun-ni hajimarimasu.*" 3. The student who sits next to her / him confirms what period that is: "*Nihongo-no jugyoo-wa 1 jikan-me desu-ne.*"	Using i-*irasshai*, have students read more about the education system in Japan (select the guide book (index) and click on the topics listed above).

Reading *Kanji:* 学 校
KANJI NOTES Class Work
Repeat the same activity as in Lesson 7's *kanji* section using the new *kanji*.

*Example Chart

Period	Subject	Time it Begins	Time it Ends
(Ex.) 1	Nihongo	8:05	8:55

Lesson 14

–te form + *imasu*	Reading Kanji: 中 高
KEY GRAMMAR POINTS Pair Work and Class Work	**KANJI NOTES** Class work
Have your students form two groups. On the Lesson 14 <u>[Verb] + *te imasu* Activity Sheet</u>*, Group A fills in the blanks with peoples' names whereas Group B is given the picture without peoples' names. One student in Group A states who there is in the picture: *~-san-to ~-san-to ~-san-ga imasu*. Then, referring to the picture they have, one student in Group A chooses one person from the picture and describes him / her: *Kono hito-wa* [name of the activity]-*o* [verb]-*te imasu*. One student in Group B guesses: *~- san desu-ne*. Have them switch roles and repeat this activity.	Repeat the same activity as in Lesson 7's *kanji* section using the new *kanji*.

Obentoo
Online Resources Discussion
Have students use various search engines to research more about boxed lunches in Japan and discuss in class.

[Verb]-te imasu Activity Sheet

Lesson 15

[verb]-*te mo ii desu-ka?*	Review
KEY GRAMMAR POINTS Class Work	*Irasshai* **website**: for students - student notebook - Resources column - Choose Your Lesson - Japanese II <u>15</u> - *Nan-to iimasu-ka?* Parts 1, 2 and 3 Game
PREPARATION: Have students make cards with the following places in *hiragana* and *katakana*: にほんの こうこう, アメリカの こうこう, デパート, としょかん, ちかてつ, えいがかん. 1. Place these cards face down. One student picks up a card. 2. The other students guess which card s/he has by asking permission questions, such as: "*Hon-o yonde-mo ii desu-ka?*"* 3. The student who holds the card answers, "*Hai, doozo.*" Or "*Aa, chotto.*" Based on whether of not the action is permissible in that particular place. 4. Another student guesses what is on the card by saying, "[name of the place] *desu-ka?*" The students keep asking questions using [Verb] –*te* + *-mo ii desu-ka?* Until someone gives the correct answer. * Other examples*: "Manga-o yonde-mo ii desu-ka?" "Juusu-o nonde-mo ii desu-ka?" "Poppu-koon-o tabete-mo ii desu-ka?" "Nete-mo ii desu-ka?"*	Have students review phrases and expressions they have learned so far.

Lesson 16

X-*no ue/shita-ni arimasu*	Visiting a Japanese Home
KEY GRAMMAR POINTS Class Work	**Online Resources** Discussion
Have students form two groups and give each group a copy of the <u>template picture of a classroom</u>*. Students in Group A draw items, such as a dictionary, textbook, comic book, pencil-case, computer, notebook, bag, and telephone, on their template picture of the classroom. Students in Group B ask students in Group A where these items are located in the picture. (Ex.) Group B: [Name of the item]-*wa doko-ni arimasu-ka?* Group A: *Sensei-no tsukue-no ue-ni arimasu.* Group B will then draw the items on their own template picture. At the end of this activity, Group A and Group B show their pictures and confirm that their answers are correct. They can switch roles and repeat this activity.	Have students use a variety of search engines and research Japanese homes and discuss their findings in class.

97

Review: Writing *Kanji*: 月 日 木 本 人 大 小
ASSIGNMENTS
Class Work
Repeat the same activity as in Lesson 10's *kanji* section including the new *kanji*.

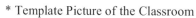
* Template Picture of the Classroom

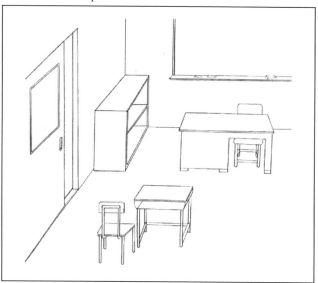

Lesson 17

te-form	Reading *Kanji*: 何
	Review *Kanji*: 月 日 木 本 人
	山 川 大 小 学 校 中 高
KEY GRAMMAR POINTS	**KANJI NOTES**
Pair Work and Class Work	Class Work
Have students list three activities that they normally do after school. Have them list them in sequential order in the *-masu* form. (Ex.) 1. Uchi-ni kaerimasu. 2. Gohan-o tabemasu. 3. Terebi-o mimasu. Then, have them present these activities using the *-te* form. (Ex) Uchi-ni kaette, gohan-o tabete, terebi-o mimasu. Finally, have the class discuss what the most common after school activities are.	Repeat the same activity as in Lesson 7's *kanji* section. Review all the *kanji* they have learned so far by using the pictures and sentences or stories they have come up with.

Lesson 18

Nani-mo, Nani-ka	Reading *Kanji*: 今 私
KEY GRAMMAR POINTS	**KANJI NOTES**
Class Work (Breakfast Survey)	Class Work
Have your students form a circle. Using the following model dialogue, find out what classmates had for breakfast. One student asks the person sitting next to her / him: A: ~-san / -kun, asa nani-ka tabemashita-ka? B: Hai, tabemashita. / Iie, nani-mo tabemasen deshita. (If the answer is "*Hai*") A: Nani-o tabemashita-ka? B: (~-to) ~-o tabemashita. Have each one write down what classmates had for breakfast. Then have them report the information to the class. (Ex) ~-san / -kun-wa asa, nani-mo tabemasen deshita. OR ~-o tabemashita. VARIATION: Have students practice this activity for drinks using the verb *nomimasu* (to drink).	Repeat the same activity as in Lesson 7's *kanji* section using the new *kanji*.

Lesson 19

Shumi	*Shumi*
KEY GRAMMAR POINTS Pair Work	Composition
Have students translate the words in the box of *shumi* into English and put the translations on cards. Stack the cards face down on the desk. Student A asks Student B, *"Shumi-wa nan desu-ka?"* Student B flips one of the cards and answers by translating the word back into Japanese. (Ex.) *Bideo-geemu-o suru-koto desu.* Variation: Have students flip more than one card and answer using *-to* (and) between each hobby. (Ex.) Bideo-geemu-o suru koto-to tenisu-o suru koto desu.	Have your students write a composition about their hobby. Have them follow the pattern below: Boku / Watashi no shumi-wa [Noun + Plain Verb] -koto desu. [Time]-ni [name of the hobby]-o shimasu. [Place]-de shimasu. Boku / Watashi-no shumi-wa [adjective] desu. Have them present their compositions to the class.

Writing *Kanji*: 何 今
WRITING PRACTICE Pair Work
Repeat the same activity as in lesson 10's *kanji* section including the new *kanji*.

Lesson 20

Particle: *-ni*	*Yoku*
KEY GRAMMAR POINTS	**VOCABULARY NOTES** Pair Work and Class Work
Review the particle *-ni* and other usages of the particle *-ni*.	Students will find out the activities that classmates do often. 1. Have each student make a list of some activities that they want to ask others. 2. Then, have students interview each other by asking: *"-~san / -kun*, [name of the activity] *-o yoku ~*[verb]*-masu-ka?* The interviewee answers: *"Hai, yoku* [verb]*-masu."* or *"Iie, anmari* [verb]*-masen"*. 3. After the interview, students can report what they found to the class. (Ex.) John *kun-wa yoku eiga-o mimasu.*

Reading *Kanji*: 火 水 金 土
KANJI NOTES Class Work
Repeat the same activity as in Lesson 7's *kanji* section using the new *kanji*. 1. Have students write the *kanji* for days of the week from Monday through Sunday on separate large sheets of paper. 2. Have one student stand in front of the class and show them one *kanji* sheet at a time, asking, *"Nan-yoobi desu-ka?"* The class answers: *"Getsu-yoobi desu."*

Lesson 21

Yokunai	*Four Seasons in Japan*
VOCABULARY NOTES Discussion	**CULTURE NOTES** **Online Resources** Presentation
Have students list the adjectives that they have learned so far and review their negative forms.	Have students use various search engines to research the four seasons in Japan. Divide the class into four groups, if possible. Assign each group a season to do a presentation on in Japanese.

Read the *Kanji*: 天 元 気
KANJI NOTES Class Work
1. Have students make a flash card for each *kanji* they have learned in this lesson. 2. Students must use their imagination. Have them draw pictures from the *kanji* 天, 元 and 気 and come up with sentences or stories that will help them remember the meaning and / or pronunciations. (Ex.) 気 - How you <u>feel</u> is the KEY [*ki*] to health. Students can vote on the best drawings or stories.

Lesson 22

Past Tense of *i*-adjectives	*Senshuu, Konshuu, Raishuu*
KEY GRAMMAR POINTS Project	**VOCABULARY** Class Work
Using the list of *i*-adjectives that students made in Lesson 21's suggested activities, have them make flash cards to memorize how to make the past tense. Write the English word on the front. Divide the back of the card into four sections and write present, negative present and past tenses. Leave the right bottom corner blank for future use.	Have a class leader come to the front of the room. The class then comes up with all time words they have learned so far. The leader writes them on the board. Then, they can review whether or not each time word takes the particle *-ni* when used in a sentence.

(Ex.)   (front)   (back)

	さむい	さむくない
Cold (adj.)	さむかった	

Lesson 23

Past Negative of *i*-adjectives	Talk about a trip you took
KEY GRAMMAR POINTS Project	**OBJECTIVES** Class Work
Pull out the *i*-adjective cards that students made in the previous lesson. Write the past negative form in the right bottom corner. Have students practice in pairs how to change *i*-adjectives into the four different forms. Students can refer to the *i*-adjectives conjugation chart in the textbook.	Have students bring in a photo from a trip they have taken. They can ask each other questions to find out about their trip. (Example Questions) 1. *Doko-ni ikimashita-ka?* 4. *Nani-o shimashita-ka?* 2. *Dare-to ikimashita-ka?* 5. *Tenki-wa doo deshita-ka?* 3. *Nan-de ikimashita-ka?* 6. *Ryokoo-wa doo deshita-ka?*

(Ex.)   (front)   (back)

	さむい	さむくない
Cold (adj.)	さむかった	さむくなかった

Lesson 24

Telephone Language	Telephone	Read the *Kanji*: 田
VOCABULARY NOTES **INTERACTIVE** **ACTIVITIES** Pair / Group Work	**CULTURE NOTES** ***i-irasshai* (online)**: telephone (activity), telephone differences, telephone numbers (activity)	**KANJI NOTES**
Have students make up a telephone dialogue. The suggested situations are: (1) inviting a friend to go to a concert, (2) inviting a	Using i-irasshai, have students read about Japanese telephones and telephone numbers and do the activities (select the	1. Have students make a flash card for each *kanji* they have learned in this lesson. 2. Do the same activity as #2 in Lesson 21's *kanji* section above. This time the *kanji* is 田. 3. Have them pull out the other *kanji* cards listed

friend to a home dinner party and (3) inviting a friend to play some sport together.	guide book (index) and click on the topics listed above).	under JAPANESE FAMILY NAMES and work in pairs to combine two *kanji* cards together and practice reading the names.

Lesson 25

-tai	*Kon/Sen/Rai-getsu*	*Kotoshi/Kyonen/Rainen*
KEY GRAMMAR POINTS Pair Work	**KEY GRAMMAR POINTS** **Online Resources** Group Work	**KEY GRAMMAR POINTS** Presentation
Have students work in pairs and list ten verbs that they have learned so far. One student says a verb and another student makes the four different *-tai* forms (present, present negative, past and past negative).	Divide the class into small groups if possible. Have students use various search engines to find ten celebrities' birthdays which are in the previous month, this month or next month. Present to the class when each celebrity's birthday is using *kon- / sen- / rai-gestu* and how old they became or will be. (Ex.) [Celebrity's name]-*san-no otanjoobi-wa* <u>*sen-getsu-no #-nichi deshita. #-sai-ni narimashita.*</u>	Have students write down three things they did last year or this year in school or outside school. (Ex.) *Kyonen / Kotoshi-wa* (activity 1) *-to* (activity 2)-*to* (activity 3)-*o shimashita.* Then, have them write down another three things they want to do this year or next year. (Ex.) *Kotoshi / Rainen-wa* (activity 4)-*to* (activity 5)-*to* (activity 6)-*o shitai desu.* Have them orally present past events and future wishes to the class. Have a representative write what was presented by the students on the board and let them see if there are any trends among the students.

Lesson 26

Doobutsuen	*-takunai desu / -tai desu*
VOCABULARY NOTES **CULTURE NOTES** **Online Resources** Group Work	**KEY GRAMMAR POINTS** Group Work
Have students study vocabulary words from DOOBUTSUEN-NO DOOBUTSU and learn how to say admission prices for adults and children. Have students use various search engines to research the zoos in Tokyo. Make small groups and assign each group to do some research on one of the zoos listed on the site. Their tasks are to find the name of the zoo, its location, how to get there, what kind of animals they can see, business hours, day(s) closed, and the admission prices. After their research, they can present it to the class. (Ex.) [name of the zoo]-*wa* [place]-*ni arimasu.* [place]-*kara* [means of transportation]-*de ikimasu.* [name of the zoo]-*ni* [lists of animals: use the particle "-*ya*" (implying "and others") to connect nouns]-*ga imasu.* [name of the zoo]-*wa* [time]-*kara* [time]-*made desu.* [day of the week]-*wa yasumi desu. Otona-wa* [price] *desu. Gakusei-wa* [price] *desu. Kodomo-wa* [price] *desu.*	Divide the class into small groups if applicable. Assign each group a place to go and have them make a list of what they want to do and what they don't want to do there. After they have decided what to do and what not to do, present to the class. Example Places: a mountain (やま), river (かわ), ocean (うみ), lake (みずうみ); London (ロンドン), Paris (パリ), Tokyo (とうきょう), New York (ニューヨーク), other cities; the mall (モール), park (こうえん), zoo (どうぶつえん), gym (たいいくかん), etc.

Kanji Review (月 日 木 本 人 大 小 何 今 火 水 金 土)
KANJI NOTES (L. 11~13, 19, 22~23)   Pair Work
Work in pairs. Student A shows the front side of flash cards of the *kanji* listed above to Student B and s/he tells the *hiragana* reading(s) and its meaning. When they are done with all the 13 cards, switch roles.

Lesson 27

Sporting Event	Read the *Kanji*: 見 行
Online Resources Group Work	**KANJI NOTES** Class Work
Divide the class into small groups if applicable. Assign each group a professional sport (MLB, NBA, NFL, NHL, etc.). Have students use various search engines to check the scores of games played the previous day. One student tells the others who played yesterday, "*Kinoo* [team 1]-*to* [team-2]-*no shiai-ga arimashita-yo.*" The other students have to guess who won by saying, "[Team 1 / 2]-*ga kachimashita-ka*?" If they guessed right, the student says "*Hai, soo desu.*" If they did not guess right, the student says "*Iie, chigaimasu.* [Team 1 / 2]-*ga kachimashita.* At the end, other students ask "*Sukoaa-wa doo deshita-ka?*" and the student tells them the score by saying "*# -tai # deshita.*"	1. Have students make a flash card for each *kanji* they have learned in this lesson. 2. Do the same activity as #2 in Lesson 21's *kanji* section explained above. This time the *kanji* are: 見 行.

Lesson 28

Non-past negative of plain form verbs	*Yomimashoo!* (Dialogue)
KEY GRAMMAR POINTS Class Work	**INTERACTIVE ACTIVITIES** Class Work
1. Have students make flash cards with the plain affirmative verb on one side and plain negative verb on the back. Students can study from these cards. Then they can time themselves, seeing how many verbs they can give the -*nai* form to (or the plain affirmative form) in one minute. 2. Students can refer to the Appendix on Japanese Verbs in the back of the textbook to see the rules for making the -*nai* form of verbs. (Verb help can also be found on the *Irasshai* website: for students - student notebook - Resources column - Grammar Helpdesk.) 3. Divide the class into 2 groups. One member from Group A shouts out a verb in the -*masu* form to Group B. The first member of Group B must then give the plain forms (affirmative and negative) of that verb. S/he gets 1 point for each correct form. Then Group B shouts out the -*masu* form of another verb. The first member of Group A must do the same. Groups / members take turns. The group with the most points at the end of a certain time limit wins.	Using the *Yomimashoo!* Dialogue in Interactive Activities, Part 2, students, in groups of 2-4, draw a *manga* (up to 8-10 frames) illustrating the dialogue on paper. They then show their work to the class, with each member reading the lines from the dialogue that go with each frame.
Kanji	
WRITING PRACTICE Class Work	
Each student writes a word using *kanji* in Section 2, *Dore desu-ka?* on the board. Write a number for each word as well. After they are all on the board, students take turns randomly reading the words. Other students listen and then say the corresponding number of that word.	

Lesson 29

Yomimashoo!	Review: Vocabulary: Phrases and Expressions
VOCABULARY Class Work	**INTERACTIVE ACTIVITY** Pair Work
Divide the class into two groups. Group 1 takes sentences 1-3 in the Yomimashoo! section and writes them out in large *kana* characters on a sheet of paper. Group 2 takes sentences 4-6 and does the same. Both groups then cut up their sentences in chunks of phrases. (Ex.) For sentence 2, there would be four phrases: 1) わたしの, 2) うちに, 3) あそびに and 4) きませんか. All phrase strips from each group are put in an envelope. Groups switch envelopes and race to see which group can put together the three sentences correctly the quickest.	This is a variation of the textbook activity. See <u>INFORMATION GAP ACTIVITY – Who's coming to the party? What are they making?</u>*

Read the *Kanji*: 来 年
KANJI NOTES
Class Work
1. Have students make a flash card for each *kanji* they have learned in this lesson.
2. Students must use their imagination. Have them draw pictures from the *kanji* 来 and 年 and come up with sentences or stories that will help them remember the meaning and / or pronunciation(s).

* INFORMATION GAP ACTIVITY - Who's coming to the party? What are they making?

Directions: Make copies of the table and Questions below and give two copies to each student. They then use one copy and fill in the chart with names of classmates they want to invite to their party and what food item that guest will bring. Use the word bank for food items. Student A asks Student B the first two questions below and fills in the chart of the other copy with the names of the people that Student B has invited. Reverse roles and Student B does the same. Student A then has three chances to ask YES / NO questions about what one particular guest is making. (See question 3 below.) If Student B answers "no" three times, Student A must ask the fourth question. Reverse roles and Student B does the same. After filling in all the information, students compare charts to check their answers.

GUEST	FOOD
1.	1.
2.	2.
3.	3.
4.	4.
5.	5.
6.	6.

Questions:

1. *Paatii-ni nan-nin kimasu-ka?* [How many people are coming to the party?]

2. *Dare-ga kimasu-ka?* [Who's coming?]

3. *~-san-wa sarada-o tsukurimasu-ka?* [Is Mr. / Ms. ~ making salad?]

4. *Ja, ~-san-wa nani-o tsukurimasu-ka?* [Well, then what is Mr. / Ms. ~ making?]

Food items:

ピザ	サラダ	サンドイッチ	ケーキ
クッキー	フライドチキン	ポテトサラダ	すし
パイ	チーズバーガー	やきとり	スープ

Lesson 30

NOUN of Chinese Origin (+ *suru*)	Review of –*tai* (want to) form from L.25
VOCABULARY NOTES Class Work	**KEY GRAMMAR POINTS** Game
Have each student come up with a sentence using NOUN + *suru* and add another piece of information (such as time, object, person, etc) to the sentence. (Ex.) *Watashi / Boku-wa heya-no sooji-o shimashita.* Student 1 states his / her sentence. Student 2 repeats that sentence using Student 1's name then states his / her own sentence. Student 3 does the same, and the activity continues until someone cannot remember all the previous sentences. That student then stops repeating all the previous sentences and starts the activity over from the beginning. Students should be encouraged to use a variety of vocabulary, phrases and verb conjugations in their sentences and not limit themselves to the nouns listed.	PREPARATION: each group needs a pair of dice and index cards onto which students write a variety of activities (Ex.) play basketball, do homework, drink prune juice, etc. - one activity per card. The numbers on the dice correspond to: 1) yesterday, 2) today, 3) tomorrow, 4) last week, 5) this week, 6) next week, 7) last month, 8) this month, 9) next month, 10) last year, 11) this year and 12) next year. GAME: Students roll the dice; they can choose to roll one or both. Then they pick a card from the stack. If they rolled a 6 (next week) and picked the card "go to the mountains," they must make a statement using the *-tai* form, depending on whether they want or don't want to do the activity. The possible sentences would be "*Raishuu yama-ni ikitai desu.*" Or "*Raishuu yama-ni ikitakunai desu.*" They must be careful of the verb tense. If they can make a grammatically correct sentence, they earn 1 point. The object is to acquire the most cards / points.

Read the *Kanji*: 一 二 三 四 五 六
KANJI NOTES
Class Work
1. Have students make a flash card for each *kanji* they have learned in this lesson.
2. Students must use their imagination. They draw pictures from the *kanji* 一, 二, 三, 四, 五 and 六 and come up with sentences or stories that will help them remember the meaning and / or pronunciation(s).

Lesson 31

Review of Grammar Points (L11, 14: -te-imasu form; L15: -te-mo ii form; L19: verb + suru-koto)	Read the *Kanji*: 七 八 九 十
KEY GRAMMAR POINTS Game	**KANJI NOTES** Class Work
PREPARATION: The facilitator prepares pictures of the verbs which students have learned (see <u>verb box</u>* below). Make a <u>pair</u> of each picture card (2" x 2" or 3" x 3"). The set of cards can be limited to however many verbs you choose. Then duplicate each set for however many groups you will divide the class into. Each group of 3-4 students gets one set of verb pair cards. GAME: Students can play a variety of "Go Fish"-type card games depending on what grammar point is being reviewed. Cards are shuffled and passed out. VARIATION 1: for Lessons 11 and 14: -te-imasu form, Student A asks Student B "Verb-te-imasu-ka?" for a picture card s/he is holding. If that student has that picture card, s/he must surrender it to Student A. The game continues until all pairs of cards are out, and the winner has the most pairs. VARIATION 2: Same as #1 above but the pattern reviewed is now "Verb -te-mo ii desu-ka?" VARIATION 3: Same as #1 and #2 above but the pattern reviewed is now "Shumi-wa [verb plain]-koto desu-ka? "	1. Have students make a flash card for each *kanji* they have learned in this lesson. 2. Students must use their imagination. They draw pictures from the *kanji* 七, 八, 九 and 十 and come up with sentences or stories that will help them remember the meaning and / or pronunciation(s).

*Verb box				
				ski
ask	date	go	play the piano	sleep
buy	dance	go home	read (a book,	swim
clean	drink	listen to music	the newspaper, etc.)	telephone
come	eat	meet (someone)	shop	write
cook	get up	play the guitar	sing	write a letter

Lesson 32

Numbers up to 999; Vocabulary: *Zenbu-de ikura desu-ka?*	Review: General Counters *hitotsu ~ too*
KEY GRAMMAR POINTS **VOCABULARY: Phrases and expressions** Pair Work	**KEY GRAMMAR POINTS** Group Work
Cut out the following 8 cards (one set for each pair of students, each student gets 4 cards), and make a copy of the table of items/ prices and sample dialog for each student. In pairs, have students practice the sample dialogue, changing the underlined parts. Student B must calculate and give Student A the correct amount. If s/he is incorrect, Student A must say "*Iie, chigaimasu,*" and Student B must calculate again.	PREPARATION: Divide the class into groups of three to four. Each group should have a pair of dice and a set of cards, each with a verb on them: *tabemasu, arimasu, kaimasu, tsukurimasu.* GAME: One student will roll the dice and pick a card. S/he has to make a sentence using the number and verb picked. (Ex.) S/he rolls a 6 and picks "*tsukurimasu.*" Sample sentence: "*Appuru-pai-o muttsu tsukurimashita.*" If s/he makes a grammatically correct sentence, s/he gets a point. The card gets returned to the bottom of the stack and the game continues.

coffee: 140 yen Bought: 3 (TOTAL: 420 yen)	melons: 430 yen Bought: 2 (TOTAL: 860 yen)	grapefruit: 350 yen Bought: 2 (TOTAL: 700 yen)	French fries (*poteto furai*): 200 yen Bought: 4 (TOTAL: 800 yen)

oranges: 110 yen Bought: 5 (TOTAL: 550 yen)	pineapples (*painappuru*): 600 yen Bought: 1 (TOTAL: 600 yen)	hamburgers: 170 yen Bought: 2 (TOTAL: 340 yen)	colas: 120 yen Bought: 6 (TOTAL: 720 yen)

(Ex.)
milk shakes (*miruku sheeki*): 100 yen Bought: 7 (TOTAL: 700 yen)

ITEMS and PRICES

(Ex.) milk shakes	100 yen	grapefruit	350 yen	oranges	110 yen
melons	430 yen	coffee	140 yen	French fries	200 yen
colas	120 yen	pineapples	600 yen	hamburgers	170 yen

SAMPLE DIALOGUE:

A: *Miruku sheeki* (milk shake)-*o kaimashita.* [I bought (milk shakes).]
B: *Soo desu-ka. Miruku sheeki-wa ikura desu-ka?* [Really? How much is a milk shake?]
A: *Hyaku-en desu.* [It's 100 yen.]
B: *Ikutsu kaimashita-ka?* [How many did you buy?]
A: *Nana-tsu kaimashita.* [I bought seven.]
B: *Aa, ja, 700-en deshita-ne.* [Oh, so the total was 700 yen, right?]
A: *Hai, soo desu.* [Yes, that's right.]

Lesson 33

-*mai*	Addressing an Envelope Japanese Style
KEY GRAMMAR POINTS Group Work	**CULTURE NOTES** **i-*irasshai* (online):** mail; mail: addressing a postcard [activity]
PREPARATION: Each group needs a pair of dice and eight index cards with different thin and flat items written on each card (a short list of items is provided in the textbook). GAME: Students form small groups and roll the dice; they can choose to roll one or both. Students pick a card from the stack. If, for example, they rolled a 6 and picked the card "CD", they must make a statement using CD and the number 6 + -*mai.* A possible sentence would be "*CD-o roku-mai kaimasu-ka?*" If they can make a grammatically correct sentence, they earn 1 point. The object is to get the most points.	Using i-*irasshai*, have students learn more about mail in Japan (select the guide book (index) and click on the topics listed above). Do an activity testing their knowledge on addressing envelopes in Japanese.
Japanese Stamps	
Online Resources	
Have students use various search engines to research and view a variety of Japanese postage stamps.	
Japanese Currency	
Online Resources	
Have students use various search engines to find photos of Japanese currency and prices of common goods in Japan.	

Lesson 34

#-ban-me Migi-kara #-ban-me desu.	Japanese Vending Machines
KEY GRAMMAR POINTS Pair Work	**CULTURE NOTES** **i-irasshai (online):** stamps, vending machine [activity]
In pairs, students write the names of seven different types of <u>doughnuts</u>* on their <u>tables</u>**. They must ask YES / NO questions to their partner to find out what doughnuts their partner wrote on their table. (Ex.) *Migi-kara ni-ban-me no doonatsu-wa chokoreeto desu-ka?* Once they find out what doughnut goes in the table, they write it in. The first student to fill in their partner's table with the correct doughnuts wins.	Using i-irasshai, have students learn more about vending machines in Japan (select the guide book (index) and click on the topics listed above). Do the activity that involves using a vending machine.

Writing *Kanji*

WRITING PRACTICE
Class Work

Each student writes the word using *kanji* in Section 2: *Dore desu-ka?* on the board. Write a number for each word as well. After they are all on the board, students take turns randomly reading the words. Other students listen and then say the corresponding number of that word.

*DOUGHNUT MENU			
cinnamon	chocolate	custard cream	jelly-filled
plain	lemon	glazed	chocolate glazed
chocolate cream	sugar	strawberry cream	mocha

**S-1's table

**S-1's partner's table

**S-2's table

**S-2's partner's table

Lesson 35

Man	#-nen mae
KEY GRAMMAR POINTS Bingo Game	**KEY GRAMMAR POINTS** Composition: "My Favorite Birthday Present"
One <u>bingo card</u>* holds nine numbers. Starting with 10,000, have students each write 24 consecutive -man numbers on small pieces of paper (Ex. 10,000 ~ 24,000). These numbers should also be written on the blackboard. Each student will randomly place nine of the numbers within the squares of their bingo cards, one number per box. Each student will say one of the numbers on the board out loud in Japanese. The number on the board should be marked so that it will not be repeated. Have students take turns reading numbers until someone gets bingo. Repeat with a new group of	1. Have students refresh their memories of what they have received for their birthday over the years. 2. Have them write about their favorite birthday presents in the past. *Boku / Watashi-no ichiban suki-na tanjoobi purezento* *Boku / Watashi-no tanjoobi-wa* (month)-*gatsu* (date)-*nichi desu #-nen mae-no tanjoobi-ni* (name of the gift item)-*o moraimashita.* (Name of the person who gave this gift)-*kara moraimashita.* (Name of the gift item)-*ga daisuki desu. Kotoshi-wa* (name of the gift item)-*ga hoshii desu.* 3. Have students present their composition to the class.

-*man* numbers if time allows.	

-*n desu*

KEY GRAMMAR POINTS
Class Work

Have students make cards with the following statements:

1. go to bed at 1:00 am everyday	4. get up at 5:00 am everyday	7. will receive a new computer
2. will buy tomorrow	5. go to Japan in Summer	8. Suzuki-sensei also comes
3. sing Japanese songs	6. eat sushi	9. keep a diary every day

Place them face down. One student turns over a card. The student who sits next to him / her comes up with a corresponding question with an –*n desu* expression. (Ex.1) Q: *Mainichi 1-ji-ni neru-n desu-ka?* A: *Hai, soo desu.* Students take turns and continue until they finish turning over all the cards.

<table>
<tr><td colspan="3" align="center">*Bingo card</td></tr>
<tr><td></td><td></td><td></td></tr>
<tr><td></td><td></td><td></td></tr>
<tr><td></td><td></td><td></td></tr>
</table>

<table>
<tr><td colspan="3" align="center">*Bingo card</td></tr>
<tr><td></td><td></td><td></td></tr>
<tr><td></td><td></td><td></td></tr>
<tr><td></td><td></td><td></td></tr>
</table>

Lesson 36

Counters: #-*hon*, #-*bon*, #-*pon*	*Iru (Irimasu)*
KEY GRAMMAR POINTS Class Work	**KEY GRAMMAR POINTS** Pair Work
Have students bring in a box which can hold many pens. Each student asks the rest of the class to give him / her a pen. Students gather pens and put them in their boxes. Students then ask others, "*Nan-bon arimasu-ka?*" Each student guesses how many pens there are by saying "# -*hon* / -*bon* / -*pon* arimasu." After all students have finished guessing their numbers, students count their pens. Who guessed closest to the actual number?	Partner A decides what s/he wants to cook for a party. Partner B is going shopping for that dish. Partner A lists the items that are needed to make the dish. Partner A tells what s/he will make by saying, "[Item]-*o tsukurimasu*." Then, Partner B has to complete the shopping list by asking, "[Item]-*ga irimasu-ka?*" Partner A would answer, "*Hai, irimasu*" or "*Iie, irimasen.*" Then Partner B adds the necessary items on his / her list. Partner B keeps asking questions until s/he obtains all the shopping list items.

Fruit as a Gift

CULTURE NOTES
i-*irasshai* (online): Fruits

Using i-*irasshai*, have students read more about the gift-giving culture in Japan (select the guide book (index) and click on the topic listed above).

Lesson 37

Dooshite, Plain form + -*kara*	Read the *Kanji*: 上 下
KEY GRAMMAR POINTS Group Work and Class Work: Travel Plan	**KANJI NOTES** Class Work
Divide students into groups of two to three to plan a trip to their <u>favorite destination</u>*. Students decide where they want to go and what they need for the trip. Have students make a list of things that they need and think of a reason to take those items. (Ex.) item: credit card; reason: for shopping. After completing their lists, have one student in each group announce an item that they will bring by saying, "Credit card-*ga irimasu*." One student from another group will ask why by	1. Have students make a flash card for each *kanji* they have learned in this lesson. 2. Students must use their imagination. Have them draw pictures from the *kanji* 上, 下 and come up with sentences or

saying, *"Dooshite desu-ka?"* The first student answers with the reason, *"Kaimono-ga shitai-kara desu."*	stories that will help them remember the meaning and / or pronunciation(s).

*Favorite Destination: _____

Item	Reason

Lesson 38

Moo and *Mada*	
VOCABULARY Class Work	
Have your students create index cards with the names of movies that have been recently released. Have them place the cards face down. One student picks one card and asks a question in Japanese using the information on the card. (Ex.) A: *Moo* [name of the movie]-*o mimashita-ka?* (Have you already seen [name of the movie]?) B: *Hai, mimashita.* (Yes, I have already seen it.) / *Iie, mada desu.* (No, not yet.) VARIATION: Students create cards with the latest pop or rock music titles using the verb *"kikimashita-ka?"*	

#-kai (#-gai)	Read the *Kanji*: 円
KEY GRAMMAR POINTS Online Resources / Group Work	**KANJI NOTES** Class Work
Divide the class into two groups. Have students go to the web site of a Japanese Department store and choose the floor guide. Print out the floor guide. Group A can look at the floor guide. One of the students in Group B asks on which floor they can find the following particular items: CDs, bags, shoes, children's clothing, men's clothing, (women's) accessories, cameras, chopsticks, and bread. (Ex.) Group B: *CD-wa nan-kai desu-ka?* Group A: *13-kai desu.* Students can take turns and ask different questions.	1. Have students make a flash card for each *kanji* they have learned in this lesson. 2. Students must use their imagination. Have them draw pictures from the *kanji* 円 and come up with sentences or stories that will help them remember the meaning and / or pronunciation(s).

Lesson 39

Past plain verb + *koto-ga arimasu*	Read the *Kanji*: 百 千
KEY GRAMMAR POINTS Bingo Game	**KANJI NOTES** Class Work
Using the Bingo template* on the next page, have your students find who has done certain activities. For example, for the box that says *karaoke*, one student asks another: *"Karaoke-o shita-koto-ga arimasu-ka?"* When students find a classmate who has done that activity, s/he can write his / her name in the parentheses on the card. The student who fills the grid first wins and presents the information to the class: (Ex.) *"John-kun-wa karaoke-o shita-koto-ga arimasu."*	1. Have students make a flash card for each *kanji* they have learned in this lesson. 2. Students must use their imagination. Have them draw pictures from the *kanji* 百 and 千 and come up with sentences or stories that will help them remember the meaning and / or pronunciation(s).

( )	( )	( )
karaoke: suru [verb]	*sushi: taberu* [verb]	*manga: yomu* [verb]
( )	( )	( )
ocha: nomu [verb]	*nihon-no ongaku: kiku* [verb]	*nihon-no ryoori: tsukuru* [verb]
( )	( )	( )
nihon-no eiga: miru [verb]	*karate: suru* [verb]	*nihon-no resutoran: iku* [verb]

Lesson 40

X-*no naka-ni*	Review	Valentine's Day (*Barentain-dee*)
KEY GRAMMAR POINTS Pair Work - Class Work	***Irasshai* website**: for students - student notebook - Resources column - Choose Your Lesson - Japanese II <u>40</u> - *Nan-to iimasu-ka?* Parts 1 and 2	**CULTURE NOTE** **Online Resources** Discussion
Have your students ask each other what they have in their book bags. A: *Kaban-no naka-ni nani-ga arimasu-ka?* B: [item 1]-*to* [item 2]-*to* [item 3]-*ga arimasu.* Have students take notes about who brings what kind of items to school. Have them discuss what the most common items are.	Have students review phrases and expressions they have learned so far.	Have students use various search engines to research Japanese Valentine's Day. Students can discuss the following: 1. When did Valentine's Day become popular? 2. What do "*giri* choco" and "*honmei* choco" mean?

Lesson 41

Body Parts	Read the *Kanji*: 万
KEY GRAMMAR POINTS Class Work	**KANJI NOTES** Class Work
Have students draw a popular character such as Hello Kitty on a card. Each student introduces the character showing the picture that they drew, saying, "*Kore-wa* [name of character] *desu.*" Students need to be familiar with the selected characters. Then, place the cards face down. One student picks a card without showing who it is. The other students ask questions describing the character using the body parts. (Ex.) "*Hana-ga arimasu-ka?* The student who has the card answers either "*Hai, arimasu.*" or "*Iie, arimasen.*" Students take turns asking one question at a time until somebody successfully guesses who the character is. Then repeat this pattern with another student selecting a character card.	1. Have students make a flash card for each *kanji* they have learned in this lesson. 2. Students must use their imagination. Have them draw pictures from the *kanji* 万 and come up with sentences or stories that will help them remember the meaning and / or pronunciation(s).

Lesson 42

Body Parts	Japanese Medicine
VOCABULARY Class Work	**Culture Note** **Online Resources**
Have students sit in a circle. One student suggests the name of a category in English. For example, if the suggested category is "Body Parts," students will take turns giving an example of a body part in Japanese. Whoever cannot think of an example for that category must come up with two example words for the next category. Students can refer to the list of words which are associated with body parts in their textbooks. Suggested categories are: office supplies, food, drinks, sports, etc.	Have students use various search engines to research medical technology in Japan. Also have students look up more about traditional Japanese medicine.

Kanji: 口 目 耳	
KANJI NOTES	
As in *kanji* activities in previous lessons, students must use their imagination. Have them draw pictures from the *kanji* 口, 目 and 耳 and come up with sentences or stories that will help them remember the meaning and/or pronunciation(s).	

Lesson 43

Describing Physical Conditions	Giving Flowers to a Sick Person
VOCABULARY Pair Work	**Culture Notes** **Online Resources** Discussion
Have students make cards in English with physical conditions on them. Then, have students practice the following sample dialogue. Using the cards, students can change the underlined part. [SAMPLE DIALOGUE] A: *Dooshita-n desu-ka?* B: <u>*Atama-ga itai-n*</u> *desu.* A: *Moo byooin-ni ikimashita-ka?* B: *Hai, ikimashita.* A: *O-daiji-ni.*	Have students use various search engines to research Japanese gift-giving rituals.

Lesson 44

Event-*no mae-ni* / *ato-de*		*Kanji*: 名 前
KEY GRAMMAR POINTS Group Work		**KANJI NOTES** Class Work
Divide the class into groups of four to six students. Have students think about what they usually do before or after a certain occasion, such as a test, a party or a sports event. Have students prepare long paper strips with sentences. For example:		As in the *kanji* activities in previous lessons, students must use their imagination. Have them draw pictures from the *kanji* 名 and 前 and come up with sentences or stories that will help them remember the meaning and / or pronunciation(s).
Paatii-no mae-ni / ryoori-o shimasu. *Tesuto-no mae-ni / benkyoo-o shimasu.* *Shiai-no mae-ni / renshuu-o shimasu.*	*Paatii-no ato-de / sooji-o shimasu.* *Tesuto-no ato-de / terebi-o mimasu.* *Shiai-no ato-de / mizu-o nomimasu.*	
Then, have them cut these sentences into two sections where indicated with a slash. Each student picks one strip with an event and asks the other students in the group, "[name]-*wa tesuto-no mae-ni nani-o shimasu-ka?*" Each person responds based on what s/he does. (Ex.) "Vocabulary cards-*o tsukurimasu.*"		

Lesson 45

Linking adjectives (-*te* form)	*Kanji*: オ
KEY GRAMMAR POINTS Group Work	**KANJI NOTES** Class Work
Divide class into groups of four to six students. Have students make adjective cards with which to practice. Make sure that students use both *i*-adjectives and *na*-adjectives that they have learned so far. Have them place these cards face down on the desk. One student turns over a card. Then the next student turns over one more card and links these two adjectives together. For example: The adjectives *ookii* and *oishii* becomes *ookikute oishii*. Note that two adjectives which have opposite meanings cannot be combined using the conjugation "*kute/de.*" (Ex.) *ookii* (big) + *chiisai* (small) = *ookikute chiisai* is not possible.	As in the *kanji* activities in previous lessons, students must use their imagination. Have them draw pictures from the kanji オ and come up with sentences or stories that will help them remember the meaning and / or pronunciation(s).

Lesson 46

Describe people in terms of physical characteristics	*Hiragana* and *Katakana* Review
INTERACTIVE ACTIVITIES Guessing Game	***Irasshai* website:** for students - student notebook - Exercises column - Matching *Hiragana* with *Katakana* Game
Have students decide on a category of people (actors, actresses, comedians, etc.), and then have each student secretly choose one famous person in that category. Each student prepares a description of the person whom s/he has chosen and writes down the description. Then, each student presents his / her description. The other students guess who the famous person is. SAMPLE HINTS: [height] Kono-hito-wa se-ga takai desu. [hair] Kono-hito-wa kami-ga kinpatsu de mijikai desu. [eye color] Kono-hito-wa me-ga chairoi desu. [personality] Ki-ga mijikai desu. Other descriptions can be included, such as where this person is from or what s/he sings, who s/he is married to/dating, etc.	Have students work on this game to review *hiragana* and *katakana* characters. Make sure that they pronounce the characters they see on the screen.

Lesson 47

Kazoku / tomodachi	*Kanji:* 先 生
INTERACTIVE ACTIVITIES Presentation	**KANJI NOTES** Class Work
Have students bring in an old family photograph or school year book. Each student gives a presentation on the photograph describing the people in it. SAMPLE PRESENTATION: *Kore-wa boku-no kazoku-no shashin desu. Furorida-ni ikimashita. 2005-nen-ni ikimashita. Kono megane-no kodomo-wa boku-no otooto desu. 5-sai deshita. Kono akai shatsu-no onna-no-hito-wa haha desu.*	As in the *kanji* activities in previous lessons, students must use their imagination. Have them draw pictures from the *kanji* 先 and 生 and come up with sentences or stories that will help them remember the meaning and / or pronunciation(s).

Lesson 48

Shitte-imasu / shirimasen	Review
VOCABULARY **VOCABULARY NOTES** Class Work: Interview	***Irasshai* website**: for students - student notebook - Resources column - Choose Your Lesson - Japanese II <u>48</u> - *Nan-to iimasu-ka?* Parts 1 and 2
Students will ask each other whether or not they know certain things. First, they must collectively decide what kinds of questions they want to ask. (Ex.) TV shows, celebrities, music, countries, food, their birthdays, teachers' full names, etc. Then, have them interview each other using an <u>interview sheet</u>* similar to the one on the next page. (Ex.) Q: *Watashi-no tanjoobi-o shitte-imasu-ka?* A: *Hai, shitte-imasu. / Iie, shirimasen.* Students should record what other students' answers are. After finishing their interviews, students can present the results to the class. "Jon-*kun-wa watashi-no tanjoobi-o shitte-imasu.*"	Students can review vocabulary words and sentence structures that they have studied so far by doing the activities. Students are encouraged to choose the *hiragana* mode for these activities.

Name of the interviewee	(Ex.) John				
(Ex.) my birthday	Yes				
(Ex.) John Denver					
(Ex.) C.S.I.					
(Ex.) *yakitori*					
(Ex.) Cranium					

Lesson 49

#-ka-getsu	[Time expression]-*ni* (review); [Place]-*de* (review)
KEY GRAMMAR POINTS Game	**KEY GRAMMAR POINTS** Class Work
This activity is played in groups of three. PREPARATION: a set of 12 index cards each with one Arabic numeral written on it (from 1-12). Cards are mixed and placed face up on a desk. One student calls out a number paired with an appropriate counter, like months (Ex.) *san-ka-getsu* = 3 months. The other two students race to pick up the card with the number three. The object is to pick up and collect as many cards as possible. After all 12 numbers are read, the cards go back on the desk, and students take turns calling out the number / counter combinations again.	On the front of an index card, have students write two Japanese sentences with information about the time (year, month, season, time of day, etc.) and place (city, state, name of hospital, etc.) where they were born. On the back of the card, have students lightly write their name in pencil in small print. The cards are shuffled and passed out, one to each student. The first student reads the card (Ex.) *Watashi-wa Arizona-de umaremashita. Fuyu-ni umaremashita.* (I was born in Arizona. I was born in winter.) The student reading the card then asks, "*Watashi-wa dare desu-ka?*" (Who am I?). The rest of the class has three chances to guess who it is. The student reading the card can give the correct answer after three incorrect guesses. From this activity, students can learn more about each other's birthplace and date.

O-miai	Funerals, Cemetery Rituals; Weddings	Reading *Kanji*: 父 母
CULTURE NOTES **Online Resources** Discussion	**i-*irasshai* (online)**	**KANJI NOTES** Class Work
Have students use various search engines to research Japanese: 1. Weddings: *o-miai*, traditions in Japanese weddings and about the ceremony itself. 2. Funeral styles: the procedures involved in the wake, Japanese funerals and burials.	Using i-*irasshai*, have students learn more about customs revolving around funerals and wedding ceremonies in Japan (select the guide book (index) and click on the topics).	Students must use their imagination. Have them draw pictures from the *kanji* 父 and 母 and come up with sentences or stories that will help them remember the meaning and / or pronunciation(s).

Lesson 50

[Place]-*ni sunde-imasu* / _____ -*no toki*
KEY GRAMMAR POINTS Project
Have students choose a celebrity and research personal / background information on him / her. They can use the chart* on the next page to write down the information they find. They can also include other similar information, and, using the grammatical patterns** in the box below the chart, have them write out sentences (preferably in *hiragana*) as though it were a short bio on that celebrity. If they can print out or cut out a picture of him / her from a magazine, small bio sheets can be made with the information they have found written below the picture. The bio sheets can be put up on a bulletin board or on walls in the Japanese classroom.

*Chart: Celebrity Name: _____

Where s/he lives now	
Where s/he was born	
If s/he is married; if so, how old s/he was when s/he got married	
At what age or time in life (Ex.) when s/he was a child, was in college, etc.) s/he did ~	
For how long s/he ~ (Ex.) was married, lived in ~, etc.	

**Grammatical Patterns

(place)-*ni sunde-imasu*   *kekkon shite-imasu / imasen*   *~ka-getsu / ~nen-kan* _____   *~sai-no toki* (things s/he did)   (event / occasion)-*no toki* (things s/he did)

Choosing a Child's Name	Japanese Homes	Reading *Kanji*: 子
CULTURE NOTES **Online Resources** Discussion	1. **Online Resources** 2. **i-*irasshai* (online):** housing situations; housing types	**KANJI NOTES** Class Work
Have students use various search engines to research the etymology and history of Japanese first names and choosing a baby's name.	1. Have students use various search engines to research Japanese homes and the Japanese lifestyle. 2. Using i-*irasshai*, have students learn more about and see photos of different Japanese house types and read more about them (select the guide book (index) and click on the topics listed above).	Students must use their imagination. Have them draw pictures from the *kanji* 子 and come up with sentences or stories that will help them remember the meaning and / or pronunciation(s).

Lesson 51

Family Members and Relatives	Traditional Japanese Calendar	My Relative
VOCABULARY NOTES Bingo Game	**CULTURE NOTES** **Online Resources** Discussion	**INTERACTIVE ACTIVITIES** **Part 2** Composition
Using the Family Members and Relatives chart in the textbook, have students fill in their <u>Bingo charts</u>* with humble and honorific terms. They will write all the words on the list on small pieces of paper and put them in a bag / box. Students take turns drawing a word from the bag / box and reading the word out loud. Continue taking turns until someone gets bingo.	Have students use various search engines to research the origin of the 12 animals of the traditional Japanese calendar.	Using the chart as a template, have students write essays (they are encouraged to write in *hiragana*) about a favorite relative. If a photo is available, the essay and photo can be pasted onto construction paper and used to decorate a bulletin board or corner of the classroom. The <u>sample essay</u>** on the next page can be copied and distributed as a model.

*Bingo Chart:

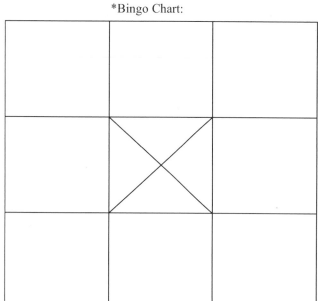

**Sample essay:

Watashi-no itoko-no namae-wa Yukina desu. 28-sai desu. Chichi-no ani- / Oji-no kodomo desu. Hokkaidoo-de umaremashita. O-tanjoobi-wa 2-gatsu 3-ka desu. Kodomo-no-toki Hokkaidoo-no Sapporo-ni sunde-imashita. Ima Tookyoo-ni sunde-imasu. Rainen kekkon shimasu. Yukina-san-wa se-ga hikukute, kami-ga mijikai desu. Tenisu-to bareebooru-ga joozu desu.

English translation: My cousin's name is Yukina. She's 28 years old. She is the child of my father's older brother / my uncle. She was born in Hokkaido. Her birthday is February 3rd. She lived in Sapporo, Hokkaido when she was a child. Now she's living in Tokyo. She's going to get married next year. She is short and has short hair. She's good at tennis and volleyball.

Lesson 52

Occupations	Occupations and Places of Work
VOCABULARY NOTES Bingo Game	**VOCABULARY NOTES** Matching Game
Using the <u>Occupation and Location list</u>*, have students fill in their Bingo chart (see Lesson 51 for template) with Japanese occupations. They will write all the words on the list on small pieces of paper and put them in a bag / box. Students take turns drawing a word from the bag / box and read the word out loud. Continue taking turns until someone gets bingo.	Using the <u>Occupation and Location list</u>*, students write the occupation and the place on two separate cards (as many as 24 cards). All cards are turned face down on a table. One student picks two cards, and makes sentences based on what is turned over. (Ex.) "*~wa ~de hatarakimasen.*" if the occupation does not match the location, and "*~wa ~de hatarakimasu.*" if it does. If it is a match, the student keeps those two cards, and the next student gets a turn. Students should only turn over two cards per turn. The object is to get the most cards.

*<u>Occupation and Location List</u>:

ten'in: mise
[clerk]
kaishain: kaisha
[company worker]
kyooju: daigaku
[professor]
kangofu: byooin
[nurse]

isha: byooin
[doctor]
ginkooin: ginkoo
[banker]
ueetaa: resutoran
[waiter]
keikan: kooban
[policeman]

seerusman: depaato
[salesman]
sensei: gakkoo
[teacher]
ueetoresu: resutoran
[waitress]
untenshu: machi-no naka
[driver]

Lesson 53

Jobs	Reading *Kanji*	*Kanji*
VOCABULARY NOTES Pair / Group Work	**KANJI NOTES** Class Work	**KANJI REVIEW** Pair Work
PREPARATION: Students must bring in a variety of ads from the Job pages of a newspaper. Using the information in the ad, they can talk about those jobs using the vocabulary from this lesson. (Ex.) *ichi-jikan ~-doru* (pay per	Students must use their imagination. Have them draw pictures from the *kanji* 言 and 話 and come up with sentences or stories	In pairs, one student silently chooses a *kanji* and tells his / her partner how many strokes it has (Ex.) *mizu* = four. S/he then writes the first stroke. The partner gets one chance to guess the *kanji*, giving the pronunciation and / or the English meaning. If s/he guesses incorrectly, the writer writes the next stroke and continues until the partner guesses

hour), (place)-*no arubaito* (type of part-time work), *~-ji kara ~-ji made* (from ~time to ~time), *shigoto-wa ~-yoobi* (the days of the part-time job), *Kono arubaito-o shitai / shitaku-nai desu.* (whether or not they want to do this job).	that will help them remember the meaning and / or pronunciation(s).	correctly. Points are given based on the number of strokes the writer did NOT have to write before the partner guessed correctly (the number of strokes in the *kanji* minus the number of strokes that had to be written before the correct answer was given. The writer should look up the correct stroke order before starting). The winner has the most points and is crowned "*Kanji* King / Queen!"
Rirekisho (Japanese Résumés)		Owing and Driving a Car in Japan
CULTURE NOTES **Online Resources** Discussion		**CULTURE NOTES** **Online Resources** Discussion
Have students use various search engines to research Japanese résumés and see samples.		Have students use various search engines to research driving in Japan.

Lesson 54

Sono ato (After that) [Length of time]-*go* ([length of time] + later)	*Sotsugyoo* (Graduation)	Reading *Kanji*: 国 語
VOCABULARY Class Work	**VOCABULARY** **Online Resources** Discussion	**KANJI NOTES** Class Work
On an index card, each student writes sentences similar to the sample sentences* below. They then write the question *Watashi-wa dare deshoo-ka?* (Who am I?), and write their name at the bottom of the card. All cards are collected, mixed and dealt out one per student. Each student reads the card, and, after listening to the information read, the class must guess who that person is.	Have students use various search engines to research school graduation ceremonies in Japan.	Students must use their imagination. Have them draw pictures from the *kanji* 国 and 語 and come up with sentences or stories that will help them remember the meaning and /or pronunciation(s).

*Sample sentences:
1. *Kotoshi / rainen /~-nen-go-ni, sotsugyoo shimasu.* (I will graduate this year/next year/in ~ years.)
2. *Sono ato, kekkon shimasu /*[name of college] *daigaku-ni ikimasu /* [place-*de*] *shigoto-o shimasu.* (After that, I will get married / go to ~ college / work at [place].)
3. [Occupation]**-*ni narimasu.* (I will become a ~.)
   ** Refer to the occupation chart or go to online Japanese dictionary websites to research job names.

Lesson 55

Shoorai, Sumimasu, Narimasu	Reading *Kanji*: 読	*Kanji*
INTERACTICE ACTIVITIES Part 1 Class Work	**KANJI NOTES** Class Work	**KANJI REVIEW** Class Work
On an index card, have each student write sentences as in the sample sentences* below. They then write the question *Watashi-wa dare deshoo-ka?* (Who am I?) and write their name at the bottom of the card. All cards are collected, mixed, and dealt out one per student. Each student reads the card, and, after listening to the information read, the class must guess who that person is.	Students must use their imagination. Have them draw pictures from the *kanji* 読 and come up with sentences or stories that will help them remember the meaning and / or pronunciation(s).	Divide the class into two teams. One person from each team goes to the board. Choosing a *kanji* from the *Kanji* Review box in the textbook, one person, the hint-giver, tells the two writers at the board: 1. "This *kanji* has # strokes." [pause], 2. "The pronunciation(s) is / are ~." [pause] and 3. "The English meaning is ~." The writers race to see who can write the correct *kanji* first. The writers and hint-givers rotate turns.

*Sample sentences:
Kodomo-no toki, ~-ni naritakatta desu. (When I was a child, I wanted to be a ~.)
Ima, ~-ni naritai desu. (Now, I want to be a ~.)
Shoorai, ~-ni sumitai desu. (In the future, I would like to live in ~.)
Kekkon shitai / shitaku-nai desu. (I want / don't want to get married.)
Kodomo-ga (#-nin) hoshii desu. (I want (#) kids.)

Lesson 56

Review of Phrases and Expressions	Religion	Reading *Kanji*: 書
***Irasshai* website**: for students - student notebook - Resources column - Choose Your Lesson - Japanese II <u>56</u> - *Nan-to iimasu-ka?* Parts 1, 2 and 3	**Online Resources** **i-*irasshai* (online)**: Buddhism and Shintoism Discussion	**KANJI NOTES** Class Work
Have students review phrases and expressions they have learned so far.	1. Have students use various search engines to research religion in Japan. 2. Using i-*irasshai*, have students learn more about various topics related to Buddhism and Shintoism (select the guide book (index) and click on monk dolls, mountains—spiritual significance, altars, chants, shrines, worship, traditions, etc.)	Students must use their imagination. Have them draw pictures from the *kanji* 書 and come up with sentences or stories that will help them remember the meaning and / or pronunciation(s).

Lesson 57

-kan		Read the *Kanji*: 聞 間
KEY GRAMMAR POINTS Class Work		**KANJI NOTES** Class Work
Have one student come to the front of the classroom and ask the other students one of the following questions. The other students will write down their answers on a piece of paper while the first student writes his / her answer on the board. A different student should read each question. QUESTIONS: 1. *Shawaa-wa nan-pun(-kan) gurai desu-ka?* (About how many minutes do you shower?) 2. *Raishuu, rekishi-no tesuto-ga arimasu. Nan-jikan benkyoo shimasu-ka?* (There is a history test next week. How many hours will you study for it?) 3. *Sukii-no renshuu-o shimasu. Nan-nichi-kan shimasu-ka?* (You will practice skiing. How many days will you practice?) 4. *Kuruma-no unten-no renshuu-o shimasu. Nan-shuu-kan shimasu-ka?* (You will practice driving (a car). How many weeks will you practice?) 5. *Nihon-ni asobi-ni ikimasu. Nan-shuu-kan ikitai desu-ka?* (You will go to Japan for vacation. How many weeks do you want to go?) 6. *Atarashii arubaito-o shimasu. Nan-shuu-kan shimasu-ka?* (You will start a new part-time job. How many weeks will you do it?) 7. *Roshiago-no benkyoo-o shimasu. Nan-nen-kan benkyoo shimasu-ka?* (You will study Russian. How many years will you study?)		1. Have students make flash cards for each *kanji* they have learned in this lesson. 2. Students must use their imagination. Have them draw pictures from the *kanji* 聞 and 間 and come up with sentences or stories that will help them remember the meaning and / or pronunciation(s). (Ex.) 聞 - I <u>hear</u> someone KICK [kiku]-ing the gate. Students can vote on the best drawings or stories.

Lesson 58

Gozen and *Gogo* Date / Time-*ni demasu / tsukimasu*	Read the *Kanji*: 時 分
VOCABULARY NOTES **KEY GRAMMAR POINTS** **Online Resources** Group Work	**KANJI NOTES** Class Work
1. Divide the students into small groups. 2. Have each group go to a travel agent's website, select a starting region and decide on a cruise. 3. Have them write down some detailed information using the <u>Cruise Information Sheet</u>* on the next page. 4. Have them report their findings to the class in Japanese and decide which cruise is the most popular.	1. Have students make flash cards for each *kanji* they have learned in this lesson. 2. Students must use their imagination. Have them draw pictures from the *kanji* 時 and 分 and come up with sentences or stories that will help them remember the meaning and / or pronunciation(s).

How many nights: _____   Price: _____
Traveling Region: _____
Traveling Cities: _____
Departure Date / Time: _____
Arrival Date / Time: _____

(Sample Script) *Kore-wa Yooroppa-no 10-ka-kan-no kuruuzu desu. 1,400-doru kara desu. Itaria-to, Girisha-to, Supein-to, Furansu-ni ikimasu. 7-gatsu 2-ka-no gogo 7-ji-ni demasu. 7-gatsu 12-nichi-no gozen 8-ji-ni tsukimasu.*
[English Translation: This is a 10-day-cruise in Europe. It costs from 1,400 dollars. You will go to Italy, Greece, Spain, and France. You will leave at 7:00 p.m. on July 2nd. You will arrive at 8:00 a.m. on July 12th.]

Lesson 59

Famous Tourist Sites in Japan	Read the *Kanji*: 雨 雪
CULTURE NOTES **Online Resources** Project and Presentation	**KANJI NOTES** Class Work
Assign each student a different tourist site in Japan listed in the CULTURE NOTES of the textbook, and have them do research to find out more about the site and report to the rest of the class. Tokyo: Tokyo City Hall, Tokyo Tower, the Imperial Palace, the National Parliament Building, Meiji-jingu Shrine Kyoto: Kinkaku-ji Temple, Heian-jingu Shrine, Kiyomizu-dera Temple, Ryoan-ji Temple	1. Have students make flash cards for each *kanji* they have learned in this lesson. 2. Students must use their imagination. Have them draw pictures from the *kanji* 雨 and 雪 and come up with sentences or stories that will help them remember the meaning and / or pronunciation(s).

Lesson 60

Japan's International Airports	Place-*ni* date / time-*ni tsukimasu* Place-*o* date / time-*ni demasu*.
CULTURE NOTES **Online Resources**: Narita International Airport, Kansai International Airport Project	**KEY GRAMMAR POINTS** **Online Resources**: Narita International Airport, Kansai International Airport Project
1. Have students go to the websites for the international airports listed above. 2. Have them find flight information for today's international arrivals and departures at each airport. 3. Have them check how many flights are coming in from the U.S. and going to the U.S. and talk about their findings.	Have students write down the arrival times of flights from the U.S. and the departure times of flights to the U.S. and report to the class in Japanese. (Ex.) 1. Hanoi-*kara-no hikooki* JL752-*wa gozen 6-ji 1-pun-ni Narita-ni tsukimashita.* (Japan Airlines flight 752 from Hanoi arrived in Narita at 6:01 a.m.) 2. Seoul-*e-no hikooki* OZ107-*wa gozen 9-ji 4-pun-ni Narita-o demashita.* (Asiana Airlines flight 107 to Seoul left Narita at 9:04 a.m.)
Shinkansen	Read the *Kanji*: 東 京 駅
VOCABULARY NOTES **Online Resources** Discussion	**KANJI NOTES** Class Work
Have students use various search engines to research bullet trains in Japan.	1. Have students make flash cards for each *kanji* they have learned in this lesson. 2. Students must use their imagination. Have them draw pictures from the *kanji* 東, 京 and 駅 and come up with sentences or stories that will help them remember the meaning and / or pronunciation(s).

Lesson 61

Item-*ga nakunaru*	Looking for Sachiko-*san*
KEY GRAMMAR POINTS Group Work	Pair Work
1. Collect about ten items from different students. Have students contribute a personal item such as a watch, an item from their bag or other school supply. 2. Have students go over the names of the items in Japanese before setting them out on a table. 3. Have students study everything there and close their eyes while the leader removes one or two items. 4. The leader then has students open their eyes and ask what is missing (*Nani-ga nakunarimashita-ka?*). 5. If someone answers correctly, change the leader and repeat the activity.	1. Make pairs. Make a copy of the <u>strip mall map</u>* below for each student. Make one copy of the figure of Sachiko for each pair. 2. Partner A has the map and the Sachiko figure and decides where Sachiko is. Partner B asks where she is. Partner A does not tell the name of the place but tells only the location of the shop. Partner B confirms where she is by telling Partner B the name of the place. When Partner B gets it right, Partner A changes the place where Sachiko is.

Sample Dialogue for Pair Work

    B: *Sumimasen. Sachiko-san-o sagashite imasu. Sachiko-san-wa doko-ni imasu-ka?*
      (Excuse me. I am looking for Sachiko. Where is she?)
    A: *Sachiko-san-wa ima <u>niku-ya-no mae</u>-no omise-ni imasu.*
      (She is now in the shop in front of the meat shop.)
    B: *Aa, soo desu-ka? Jaa, Sachiko-san-wa <u>pan-ya</u>-ni imasu-ne.*
      (Is that so? Then, she is at the bakery, isn't she?)
    A: *Hai, soo desu.* (Yes, that's right.)

*Strip Mall Map

bookstore	bakery	shoe store	clothes shop	restaurant	coffee shop

sandwich shop	meat shop	fish store	watch shop	cake shop	camera shop

Sachiko

Lesson 62

Counters	Past Adjectives
KEY GRAMMAR POINTS Pair Work	**KEY GRAMMAR POINTS** Pair Work
Prepare 24 index cards and write a counter word on one side and its category in English on the other side (Ex.) Side A: *-fun, - pun*; Side B: minutes. Shuffle the cards and divide them into two. Each person has 12 cards. Have students look only at the English category side (Side B) and ask a question using the counter word for the category. They can look at the other side of the card only if they cannot come up with the counter word for the category. (Ex.) [degrees]	1. Using the adjective flash cards students made in Lesson 23, have students go over making the past tense, both affirmative and negative. 2. Give them a category to talk about such as restaurants, movies, books, TV shows, places to go, people, classes or music, and have them create a casual conversation to exchange information. Sample Dialogue: A: *B-san-wa moo* [a movie title]-*o mimashita-ka?* (Have you already seen [a movie title]?) B: *Iie, mada-desu-kedo. Doo deshita-ka?* (No, not yet. How was it?) A: *Totemo omoshirokatta desu-yo. Senshuu, eiga-o mimashita-ka?* (It was very interesting. Did you see any movies last week?)

A: *Kyoo-wa nan-do desu-ka?* (What is the temperature today?) B: *65-do desu.* (It's 65 degrees.)	B: *Hai,* [a movie title]-*o mimashita. Nagaku-te tsumaranakatta desu-yo.* (Yes, I saw [a movie title]. It was long and boring.)

-~*kara #-ban-me*

KEY GRAMMAR POINTS
Game

1. Make two copies of the <u>grid</u>* below for each student (one grid is for the student's own words; the other is for their partner's words).
2. Without their partner seeing their grid, have each student write five words in *hiragana* or *katakana* either from left to right or top to bottom. Use one box for each syllable. They can start writing a word from anywhere within the grid unless they run out of boxes (the entire word must fit comfortably within the grid in a straight line).
3. Partner A tells one syllable at a time and its location on the grid (sample provided below*). Partner B writes that character in the appropriate box on his / her second grid. The partners will take turns telling one syllable at a time to each other. They can start guessing what the word is whenever they can figure it out. Whoever guesses all of the five words fastest wins the game.

*SAMPLE: If the word "えんぴつ" is written in the second row from column 3 through 6, Partner A would say, "*Ue-kara 2-ban-me desu. Hidari-kara 4-ban-me-no hiragana-wa 'n' desu.*" (It's the second from the top. The *hiragana* in the fourth block from the left is 'n'.)

*Grid

	1	2	3	4	5	6	7	8	9	10
1										
2										
3										
4										
5										
6										
7										
8										
9										
10										

Lesson 63

Grammar Review (L57~63)	*Kanji* Review
Irasshai website: for students - student notebook - Resources column - Choose Your Lesson - Japanese II <u>63</u> - *Nan-to iimasu-ka?* Parts 1, 2 and 3	Pair Work
Students can go to the website and review the grammatical items they learned from Lesson 57 through 61.	Make pairs. Using flash cards, Partner A can test Partner B's knowledge of the *kanji* they have learned in this course. Partner A shows the *kanji* side of the card and Partner B tells its reading and meaning. If Partner B does not know a *kanji*, set the card aside to do a second round. When Partner B is done, they can switch roles.

Volume 2
Workbook Answer Keys

Workbook Assignment Answer Keys
Particle Practice Answer Keys
Reading and Writing Practice Answer Keys

PRELIMINARY LESSON 1

PART 1

1. **Read all of the notes for Preliminary Lesson 1.**
2. **Review the vocabulary.**

PART 2

1. **Review all hiragana.**
2. **Preview the vocabulary and notes for Preliminary Lesson 2.**

PRELIMINARY LESSON 2

PART 1

1. **Read all of the notes for Preliminary Lesson 2.**
2. **Review the vocabulary.**

PART 2

1. **Review all hiragana.**
2. **Preview the vocabulary and notes for Lesson 1 of this text.**

LESSON 1

PART 1

1. **Read all of the notes for Lesson 1.**
2. **Review the vocabulary.**
3. **Kakimashoo!**

    1. music おんがく [ongaku] 2. foods たべもの [tabemono] 3. Japanese にほんご [nihongo] 4. (school) subject かもく [kamoku] 5. English えいご [eigo] 6. can (do) a little すこし できます [sukoshi dekimasu] 7. like, is/are pleasing すきです [suki desu] 8. don't really like あんまり すき じゃない です [anmari suki ja nai desu] 9. fish さかな [sakana] 10. meat にく [niku] 11. vegetables やさい [yasai] 12. movies えいが [eiga] 13. can't really (do) あんまり できません [anmari dekimasen] 14. math すうがく [suugaku] 15. history れきし [rekishi]

PART 2

1. **Kotaete kudasai.**

    1. O-namae-wa? (What's your name?) → *Name* です。 [*Name* desu.] (I'm ~.) 2. Nan-nen-sei desu-ka? (What grade are you in?) → *Grade* です。 [*Grade* desu.] (I'm in the ~ grade.) 3. Gakkoo-wa doko desu-ka? (What school do you go to/Where's your school?) → *School name/City* です。 (I go to *school name/* My school is in *city*.) 4. Nan-sai desu-ka? (How old are you?) → *Age* です。 (I'm # years old.) 5. Tabemono-wa nani-ga ichiban suki desu-ka? (What is your favorite food?) → *Favorite food* です。 (I like *favorite food* best.) 6. Supootsu-wa nani-ga dekimasu-ka? (What sports can you play?) → *Sport*が できます。 (I can play *sport*.)

2. **Preview the vocabulary and notes for Lesson 2.**

LESSON 2

PART 1

1. **Read all of the notes for Lesson 2.**
2. **Study the vocabulary.**
3. **Kakimashoo!**

    1. いつ (when) 2. おたんじょうび (birthday) 3. プール (swimming pool) 4. から (from) 5. まで (until) 6. がつ (~month) 7. ピクニックに いきます (go on a picnic) 8. なつ やすみ (summer vacation) 9. ホームステイ (homestay)

PART 2

1. **Kakimashoo!**

    1. テニスを します (play tennis) 2. ドライブに いきます (go for a drive) 3. サッカーを します (play soccer) 4. バレーボールを します (play volleyball) 5. スキーを します (ski) 6. ゴルフを します (play golf)

2. **Preview the vocabulary and notes for Lesson 3.**

LESSON 3

PART 1

1. **Read all of the notes for Lesson 3.**
2. **Study the vocabulary.**

PART 2

1. **Eigo-de nan-to iimasu-ka?**

kutsu-ya (shoe store)	daigaku (college, university)	eki (station)
panya (bakery)	chuugakkoo (middle school)	kamera-ya (camera store)
hon-ya (bookstore)	tokei-ya (watch/clock shop)	yuubinkyoku (post office)
kooen (park)	depaato (department store)	fuku-ya (clothes shop)
hoteru (hotel)	niku-ya (meat shop)	shoogakkoo (elementary school)
toshokan (library)	sakana-ya (fish shop)	kookoo (high school)
ginkoo (bank)	yao-ya (vegetable store)	keeki-ya (cake shop)
chikatetsu (subway)	eigakan (movie theater)	suupaa (supermarket)

2. **Preview the vocabulary and notes for Lesson 4.**

LESSON 4

PART 1

1. **Read all of the notes for Lesson 4.**
2. **Study the vocabulary.**
3. **Kakimashoo!**

1. ペット (pet) 2. いぬ (dog) 3. かわいい (cute) 4. しゃしん (photograph) 5. だれ (who) 6. ねこ (cat) 7. おかあさん (someone's mother) 8. いもうと (my younger sister) 9. かぞく (my family) 10. ちち (my father) 11. かっています (keep a *pet*) 12. ごきょうだい (someone's brothers and sisters)

PART 2

1. **Watashi-no petto** (My Pet) [Sample answers]
   わたしは　ペットを　かっています。ペットは いぬ／ねこ です。なまえは スパイク／ ウィスカーズ です。くろい／しろい／ちゃいろとしろ です。おおきい／ちいさい です。にく／ さかなを たべます。にほんごが できます／すこしできます／できません／ぜんぜんできません。
   [*Roomaji* version] Watashi-wa petto-o katte-imasu. Petto-wa inu/neko desu. Namae-wa Supaiku/ Wisukaazu desu. Kuroi/Shiroi/Chairo-to shiro desu. Ookii/Chiisai desu. Niku/Sakana-o tabemasu. Nihongo-ga dekimasu / sukoshi dekimasu / dekimasen / zenzen dekimasen.
   (English translation) I have a pet. The pet is a dog/cat. His/her name is Spike/Whiskers. He/she is black/white/brown and white. He/she is big/small. He/she eats meat/fish. He/she understands Japanese/ understands Japanese a little/doesn't understand Japanese/doesn't understand Japanese at all.

2. **Preview the vocabulary and notes for Lesson 5.**

LESSON 5

PART 1

1. **Read all of the notes for Lesson 5.**
2. **Study the vocabulary.**
3. **Wakaru? Wakarimasu-ka?**

する	do	よむ	read	できる	be able/can
ちがう	be different/wrong	みる	see/watch	たべる	eat
いく	go	くる	come	うたう	sing
いる	is/are; has/have *animate*	おきる	wake up/get up	のむ	drink
きく	listen/hear/ask	かえる	return	かう	buy
ある	is/are; has/have *inanimate*	ねる	go to bed	なる	become

PART 2

1. **Kakimashoo!**

1. はやい (early/fast) 2. ねむい (sleepy) 3. いただきます。 (I will receive *this food/drink*.) 4. どうですか。 (How is it?) 5. おそい (late/slow) 6. いま (now) 7. おいしい (delicious) 8. あさごはん (breakfast) 9. まいにち (every day) 10. はやい (early/fast)

2. **Preview the vocabulary and notes for Lesson 6.**

LESSON 6

PART 1
1. **Read all of the notes for Lesson 6.**
2. **Learn the new vocabulary.**

PART 2
1. **Kakimashoo!** [Sample answers]

   どこの くに ですか。 1. この くには *name of a country* から とおい です。 2. おおきい／ちいさい です。 3. *Name of a country* に ちかい です。 4. この くには *name of a country* じゃない です。 5. この くにでは *name of a language* を はなします。

   [*Roomaji* version] Doko-no kuni desu-ka? 1. Kono kuni-wa *name of a country*-kara tooi desu. 2. Ookii/Chiisai desu. 3. *Name of a country*-ni chikai desu. 4. Kono kuni-wa *name of a country* ja nai desu. 5. Kono kuni-de-wa *name of a language*-o hanashimasu.

   (English translation) What country is it? 1. This country is far from *name of a country*. 2. It is big / small. 3. It is near *name of a country*. 4. This country is not *name of a country*. 5. They speak *name of a language* in this country.

2. **Preview the vocabulary and notes for Lesson 7.**

LESSON 7

PART 1
1. **Read all of the notes for Lesson 7.**
2. **Learn the new vocabulary.**
3. **Prepare for an interactive activity.**

PART 2
1. **Kakimashoo!** [Sample answers]

   どこの くに ですか。 1. この くには おおきい／ちいさい です。 2. *Name of a continent*＊ に あります。 3. この くにでは *name of a language* を はなします。 4. アメリカにちかい ／ から とおい です。 5. *Name of a country* に ちかい です。 6. *Name of a country* の きた／みなみ／ひがし／ にし です。 7. *Name of a country* じゃない です。

   ＊ CONTINENTS: アフリカ Afurika (Africa), アジア Ajia (Asia), オーストラリア Oosutoraria (Australia), ヨーロッパ Yooroppa (Europe), きたアメリカ Kita Amerika (North America), みなみアメリカ Minami Amerika (South America)

   [*Roomaji* version] Doko-no kuni desu-ka? 1. Kono kuni-wa ookii/chiisai desu. 2. *Name of a continent*-ni arimasu. 3. Kono kuni-de-wa *name of a language*-o hanashimasu. 4. Amerika-ni chikai /-kara tooi desu. 5. *Name of a country*-ni chikai desu. 6. *Name of a country*-no kita/minami/higashi/nishi desu. 7. *Name of a country* ja nai desu.

   (English translation) What country is it? 1. This country is big/small. 2. It is in *name of a continent*. 3. They speak *name of a language* in this country. 4. It is near/far from the U.S. 5. It is near *name of a country*. 6. It is north/south/east/west of *name of a country*. 7. It is not *name of a country*.

2. **Yomimashoo!**

   1. Monday 2. January 3. March 4. what month? 5. Sunday 6. Tuesday 7. birthday 8. 11th 9. 23rd 10. 2nd 11. 3rd

3. **Preview the vocabulary and notes for Lesson 8.**

LESSON 8

PART 1
1. **Read all of the notes for Lesson 8.**
2. **Learn the new vocabulary.**
3. **Dekimasu-ka?**

   Nihon-wa chiisai desu-kedo totemo kirei-na kuni desu. (Japan is very small but is a very pretty country.)

PART 2
1. **Kakimashoo!**

   1. しま (island) 2. みずうみ (lake) 3. やま (mountain) 4. うみ (ocean, sea) 5. かわ (river)

2. **Yomimashoo!**

   1. Thursday 2. book 3. Japan 4. Japanese language 5. person, people 6. three people 7. American people 8. Japanese people 9. woman 10. 3rd 11. Tuesday 12. Monday 13. January 14. 20th 15. 2nd 16. 14th 17. what month? 18. Sunday 19. birthday 20. 11th

3. Preview the vocabulary and notes for Lesson 9.

LESSON 9

PART 1

1. Read all of the notes for Lesson 9.

2. Learn the new vocabulary.

3. Yomimashoo!

1. small   2. Japanese book   3. 2nd 4. what month?   5. Japan   6. elementary school   7. very pleasing, like a lot   8. Monday   9. three people   10. birthday   11. woman   12. college, university   13. Thursday   14. Japanese people   15. Sunday   16. 23rd 17. big

PART 2

1. Kakimashoo! [Sample answers]

1. わたしの くるまは いちばん ふるい です。 Watashi-no kuruma-wa ichiban furui desu. (My car is the oldest.)

2. あの デパートは いちばん おおきい です。 Ano depaato-wa ichiban ookii desu. (That department store is the biggest.)

3. わたしの まちは いちばん しずか です。 Watashi-no machi-wa ichiban shizuka desu. (My town is the quietest.)

4. にほんごの じゅぎょうは いちばん おもしろい です。 Nihongo-no jugyoo-wa ichiban omoshiroi (Japanese class is the most interesting.) desu.

5. ティムせんせいの ネクタイは いちばん へん です。 Timu-sensei-no nekutai-wa ichiban hen desu. (Tim-sensei's neckties are the strangest.)

2. Preview the vocabulary and notes for Lesson 10.

LESSON 10

PART 1

1. Read all of the notes for Lesson 10.

2. Learn the new vocabulary.

3. Complete Writing Practice ❶ Study, trace and write.

PART 2

1. Complete the remainder of the Writing Practice.

2. Preview the vocabulary and notes for Lesson 11.

WRITING PRACTICE

❶ **Study, trace and write.**

❷ **Dore desu-ka?**

1. getsu 月 -yoobi 日   2. juu-ichi-nichi 日   3. nan-gatsu 月   4. futsuka 日   5. tanjoobi 日   6. mainichi 日   7. ichi-gatsu 月   8. nichi 日 -yoobi 日

❸ **Kakimashoo!**

1. いちがつ 月   2. なんがつ 月   3. まいにち 日   4. げつ 月 ようび 日   5. じゅういちにち 日   6. ふつか 日   7. にち 日 ようび 日   8. たんじょうび 日

❹ **Dekimasu-ka?**

1. なん 月 でしたか。 Nan-gatsu deshita-ka? (What month was it?)

2. 月 よう 日 にいきました。 Getsu-yoobi-ni ikimashita. (I/You/He/She/They went on Monday.)

3. 日 よう 日 ですか。 Nichi-yoobi desu-ka? (Is it Sunday?)

4. みっ 日 じゃないです。 Mikka ja-nai desu. (It's not the 3rd.)

❺ **More writing practice**

LESSON 11

PART 1

1. Read all of the notes for Lesson 11.

2. Complete Writing Practice ❶ Study, trace and write.

PART 2

1. Complete the remainder of the Writing Practice.

2. Preview the vocabulary and notes for Lesson 12.

WRITING PRACTICE

❶ **Study, trace and write.**

❷ **Dore desu-ka?**

1. <u>moku</u> 木 -yoo<u>bi</u> 日　2. nan-<u>gatsu</u> 月　3. futa<u>ri</u> 人　4. <u>nihon-jin</u> 日本人　5. juu-ichi-<u>nichi</u> 日

6. san-<u>nin</u> 人　7. ichi-<u>gatsu</u> 月　8. <u>nichi</u> 日 -yoo<u>bi</u> 日　9. <u>hon</u> 本　10. amerika-<u>jin</u> 人

11. <u>getsu</u> 月 -yoo<u>bi</u> 日　12. futsu<u>ka</u> 日　13. tanjoo<u>bi</u> 日　14. hito<u>ri</u> 人　15. mik<u>ka</u> 日　16. <u>hito</u> 人

❸ **Kakimashoo!**

1. <u>ひと</u> 人　2. <u>ほん</u> 本　3. <u>ふつか</u> 日　4. アメリカ<u>じん</u> 人　5. なん<u>がつ</u> 月　6. たんじょう<u>び</u> 日

7. <u>ふた り</u> 人　8. <u>じゅういちにち</u> 日　9. <u>にほんじん</u> 日本人　10. <u>いちがつ</u> 月　11. <u>ひと り</u> 人

12. <u>にち</u> 日 よう<u>び</u> 日　13. <u>もく</u> 木 よう<u>び</u> 日　14. <u>みっか</u> 日　15. <u>げつ</u> 月 よう<u>び</u> 日　16. さん<u>にん</u> 人

❹ **Dekimasu-ka?**

1. <u>日本</u>のだいがくですか。Nihon-no daigaku desu-ka? (Is it a Japanese university?)

2. <u>木</u>よう<u>日</u>にしました。Moku-yoobi-ni shimashita. (I did on Thursday.)

3. おんなの<u>人</u>がさん<u>人</u>います。Onna-no hito-ga san-nin imasu. (There are three women.)

4. <u>月</u>よう<u>日</u>にいきました。Getsu-yoobi-ni ikimashita. (I went on Monday.)

❺ **More writing practice**

LESSON 12

PART 1

1. **Read all of the notes for Lesson 12.**
2. **Prepare for an interactive activity.**
3. **Complete Writing Practice ❶ Study, trace and write.**

PART 2

1. **Complete the remainder of the Writing Practice.**
2. **Preview the vocabulary and notes for Lesson 13.**

WRITING PRACTICE

❶ **Study, trace and write.**

❷ **Dore desu-ka?**

1. <u>moku</u> 木 -yoo<u>bi</u> 日　2. <u>shoo</u> 小 gakkoo　3. futa<u>ri</u> 人　4. tanjoo<u>bi</u> 日　5. hito<u>ri</u> 人　6. <u>nihon-jin</u> 日本人

7. <u>oo</u> 大 kii　8. san-<u>nin</u> 人　9. mai<u>nichi</u> 日　10. <u>hito</u> 人　11. ichi-<u>gatsu</u> 月　12. <u>nichi</u> 日 -yoo<u>bi</u> 日

13. <u>hon</u> 本　14. amerika-<u>jin</u> 人　15. <u>dai</u> 大 gaku　16. nan-<u>gatsu</u> 人　17. <u>getsu</u> 月 -yoo<u>bi</u> 日　18. futsu<u>ka</u> 日

19. <u>chii</u> 小 sai　20. juu-ichi-<u>nichi</u> 日

❸ **Kakimashoo!**

1. <u>ひと</u> 人　2. <u>ほん</u> 本　3. <u>おお</u> 大 きい　4. アメリカ<u>じん</u> 人　5. なん<u>がつ</u> 月　6. たんじょう<u>び</u> 日

7. <u>ちい</u> 小 さい　8. <u>じゅういちにち</u> 日　9. <u>ふた り</u> 人　10. <u>だい</u> 大 がく　11. <u>ひと り</u> 人　12. <u>にち</u> 日 よう<u>び</u> 日

13. さん<u>にん</u> 人　14. まい<u>にち</u> 日　15. <u>げつ</u> 月 よう<u>び</u> 日　16. <u>にほんじん</u> 日本人

17. <u>もく</u> 木 よう<u>び</u> 日　18. いち<u>がつ</u> 月　19. <u>ふつか</u> 日　20. <u>しょう</u> 小 がっこう

❹ **Dekimasu-ka?**

1. この<u>大</u>がくは<u>大</u>きいです。Kono daigaku-wa ookii desu. (This university is big.)

2. <u>日</u>よう<u>び</u><u>日</u>のパーティーにアメリカ<u>人</u>がふた<u>人</u>と<u>日本人</u>がろく<u>人</u>きました。
Nichi-yoobi-no-paatii-ni amerika-jin-ga futari-to nihon-jin ga roku-nin kimashita. (Two Americans and six Japanese came to Sunday's party.)

3. 3<u>月</u>23<u>日</u>に<u>日本人</u>がひと<u>人</u><u>小</u>がっこうにきました。San-gatsu ni-juu-san-nichi-ni nihon-jin-ga hitori shoogakkoo-ni kimashita. (A Japanese person came to the elementary school on March 23rd.)

4. <u>木</u>よう<u>日</u>に<u>大</u>がくの<u>本</u>やで<u>大</u>きい<u>日本</u>ごの本をかいました。わたしはこの<u>本</u>が<u>大</u>すきです。
Moku-yoobi-ni daigaku-no hon-ya-de ookii nihongo-no hon-o kaimashita. Watashi-wa kono hon-ga daisuki desu. (On Thursday I bought a big Japanese book at the college bookstore. I really like this book.)

❺ **More writing practice**

LESSON 13

PART 1

1. **Read all of the notes for Lesson 13.**
2. **Learn the new vocabulary.**
3. **Yomimashoo!**

1. small　2. Japanese book　3. 5th　4. what month?　5. Japan　6. elementary school

7. very pleasing, like a lot   8. Monday   9. four people   10. Canadian people   11. birthday   12. man   13. college student   14. Thursday   15. Japanese people   16. Sunday   17. June

PART 2

1. Watashi-no-sukejuuru [Sample answers]

1. がっこうは はちじに はじまります。Gakkoo-wa hachiji-ni hajimarimasu. (School starts at 8:00.)

2. いちじかんめは すうがく です。Ichi-jikan-me-wa suugaku desu. (First period is math.)

3. にほんごは よじかんめ です。Nihongo-wa yo-jikan-me desu. (Japanese is fourth period.)

4. れきしは にじに はじまります。Rekishi-wa ni-ji-ni hajimarimasu. (History starts at 2:00.)

5. がっこうは さんじはんに おわります。Gakkoo-wa san-ji-han-ni owarimasu. (School ends at 3:30.)

6. にほんごが いちばん すきです。Nihongo-ga ichiban suki desu. (I like Japanese the best.)

2. Preview the vocabulary and notes for Lesson 14.

LESSON 14

PART 1

1. Read all of the notes for Lesson 14.

2. Learn the new vocabulary.

3. Dekimasu-ka?

1. たべて Nakayama-san-wa tabete-imasu. (Mr./Ms. Nakayama is eating.)

2. のんで Neko-wa miruku-o nonde-imasu. (The cat is drinking milk.)

3. みて Yukari-san-wa terebi-o mite-imasu. (Yukari is watching T.V.)

4. おきて Akiko-chan-wa okite-imasu. (Akiko is up.)

5. はいって Sumisu-san-wa nihongo-bu-ni haitte-imasu. (Mr./Ms. Smith is in the Japanese language club.)

6. きて Sensei-ga kite-imasu. (The teacher is here.)

7. はいって Sensei-wa kyooshitsu-ni haitte-imasu. (The teacher is in the classroom.)

8. はなして Taroo-kun-wa tomodachi-to hanashite-imasu. (Taro is talking with his friends.)

9. ねて Akiko-san-wa nete-imasu. (Akiko is asleep.)

10. うたって Masayo-san-wa uta-o utatte-imasu. (Masayo is singing a song.)

Sample sentence: スミスさんは やきゅうを しています。Sumisu-san-wa yakyuu-o shite-imasu. (Mr./Ms. Smith is playing baseball.)

PART 2

1. Yomimashoo!

1. small   2. Japanese book   3. 5th   4. what month?   5. tall mountain   6. elementary school   7. very pleasing, like a lot   8. Monday   9. 4 people   10. Canadian people   11. how many people?   12. man   13. junior high school   14. Thursday   15. inside   16. Sunday   17. June   18. 30th   19. not big   20. high school student

2. Preview the vocabulary and notes for Lesson 15.

LESSON 15

PART 1

1. Read all of the notes for Lesson 15.

2. Learn the new vocabulary.

3. Yomimashoo!

1. Sono ookii hoteru-wa takai desu-yo. (That big hotel is expensive.)   2. Ano kookoo-wa chiisai desu-ne. (That high school is small, isn't it?)   3. San-gatsu ni-juu-go-nichi-wa nihon-no tomodachi-no tanjoobi desu. (March 25th is my Japanese friend's birthday.)   4. Ano hito-wa nihon-jin desu-ka? (Is that person a Japanese?)   5. Ano chuugakkoo-no naka-wa kirei desu-yo. (The inside of that junior high school is pretty.)

PART 2

1. Kakimashoo!

1. 人 (person)   2. 本 (book)   3. 大きい (big)   4. 日本人 (Japanese person)   5. 小さい (small)   6. 木よう日 (Thursday)   7. 3 月 (March)   8. 小がっこう (elementary school)   9. 大すき (really like)   10. 3 日 (3rd)

2. Preview the vocabulary and notes for Lesson 16.

LESSON 16

PART 1

1. Read all of the notes for Lesson 16.

2. Learn the new vocabulary.

3. Kakimashoo!

PART 2

1. Kakimashoo!

1. 日本人 (Japanese person) 2. 木よう日 (Thursday) 3. 大きい (big) 4. 人 (person/people)

5. 小がっこう (elementary school) 6. 本 (book) 7. 9 月 (September) 8. 小さい (small)

9. 大がく (college, university) 10. 2日 (2nd)

2. Preview the vocabulary and notes for Lesson 17.

LESSON 17

PART 1

1. Read all of the notes for Lesson 17.

2. Learn the new vocabulary.

3. Kakimashoo! [Sample diary]

11月 5日 （木よう日）

きょうは はれ／くもり／あめ／ゆき でした。
わたしは あさ しちじに おきて、あさごはんを たべて、がっこうに いって、 日本ごを
べんきょう して、しゅくだいを して、うちに かえりました。

[*Roomaji* version] 11-gatsu 5-ka (Moku-yoobi) Kyoo-wa hare/kumori/ame/yuki deshita. Watashi-wa asa shichi-j-ni okite, asa gohan-o tabete, gakkoo-ni itte, nihongo-o benkyoo shite, shukudai-o shite, uchi-ni kaerimashita.

(English translation) November 5th (Thursday) Today was clear/cloudy/rainy/snowy. This morning I woke up at 7:00, ate breakfast, went to school, studied Japanese, did homework and came home.

PART 2

1. Yomimashoo!

1. Nan-nin imasu-ka? (How many people are there?) 2. Sono ookii hoteru-wa takai desu-yo. (That big hotel is expensive.) 3. Nan-no hon desu ka? (What kind of book is it?) 4. San-gatsu ni-juu-go-nichi-wa Nihon-no tomodachi-no tanjoobi desu. (March 25th is my Japanese friend's birthday.) 5. Moku-yoobi-ni shimashita. (I did it on Thursday.) 6. Gakkoo-ga mittsu arimasu. (There are three schools.) 7. Nakakawa-san-wa chiisai daigaku-ni ikimashita. (Mr./Ms. Nakakawa went to a small college.)

2. Preview the vocabulary and notes for Lesson 18.

LESSON 18

PART 1

1. Read all of the notes for Lesson 18.

2. Learn the new vocabulary.

3. Dekimasu-ka?

私は今日小さい日本ごの本をかいました。 Watashi-wa kyoo chiisai nihongo-no hon-o kaimashita.
(Today I bought a small Japanese book.)

PART 2

1. Wakarimasu-ka?

1. Kyoo-wa nani-mo shimasen deshita. (I didn't do anything today.) 2. Dare-ka arubaito-o shimasu ka? (Will anyone do a part-time job?) 3. Dare-mo imasen. (Nobody is there.) 4. Ano hito-wa nani-ka yonde-imasu. (That person is reading something.) 5. Tsukue-no naka-ni nani-mo arimasen. (There's nothing in the desk.) 6. Dare-ka wakarimasu-ka? (Does anyone know/understand?)

2. Preview the vocabulary and notes for Lesson 19.

LESSON 19

PART 1

1. Read all of the notes for Lesson 19.

2. Learn the new vocabulary.

3. Complete Writing Practice ❶ Study, trace and write.

PART 2

1. Complete the remainder of the Writing Practice.

2. Preview the vocabulary and notes for Lesson 20.

WRITING PRACTICE

❶ **Study, trace and write.**

❷ **Dore desu-ka?**

1. mai<u>nichi</u> 日 2. <u>hito</u> 人 3. <u>dai</u> 大 suki 4. <u>nihon-jin</u> 日 本 人 5. <u>chii</u> 小 -sai 6. san-<u>nin</u> 人 7. <u>nan</u> 何 -<u>gatsu</u> 月 8. tanjoo<u>bi</u> 日 9. <u>hon</u> 本 dana 10. <u>ima</u> 今 11. <u>getsu</u> 月 -yoo<u>bi</u> 日 12. <u>nan</u> 何 -<u>nin</u> 人 13. <u>moku</u> 木 -yoo<u>bi</u> 日 14. <u>kyoo</u> 今日 15. itsu<u>ka</u> 日 16. <u>shoo</u> 小 gakkoo 17. <u>nan</u> 何 -<u>nichi</u> 日 18. futa<u>ri</u> 人 19. <u>oo</u> 大 kii 20. <u>konnichi</u> 今日 -wa

❸ **Kakimashoo!**

1. <u>ひと</u> 人 2. <u>ほん</u> 本 だな 3. <u>おお</u> 大 きい 4. <u>なんにち</u> 何 日 5. <u>なんがつ</u> 何 月 6. たんじょう<u>び</u> 日 7. <u>ちい</u> 小 さい 8. <u>こんにち</u> 今日 は 9. ふた<u>り</u> 人 10. <u>だい</u> 大 すき 11. <u>きょう</u> 今日 12. <u>まいにち</u> 日 13. <u>さんにん</u> 人 14. <u>なんにん</u> 何 人 15. <u>げつ</u> 月 よう<u>び</u> 日 16. <u>にほんじん</u> 日 本 人 17. <u>もく</u> 木 よう<u>び</u> 日 18. <u>いま</u> 今 19. いつ<u>か</u> 日 20. <u>しょう</u> 小 がっこう

❹ **Dekimasu-ka?**

1. あの<u>人</u>は<u>日本人</u>ですか。 Ano hito-wa nihon-jin desu-ka? (Is that person Japanese?)

2. <u>月</u>よう<u>日</u>はともだちのたんじょう<u>日</u>です。 Getsu-yoobi-wa tomodachi-no tanjoobi desu. (Monday is my friend's birthday.)

3. この<u>日本</u>ごの本が<u>大</u>すきです。 Kono nihongo-no hon-ga daisuki desu. (I really like this Japanese book.)

4. トムさんは<u>大</u>きいねこと<u>小</u>さいいぬをかっています。 Tomu-san-wa ookii neko-to chiisai inu-o katte-imasu. (Tom has a big cat and a small dog.)

5. <u>木</u>よう<u>日</u>にともだちがふた<u>人</u> <u>日本</u>にいきます。 Moku-yoobi-ni tomodachi-ga futari Nihon-ni ikimasu. (On Thursday, two of my friends will go to Japan.)

❺ **More writing practice**

LESSON 20

PART 1

1. **Read all of the notes for Lesson 20.**
2. **Learn the new vocabulary.**
3. **Non-stop talking exercise**

PART 2

Kakimashoo! [Sample letter]

1. 私のなまえはデーナミラーです。 2.じゅうななさいです。 3. たんじょう日はいち月むい日です。 4.こうこうにねんせいです。 5.私のかぞくはご人です。 6.小さいいぬをかっています。 なまえはラッキーです。 7.私のしゅみはバスケットボールです。 8.しゅうまつにテレビをみて、ともだちとあそんで、バスケットボールをします。 どんなスポーツがすきですか。 しゅうまつに何をしますか。

[*Roomaji* version] 1. Watashi-no namae-wa Deena Miraa desu. 2. Juu-nana-sai desu. 3. Tanjoobi-wa ichi-gatsu muika desu. 4. Kookoo ni-nen-sei desu. 5. Watashi-no kazoku-wa go-nin desu. 6. Chiisai inu-o katte-imasu. Namae-wa Rakkii desu. 7. Watashi-no shumi-wa basukettoboru desu. 8. Shuumatsu-ni terebi-o mite, tomodachi-to asonde, basukettobooru-o shimasu. Donna supootsu-ga suki desu-ka? Shuumatsu-ni nani-o shimasu-ka?

(English translation) 1. My name is Dana Miller. 2. I'm 17 years old. 3. My birthday is January 6th. 4. I'm a high school junior. 5. There are five people in my family. 6. I have a small dog. His name is Lucky. 7. My hobby is (playing) basketball. 8. On weekends, I watch T.V., play with my friends, and play basketball. What kind of sports do you like? What do you do on weekends?

REVIEW LESSON 1

PART 1

1. **Read all of the notes for Review Lesson 1.**
2. **Review the vocabulary.**
3. **Writing practice - What would you say?**

1. ちりの じゅぎょうは なんようび ですか。 Chiri-no jugyoo-wa nan-yoobi desu-ka? 2. れきしの じゅぎょうは すいようびと きんようび です。 Rekishi-no jugyoo-wa sui-yoobi-to kin-yoobi desu.

3. スポーツは なにが いちばん すき ですか。 Supootsu-wa nani-ga ichiban suki desu-ka? 4. カラオケ は あまり じょうずじゃない です。 Karaoke-wa amari joozu ja nai desu.

PART 2

1. **Writing gairaigo**

1. サッカー (e) 2. コーラ (c) 3. ケーキ (g) 4. コーヒー (a) 5. ミルク (d) 6. ペン (b)

128

7. ホッチキス (h)　8. ファックス (f)

2. Dialogue

[*Roomaji* version] Keiko: Miho-san, gorufu-ga dekimasu-ka?　Miho: Hai, heta desu-kedo, suki desu-yo. Keiko: Ja, do-yoobi-ni issho-ni gorufu-o shimasen-ka?　Miho: A, ii desu-ne. Shimashoo! Nan-ji-ni shimashoo-ka? Keiko: 2-ji-ni shimasen-ka?　Miho: Hai, soo shimashoo!

(English translation) Keiko: Miho, can you play golf?　Miho: Yes, I like it although I'm not good at it. Keiko: Then, won't you play golf with me on Saturday?　Miho: That sounds good. Let's (play together). What time shall we play?　Keiko: (Why) don't we play at 2:00?　Miho: Yes, let's do that.

1. golf　2. No, she did not.　3. Yes, she does.　4. Saturday　5. 2:00

3. Nihongo-de kaite kudasai. [Sample answers]

1. Boku/Watashi-no machi-wa (My town): ちいさいです (a) ／ おおきいです (b) ／ しずかです (c)

2. Karaoke-wa (Karaoke): むずかしいです (d) ／ おもしろいです (f) ／ つまらないです (g)

3. Nihongo-no jugyoo-wa (My Japanese class): むずかしいです (d) ／ かんたんです (e) ／ おもしろいです (f) ／ つまらないです (g)

4. Gakkoo-no konpyuutaa-wa (School's computers): はやいです (h) ／ おそいです (i) ／ あたらしいです (j) ／ ふるいです (k) ／ あかいです (n) ／ くろいです (o) ／ あおいです (p)

5. Boku/Watashi-no kaban-wa (My bag): ちいさいです (a) ／ おおきいです (b) ／ あたらしいです (j) ／ ふるいです (k) ／ あかいです (n) ／ くろいです (o) ／ あおいです (p)

a. ちいさい chiisai	e. かんたん kantan	i. おそい osoi	m. おいしい oishii
b. おおきい ookii	f. おもしろい omoshiroi	j. あたらしい atarashii	n. あかい akai
c. しずか shizuka	g. つまらない tsumaranai	k. ふるい furui	o. くろい kuroi
d. むずかしい muzukashii	h. はやい hayai	l. いい ii	p. あおい aoi

REVIEW LESSON 2

PART 1

1. **Read all of the notes for Review Lesson 2.**
2. **Review the vocabulary.**
3. **Writing practice - What would you say?**

1. どの ふく に しましょうか。Dono fuku-ni shimashoo-ka?　2. これに しましょう。Kore-ni shimashoo!　3. しゅうまつの てんきは どう ですか。Shuumatsu-no tenki-wa doo desu-ka?　4. あしたは あめ みたい です。Ashita-wa ame mitai desu.

PART 2

1. **Katakana writing practice**

1. konpyuutaa (computer)　2. chokoreeto (chocolate)　3. juusu (juice)　4. wain (wine)　5. naifu (knife) 6. beddo (bed)　7. botan (button)　8. remon (lemon)

2. **Reading practice**

[*Roomaji* version] Shuumatsu ane-to depaato-ni kaimono-ni ikimashita. Ane-wa kuroi kutsu-to murasaki-no kutsushita-o kaimashita. Kutsushita-wa 900-en deshita. Chotto takai desu-kedo, totemo kirei desu. Watashi-wa kawaii burausu-to midori-no sukaato-o kaimashita.

(English translation) I went shopping with my older sister this weekend. My sister bought black shoes and purple socks. The socks were 900 yen. It is a little expensive, but they are very pretty. I bought a cute blouse and a green skirt.

1. her (older) sister　2. to the department store　3. a cute blouse and a green skirt　4. black shoes and 900 yen (a little expensive), pretty purple socks

REVIEW LESSON 3

PART 1

1. **Read all of the notes for Review Lesson 3.**
2. **Review the vocabulary.**
3. **Writing practice - What would you say?**

1. パーティーに なんで いきますか。Paatii-ni nan-de ikimasu-ka?　2. ちかてつで いきましょう。Chikatetsu-de ikimashoo!　3. はやし さんは いま ほんやの なかに います。Hayashi-san-wa ima hon-ya-

no naka-ni imasu. 4. ゆうびんきょくは ここから ちかい ですか。 Yuubinkyoku-wa koko-kara chikai desu-ka? 5. あるいて なんぷん ぐらい ですか。 Aruite nan-pun gurai desu-ka?

PART 2
Reading practice

[*Roomaji* version] Watashi-no namae-wa Wendii desu. Watashi-no migi-ni haha-ga imasu. Haha-no namae-wa Nanshii desu. Watashi-no hidari-ni chichi-ga imasu. Chichi-no namae-wa Jimu desu. Haha-no ushiro-ni ani-ga imasu. Ani-no namae-wa Tomu desu. Imooto-wa ani-no hidari-ni imasu. Imooto-no namae-wa Arisu desu.

(English translation) My name is Wendy. To my right is my mother. My mother's name is Nancy. To my left is my father. My father's name is Jim. Behind my mother is my older brother. My older brother's name is Tom. To my brother's left is my younger sister. My younger sister's name is Alice.

A. Top row from left to right: Alice, Tom; bottom row from left to right: Jim, Wendy, Nancy

B. 1. Okaasan-no ushiro-ni dare-ga imasu-ka? (Who is behind the mother?) →
      トムさん／おにいさん Tomu-san/oniisan

   2. Imootosan-no mae-ni dare-ga imasu-ka? (Who is in front of the younger sister?) →
      ウェンディーさん Wendii-san

   3. Wendii-san-no migi-ni dare-ga imasu-ka? (Who is to the right of Wendy?) →
      ナンシーさん／おかあさん Nanshii-san/okaasan

   4. Oniisan-no hidari-ni dare-ga imasu-ka? (Who is to the left of the older brother?) →
      アリスさん／いもうとさん Arisu-san/imooto-san

REVIEW LESSON 4
PART 1
1. **Read all of the notes for Review Lesson 4.**
2. **Review the vocabulary.**
3. **Writing practice - What would you say?**

   1. きょうはなん月なん日ですか。 Kyoo-wa nan-gatsu nan-nichi desu-ka? 2. なんのクラブにはいっていますか。 Nan-no kurabu-ni haitte imasu-ka? 3. もういちどゆっくりいってください。 Moo ichido yukkuri itte kudasai. 4. でんわばんごうをおしえてください。 Denwa bangoo-o oshiete kudasai. 5. このきょうかしょをつかってもいいですか。 Kono kyookasho-o tsukatte-mo ii desu-ka?

PART 2
1. **Sentence completion**

   1. しま shima, ほんしゅう Honshuu (The largest island in Japan is Honshuu.); グリーンランド Guriinrando (Greenland) (The largest one in the world is Greenland.) 2. 山（やま）yama, ふじ山（さん）Fuji-san (Mt. Fuji) (The tallest mountain in Japan is Mt. Fuji.); マッキンリー山（ざん）Makkinrii-zan (Mt. McKinley) (The tallest one in America is Mt. McKinley.) 3. 川（かわ）kawa , ミシシッピー川（がわ）Mishishippii-gawa (the Mississippi River) (The longest river in America is the Mississippi River.); ナイル川（がわ）Nairu-gawa (the Nile River) (The longest one in the world is the Nile River.) 4. みずうみ mizuumi, びわこ Biwa-ko (Lake Biwa) (The largest lake in Japan is Lake Biwa.); スペリアこ Superia-ko (Lake Superior) (The largest one in America is Lake Superior.)

2. **Reading practice**

   [*Roomaji* version] Yuka: Oniichan-no gakkoo-no tomodachi-no Mariusu-san-wa dochira-kara? Kenji: Kanada-kara da-yo. Yuka: Hee. Kanada-no dochira-kara? Kenji: Kanada-no Kebekku-kara. Yuka: Aa, soo. Mariusu-san-wa nani-go-o hanasu-no? Kenji: Furansugo-to eigo-o hanasu-yo. Yuka: Nihongo-wa? Kenji: Nihongo-mo sukoshi dekiru-yo. Yuka: Waa, kakkoii!

   (English translation) Yuka: Where is your school friend Marius from? Kenji: From Canada. Yuka: Oh, from where in Canada? Kenji: From Quebec in Canada. Yuka: Is that so? What language does he speak? Kenji: He speaks French and English. Yuka: How about Japanese? Kenji: He can also speak Japanese a little. Yuka: Wow, (that's) cool.

   1. at his school. 2. He's from (Quebec,) Canada. 3. He speaks French, English and a little Japanese.
   4. She thinks he's cool.

REVIEW LESSON 5

PART 1
1. **Read all of the notes for Review Lesson 5.**
2. **Review the vocabulary.**
3. **Writing practice - What would you say?**

1. ただいま。Tadaima. おかえりなさい。O-kaerinasai. 2. いってきます。Itte-kimasu.
いってらっしゃい。Itterasshai. 3. だれもきませんでした。Dare-mo kimasen deshita. 4. しゅみは
なんですか。Shumi-wa nan desu-ka? 5. なにもたべませんでした。Nani-mo tabemasen deshita.
6. なにかのみますか。Nani-ka nomimasu-ka? 6. まりこさんのへやはきれいですね。
Mariko-san-no heya-wa kirei desu-ne.

PART 2
1. **Reading comprehension**

[*Roomaji* version] Boku-no shumi-wa manga-o atsumeru koto-to eiga-o miru koto desu. Amerika-no furui manga-ga suki desu-kedo, Nihon-no manga-mo suki desu. Eiga-wa akushon eiga-ga ichiban suki desu. Yoku gaarufurendo-to eiga-o mimasu. Gaarufurendo-wa rabu stoorii-ga suki desu.

(English translation) My hobby is collecting comics and watching movies. I like old American comics, but I also like Japanese comics. I like action movies the best. I often watch movies with my girlfriend. She likes love stories.

1. collecting manga (comics) and watching movies   2. He likes old comics.   3. He likes action movies.
4. his girlfriend   5. love stories

2. **Sentence writing practice** [Sample answers]

1. くじにおきて、ジュースをのみます。Ku-ji-ni okite, juusu-o nomimasu. (I wake up at 9:00 and drink juice.)   2. ともだちにあって、えいがかんにいきます。Tomodachi-ni atte, eigakan-ni ikimasu. (I will meet my friends and go to a movie theater.)   3. 本やにいって、本をかいます。Hon-ya-ni itte, hon-o kaimasu. (I will go to the bookstore and buy a book.)   4. うちにかえって、テレビをみます。Uchi-ni kaette, terebi-o mimasu. (I will return home and watch TV.)   5. ペンパルにてがみをかいて、じゅうにじにねます。Pen-paru-ni tegami-o kaite, juu-ni-ji-ni nemasu.

3. **Preview the vocabulary and notes for Lesson 21.**

LESSON 21

PART 1
1. **Read all of the notes for Lesson 21.**
2. **Learn the new vocabulary.**
3. **Yomimashoo!**

PART 2
1. **Tegami-o kakimashoo!** [Sample letter]

10月5日 金よう日

まりこさんへ
お元気ですか。私は元気です。きょうはいい天気です。こうえんにいってともだちと
フリスビーをします。フリスビーはとてもたのしいです。
日よう日に あにと デパートに いきました。私は あかい セーターを かいました。
まりこさんは しゅうまつ かいものに いきますか。かいものが すき ですか。
じゃ、また、てがみをください。
さようなら
ジュリー

[*Roomaji* version] juu-gatsu itsuka, kinyoobi
Mariko-san-e
O-genki desu-ka? Watashi-wa genki desu. Kyoo-wa ii tenki desu. Kooen-ni itte tomodachi-to furisubii-o shimasu. Furisubii-wa totemo tanoshii desu. Nichi-yoobi-ni ani-to depaato-ni ikimashita. Watashi-wa akai seetaa-o kaimashita. Mariko-san-wa shuumatsu kaimono-ni ikimasu-ka? Kaimono-ga suki desu-ka? Ja, mata, tegami-o kudasai. Sayoonara. Jurii
(English translation) Friday, October 5th
Dear Mariko,
How are you? I'm fine. It's fine weather today. I will go to the park and play Frisbee with my friends.

Playing Frisbee is really fun. On Sunday, I went to the department store with my older brother. I bought a red sweater. Mariko, do you go shopping on weekends? Do you like shopping? Well, please write again. Good-bye. Julie

2. Preview the vocabulary and notes for Lesson 22.

LESSON 22

PART 1

1. **Read all of the notes for Lesson 22.**
2. **Learn the new vocabulary.**
3. **Complete Writing Practice ❶ Study, trace and write.**

PART 2

1. **Complete the remainder of the Writing Practice.**
2. **Preview the vocabulary and notes for Lesson 23.**

WRITING PRACTICE

❶ **Study, trace and write.**

❷ **Dore desu-ka?**

1. o-<u>mizu</u> 水 2. <u>hito</u> 人 3. <u>dai</u> 大 gaku 4. <u>nihon</u>-jin 日本人 5. <u>chii</u> 小 sai 6. yo-<u>nin</u> 人 7. <u>nan</u>-gatsu 何月 8. <u>sui</u> 水 -yoobi 日 9. <u>hon</u> 本 10. <u>ima</u> 今 11. <u>ka</u> 火 -yoobi 日 12. <u>nan</u>-nin 何人 13. <u>moku</u> 木 -yoobi 日 14. <u>kyoo</u> 今日 15. futsu<u>ka</u> 日 16. <u>shoo</u> 小 gakkoo 17. <u>nan</u>-nichi 何 日 18. futa<u>ri</u> 人 19. <u>oo</u> 大 kii 20. <u>konnichi</u> 今日 -wa

❸ **Kakimashoo!**

1. <u>ひと</u> 人 2. <u>ほん</u> 本 3. <u>おお</u> 大 きい 4. <u>なんにち</u> 何日 5. <u>なんがつ</u> 何月 6. <u>すい</u> 水 よう び 日 7. <u>ちい</u> 小 さい 8. <u>こんにち</u> 今日 は 9. ふた<u>り</u> 人 10. <u>だい</u> 大 がく 11. <u>きょう</u> 今日 12. おみず 水 13. よにん 人 14. <u>なんにん</u> 何人 15. <u>か</u> 火 ようび 日 16. にほんじん 日本人 17. <u>もく</u> 木 ようび 日 18. <u>いま</u> 今 19. ふつか 日 20. <u>しょう</u> 小 がっこう

❹ **Dekimasu-ka?**

1. あの <u>人</u>は カナダ<u>人</u> ですか。 Ano-hito-wa Kanada-jin desu-ka? (Is that person a Canadian?)
2. <u>今日</u>は <u>火</u>よう<u>日</u> です。 Kyoo-wa ka-yoobi desu. (Today is Tuesday.)
3. あの <u>大</u>がくの <u>日本</u>ごの せんせいは <u>日本人</u> じゃ ない です。 Ano daigaku-no nihongo-no sensei-wa nihon-jin ja nai desu. (The Japanese teacher at that university is not Japanese.)
4. <u>月</u>よう<u>日</u>と <u>火</u>よう<u>日</u>と <u>水</u>よう<u>日</u>は はれ でした。<u>木</u>よう<u>日</u>は あめ でした。 Getsu-yoobi-to ka-yoobi-to sui-yoobi-wa hare deshita. Moku-yoobi-wa ame deshita. (It was fine (weather) on Monday, Tuesday, and Wednesday. It rained on Thursday.)
5. <u>今</u> <u>何</u>じ ですか。 Ima nan-ji desu-ka? (What time is it now?)
6. 私のくるまは <u>小</u>さい ですけど <u>大</u>すき です。 Watashi-no kuruma-wa chiisai desu-kedo, daisuki desu. (My car is small, but I really like it.)
7. ここの お<u>水</u>は おいしい です。 Koko-no o-mizu-wa oishii desu. (The water here is tasty.)

❺ **More writing practice**

LESSON 23

PART 1

1. **Read all of the notes for Lesson 23.**
2. **Complete Writing Practice ❶ Study, trace and write.**

PART 2

1. **Complete the remainder of the Writing Practice.**
2. **Preview the vocabulary and notes for Lesson 24.**

WRITING PRACTICE

❶ **Study, trace and write.**

❷ **Dore desu-ka?**

1. <u>nan</u>-gatsu 何月 2. <u>oo</u> 大 kii 3. <u>ima</u> 今 4. <u>konnichi</u> 今日 -wa 5. <u>chii</u> 小 sai 6. san-<u>nin</u> 人 7. <u>kin</u> 金 -yoobi 日 8. o-<u>mizu</u> 水 9. <u>nan</u>-nin 何人 10. <u>dai</u> 大 suki 11. o-<u>kane</u> 金 12. <u>hon</u> 本 dana 13. <u>ka</u> 火 -yoobi 日 14. <u>kyoo</u> 今日 15. <u>do</u> 土 -yoobi 日 16. <u>shoo</u> 小 gakkoo 17. <u>nan</u>-nichi 何日 18. <u>sui</u> 水 -yoobi 日 19. <u>hito</u> 人 20. <u>nihon</u>-jin 日本人

❸ **Kakimashoo!**

1. <u>ちい</u> 小 さい 2. <u>ほん</u> 本 だな 3. <u>おお</u> 大 きい 4. <u>なんにち</u> 何日 5. <u>なんがつ</u> 何月 6. おみず 水

7. ひと 人 8. こんにち 今日 は 9. すい 水 ようび 日 10. だい 大 すき 11. きょう 今日

12. きん 金 ようび 日 13. いま 今 14. なんにん 何人 15. おかね 金 16. にほんじん 日本人

17. か 火 ようび 日 18. さんにん 人 19. ど 土 ようび 日 20. しょう 小 がっこう

❹ Dekimasu-ka?

1. 今日は 何よう日 ですか。 Kyoo-wa nan-yoobi desu-ka? (What day is today?) 2. 金よう日が すき です。 Kin-yoobi-ga suki desu. (I like Fridays.) 3. 火よう日と 水よう日は ゆき でした。 Ka-yoobi-to sui-yoobi-wa yuki deshita. (It snowed on Tuesday and Wednesday.) 4. 大がくに 日本ごの せんせいが ふた人 います。 Daigaku-ni nihongo-no sensei-ga futari imasu. (There are two Japanese professors at the university.) 5. 土よう日と 日よう日は うちで 日本ごの べんきょうを します。 Do-yoobi-to nichi-yoobi-wa uchi-de nihongo-no benkyoo-o shimasu. (On Saturday and Sunday I will study Japanese at home.)

❺ More writing practice

LESSON 24

PART 1

1. **Read all of the notes for Lesson 24.**
2. **Learn the new vocabulary.**

PART 2

1. **Rusuban denwa-no messeeji** (telephone answering machine message) [Sample answer]

もしもし。けんじくん、*name*です。どようびは いそがしいですか。ブラウンさんと コンサート に いきますけど、けんじくんも いっしょに いきませんか。ジャズの コンサートです。しちじ はんに はじまります。あとで でんわ ください。じゃ、さようなら。

[*Roomaji* version] Moshi moshi. Kenji-kun, *name* desu. Do-yoobi -wa isogashii desu-ka? Buraun-san-to konsaato-ni ikimasu-kedo, Kenji-kun-mo issho-ni ikimasen-ka? Jazu-no konsaato desu. Shichiji-han-ni hajimarimasu. Ato-de denwa kudasai. Ja, sayoonara.

(English translation) Hello? Kenji, this is *name*. Are you busy on Saturday? I'm going to a concert with Ms. Brown, so won't you come with us? It's a jazz concert. It starts at 7:30. Give me a call later. Ok, good-bye!

2. **Preview the vocabulary and notes for Lesson 25.**

LESSON 25

PART 1

1. **Read all of the notes for Lesson 25.**
2. **Learn the new vocabulary.**
3. **Yasumi-ni nani-o shitai desu-ka?**

1. やすみに ともだちと かいものを したい です。 Yasumi-ni tomodachi-to kaimono-o shitai desu. (During break, I want to go shopping with my friends.)
2. やすみに えいがを みたい です。 Yasumi-ni eiga-o mitai desu. (During break, I want to see movies.)
3. やすみに かぞくと りょこうを したい です。 Yasumi-ni kazoku-to ryokoo-o shitai desu. (During break, I want to go on a trip with my family.)

PART 2

1. **Yomimashoo!**

1. てんき tenki (weather) 2. なんがつなんにち nan-gatsu nan-nichi (what day, what month?)

3. かようび ka-yoobi (Tuesday) 4. げんき genki (healthy, fine) 5. きんようび kin-yoobi (Friday)

6. おみず o-mizu (water) 7. わたし watashi (me, I) 8. どようび do-yoobi (Saturday) 9. おかね o-kane (money) 10. すいようび sui-yoobi (Wednesday) 11. にほんじん nihon-jin (Japanese person)

12. もくようび moku-yoobi (Thursday) 13. さんがつ san-gatsu (March) 14. ちいさいしょうがっこう chiisai shoogakkoo (small elementary school) 15. こんげつ kon-getsu (this month)

2. **Preview the vocabulary and notes for Lesson 26.**

LESSON 26

PART 1

1. **Read all of the notes for Lesson 26.**
2. **Learn the new vocabulary.**
3. **Kanji review**

4. Kakimashoo!

1. 日本人 (Japanese person) 2. 木よう日 (Thursday) 3. 大きい (big) 4. 人 (person) 5. 月よう日 (Monday) 6. 本 (book) 7. 1人 (one person) 8. 小さい (small) 9. 大がく (college) 10. 2日 (2ⁿᵈ) 11. 大さか (Osaka) 12. 3人 (3 people) 13. 小がっこう (elementary school) 14. 9月 (September) 15. 大すき (like a lot)

PART 2

1. Kanji review

2. Kakimashoo!

1. 何 (What?) 2. 今 (now) 3. 火よう日 (Tuesday) 4. お水 (water) 5. 金よう日 (Friday) 6. 何よう日 (What day?) 7. お金 (money) 8. 土よう日 (Saturday) 9. 何日 (What day of the month?) 10. 今日は 。 (Hello./ Good afternoon.) 11. 水よう日 (Wednesday) 12. 何人 (How many people?) 13. 今月 (this month) 14. 今日 (today) 15. 何の本ですか。 (What kind of book is it?)

3. Preview the vocabulary and notes for Lesson 27.

LESSON 27

PART 1

1. Read all of the notes for Lesson 27.

2. Learn the new vocabulary.

3. Dekimasu-ka?

1. Itsu juudoo-no renshuu-o shimasu-ka? (When do you practice judo?)
2. Kinoo-no yakyuu-no shiai-wa Raionzu-ga kachimashita-ka? (Did the Lions win yesterday's baseball game?)

PART 2

1. Kakimashoo! [Sample answers]

サッカーの チームは パンダーズが いちばんすき です。 つよい/よわいです。 きのう/せんしゅう/もくようび/せんしゅうのげつようび の しあいは パンダーズが かちました/まけました。 スコアは 5 たい 3 でした。

[*Roomaji* version] Sakkaa-no chiimu-wa Pandaazu-ga ichiban suki desu. Tsuyoi/Yowai desu. Kinoo/Senshuu/ Moku-yoobi/Senshuu-no getsu-yoobi-no shiai-wa Pandaazu-ga kachimashita/makemashita. Sukoa-wa 5-tai 3 deshita.

(English translation) As for soccer teams, I like the Pandas the best. They are strong/weak. Yesterday/Last week/On Thursday/Last Monday, the Pandas won/lost the game. The score was five to three.

2. Preview the vocabulary and notes for Lesson 28.

LESSON 28

PART 1

1. Read all of the notes for Lesson 28.

2. Learn the new vocabulary.

3. Complete Writing Practice ❶ Study, trace and write.

PART 2

1. Complete the remainder of the Writing Practice.

2. Preview the vocabulary and notes for Lesson 29.

WRITING PRACTICE

❶ **Study, trace and write.**

❷ **Dore desu-ka?**

1. o-<u>mizu</u> 水 2. <u>oo</u> 大 kii 3. <u>nan-nin</u> 何人 4. <u>nihon</u>-jin 日本人 5. <u>itsuka</u> 日 6. kyuu-<u>nin</u> 人
7. <u>nan-gatsu</u> 何月 8. <u>i</u> 行 kimashita 9. o-<u>kane</u> 金 10. <u>nan-nichi</u> 何日 11. <u>getsu</u> 月 -yoobi 日
12. <u>dai</u> 大 suki 13. <u>moku</u> 木 -yoobi 14. <u>kyoo</u> 今日 15. <u>chii</u> 小 sai 16. <u>shoo</u> 小 gakkoo 17. <u>ima</u> 今
18. <u>mi</u> 見 te-imasu 19. <u>hito</u> 人 20. <u>konnichi</u> 今日 -wa

❸ **Kakimashoo!**

1. 人 2. お金 3. 大きい 4. 何日 5. 何月 6. 行きました 7. 小さい 8. 今日は 9. 見ています
10. 大すき 11. 今日 12. お水 13. きゅう人 14. 何人 15. 月よう日 16. 日本人 17. 木よう日
18. 今 19. いつ日 20. 小がっこう

❹ **Dekimasu-ka?**

1. まい日 日本の テレビを 見ます。(Every day I watch Japanese T.V.) 2. 今 何の 本を よんでいます
か。(What book are you reading now?) 3. 3月 19日は アメリカの ともだちの たんじょう日 です。
(March 19th is my American friend's birthday.) 4. トムさんは 大きい ねこと 小さい いぬを かって
います。 (Tom has a big cat and a small dog.) 5. 今日は えいがを 見て ひるごはんを たべて
ドライブに 行く。(Today I'm going to see a movie, eat lunch, and go for a drive.) 6. 木よう日に
ともだちが 2人 日本に 行きます。(On Thursday, two of my friends are going to Japan.)

❺ **More writing practice**

LESSON 29

PART 1

1. **Read all of the notes for Lesson 29.**
2. **Learn the new vocabulary.**
3. **Dekimasu-ka?**

わたしの うちに あそびに きませんか。Watashi-no uchi-ni asobi-ni kimasen-ka? (Won't you come to
my house for a visit?)

PART 2

1. **Shitsumon-ni kotaete kudasai.**

1. Dare-ga denwa-o shimashita-ka? (Who made a phone call?) ➔ 中川 さんが でんわを しました。
Nakagawa-san-ga denwa-o shimashita. (Ms. Nakagawa made the phone call.) 2. Paatii-wa itsu desu-ka?
(When is the party?) ➔ 今日のよる です。Kyoo-no yoru desu. (It is tonight.) 3. Takayama-san-wa
hima desu-ka? (Is Mr./Ms. Takayama free?) ➔ はい、ひま です。Hai, hima desu. (Yes, she is free.)
4. Dare-ga paatii-ni kimasu-ka? (Who is coming to the party?) ➔ 本田さんと 山本さんと 田中さんが
来ます。Honda-san-to Yamamoto-san-to Tanaka-san-ga kimasu. (Mr./Ms. Honda, Mr./Ms. Yamamoto,
and Mr./Ms. Tanaka are coming.) 5. Paatii-wa nan-ji-kara desu-ka? (What time does the party start?) ➔
しちじ から です。Shichi-ji-kara desu. (It is from 7:00.)

2. **Preview the vocabulary and notes for Lesson 30.**

LESSON 30

PART 1

1. **Read all of the notes for Lesson 30.**
2. **Review the negative of the plain form.**

English	Negative	English	Negative	English	Negative
4. read	yomanai	9. go	ikanai	14. listen, hear	kikanai
5. eat	tabenai	10. drink	nomanai	15. buy	kawanai
6. see, look at	minai	11. forget	wasurenai	16. enter, join	hairanai
7. do	shinai	12. is, am, are	nai	17. return	kaeranai
8. understand	wakaranai	13. teach	oshienai		

PART 2

1. **Wakarimasu-ka?**

1. Kyonen-wa nani-o shimashita-ka? (What did you do last year?) 2. Raishuu-no tenki-wa doo desu-ka?
(How will next week's weather be?) 3. Senshuu-no getsu-yoobi-ni kimashita. (I came last Monday.)
4. Kyoo watashi-wa isogashii desu. (I am busy today.) 5. Kongetsu-wa go-gatsu ja nai desu. (This month is
not May.) 6. Kotoshi-mo sekai ryokoo-o shitai desu. (I want to travel around the world this year, too.)

2. **Preview the vocabulary and notes for Lesson 31.**

LESSON 31

1. **Read all of the notes for Lesson 31.**
2. **Kanji review**

READINGS	MEANINGS	READINGS	MEANINGS
1. GETSU, GATSU	month, moon	7. kawa	river
2. NICHI, bi, ~ka	day, sun	8. DAI; oo(kii)	big, large, great
3. MOKU	tree, wood	9. SHOO; ko, chii(sai)	small, little
4. HON	book, origin, source	10. GAKU	learning, science
5. NIN, JIN; hito, ~ri	person	11. KOO	school
6. SAN; yama	mountain	12. CHUU; naka	middle, inside, within

13. KOO; taka(i)	high, expensive	21. TEN	sky, heaven
14. nan, nani	what?, how many?	22. GEN	beginning, foundation
15. KON; ima	now, the present	23. KI	spirit, energy
16. watashi	I, privacy	24. ta [da]	rice field, paddy
17. KA	fire	25. mi(ru)	see, look at, watch
18. SUI; mizu	water	26. i(ku)	go
19. KIN; kane	gold; money	27. RAI; ku(ru), ki(masu)	come
20. DO	earth, soil	28. NEN; toshi	year

LESSON 32

PART 1

1. **Read all of the notes for Lesson 32.**
2. **Learn the new vocabulary.**
3. **Prepare for an interactive activity.**
4. **Yomimashoo!**

   1. やっつ／yattsu 2. むっつ／muttsu 3. ふたつ／futatsu 4. ここのつ／kokonotsu 5. よっつ／yottsu 6. ななつ／nanatsu 7. みっつ／mittsu 8. ひとつ／hitotsu 9. いつつ／itsutsu

PART 2

1. **Yomimashoo!**

   1. なにを みて いますか。 Nani-o mite-imasu-ka? (What are you looking at?) 2. らいげつは やまに いきたい です。 Rai-getsu-wa yama-ni ikitai desu. (I want to go to the mountains next month.) 3. どっち が おおきい ですか。 Dotchi-ga ookii desu-ka? (Which one is bigger?) 4. この ちいさい ほんを みて ください。 Kono chiisai hon-o mite kudasai. (Please look at this small book.) 5. らいねん にほんから たなかさんが きます。 Rai-nen Nihon-kara Tanaka-san-ga kimasu. (Mr./Ms. Tanaka is coming from Japan next year.)

2. **Preview the vocabulary and notes for Lesson 33.**

LESSON 33

PART 1

1. **Read all of the notes for Lesson 33.**
2. **Learn the new vocabulary.**
3. **Kakimashoo!**

   1. 日本人 2. 木よう日 3. 大きい 4. 人 5. 月よう日 6. 本 7. 1人 8. 小さい 9. 大がく 10. 2日 11. 大さか 12. 3人 13. 小がっこう 14. 9月 15. 大すき

PART 2

1. **Kanji review**
2. **Kakimashoo!**

   1. 何 2. 今 3. 火よう日 4. お水 5. 金よう日 6. 何よう日 7. お金 8. 土よう日 9. 何日 10. 今日は 11. 水よう日 12. 何人 13. 今月 14. 今日 15. 何の本ですか。

3. **Preview the vocabulary and notes for Lesson 34.**

LESSON 34

PART 1

1. **Read all of the notes for Lesson 34.**
2. **Complete Writing Practice ❶ Study, trace and write.**
3. **Kakimashoo!** [Sample answers]

   1. (B) ひだりから 三ばんめの ドーナッツを 八つ ください。 Hidari-kara san-ban-me no doonatsu-o yattsu kudasai. (Please give me eight of the doughnuts that are third from the left.) 2. (F) みぎから 二ばんめの ドーナッツを 七つ ください。 Migi-kara ni-ban-me no doonatsu-o nanatsu kudasai. (Please give me seven of the doughnuts that are second from the right.) 3. (A) ひだりから 六ばんめの ドーナッツを 九つ ください。 Hidari-kara roku-ban-me-no doonatsu-o kokonotsu kudasai. (Please give me nine of the doughnuts that are sixth from the left.) 4. (D) ひだりから 四ばんめの ドーナッツを 四つ ください。 Hidari-kara yon-ban-me-no doonatsu-o yottsu kudasai. (Please give me four of the doughnuts that are fourth from the left.) 5. (E) みぎから 七ばんめの ドーナッツを 五つ ください。 Migi-kara nana-ban-me-no doonatsu-o itsutsu kudasai. (Please give me five of the doughnuts that are seventh from the right.)

PART 2

1. Complete the remainder of the Writing Practice.

2. Preview the vocabulary and notes for Lesson 35.

WRITING PRACTICE

❶ **Study, trace and write.**

❷ **Dore desu-ka?**

1. <u>chii</u> 小 sai 2. <u>kyoo</u> 今日 3. <u>koo</u>koo 校 4. <u>shoogakkoo</u> 小学校 5. <u>mi</u> 見 mashita 6. <u>i</u> 行 kimasen

7. <u>nan</u> 何 -<u>gatsu</u> 月 8. hachi-<u>nin</u> 人 9. nihon-<u>jin</u> 日本人 10. <u>moku</u> 木 -yoobi 日 11. <u>getsu</u> 月 -yoobi 日

12. <u>daigaku</u> 大学 13. <u>nan-nichi</u> 何 日 14. <u>oo</u> 大 kii 15. o-<u>mizu</u> 水 16. o-<u>kane</u> 金 17. <u>mi</u> 見 te-imasu

18. <u>ima</u> 今 19. <u>konnichi</u> 今日 -wa 20. <u>hito</u> 人

❸ **Kakimashoo!**

1. 人 2. お金 3. 大きい 4. 何日 5. 何月 6. 行きません 7. 小さい 8. 今日は 9. 見ています

10. 大学 11. 今日 12. お水 13. 8人 14. こう校 15. 月よう日 16. 日本人 17. 木よう日 18. 今

19. 見ました 20. 小学校

❹ **Dekimasu-ka?**

1. この ちかくに <u>大学</u>が ありますか。(Is there a university near here?) 2. ジェシカさんは <u>小</u>さい いぬと <u>大</u>きい ねこを かっています。(Jessica has a small dog and a big cat.) 3. <u>今日</u>は どこに 行きたい ですか。(Where do you want to go today?) 4. <u>土</u>よう<u>日</u>に <u>何</u>の えいがを 見ましたか。(What movie did you see on Saturday?) 5. <u>今月</u>の 19 <u>日</u>は <u>水</u>よう<u>日</u>です。(The 19th of this month is a Wednesday.) 6. <u>金</u>よう<u>日</u>に <u>学校</u>の ともだちが <u>日本</u>に <u>行</u>きます。(On Friday, my friends from school are going to Japan.)

❺ **More writing practice**

LESSON 35

PART 1

1. Read all of the notes for Lesson 35.

2. Learn the new vocabulary.

3. Complete Writing Practice ❷ Study, trace and write.

PART 2

1. Complete the remainder of the Writing Practice.

2. Preview the vocabulary and notes for Lesson 36.

WRITING PRACTICE

❶ **Dore desu-ka?**

1. <u>taka</u> 高 i 2. <u>hito</u> 人 3. <u>nan</u> 何 -nin 人 4. o-<u>mizu</u> 水 5. <u>naka</u> 中 6. <u>konnichi</u> 今日 -wa 7. <u>nan-gatsu</u> 何月 8. <u>mi</u> 見 masen 9. o-<u>kane</u> 金 10. <u>chuugakkoo</u> 中学校 11. <u>oo</u> 大 kii 12. <u>moku</u> 木 yoobi 日

13. <u>daigaku</u> 大学 14. <u>kyoo</u> 今日 15. <u>chii</u> 小 sai 16. <u>koo</u>koo 高校 17. <u>ima</u> 今 18. <u>i</u> 行 ku 19. <u>nihon-jin</u> 日本人 20. shichi-<u>nin</u> 人

❷ **Study, trace and write.**

❸ **Kakimashoo!**

1. 何人 2. 今 3. 高校 4. 中学校 5. 何月 6. 行く 7. 小さい 8. 今日は 9. 見ません

10. 大学 11. 今日 12. お水 13. 7人 14. 人 15. 高い 16. 日本人 17. 木よう日 18. お金

19. 中 20. 大きい

❹ **Dekimasu-ka?**

1. <u>中</u>川さんは <u>小</u>さい <u>大学</u>に <u>行</u>きました。(Mr./Ms. Nakagawa went to a small university.) 2. あの <u>高校</u>の <u>中</u>は きれい ですよ。(It's pretty inside that high school.) 3. <u>今日</u> <u>学校</u>で <u>何</u>を しましたか。(What did you do in school today?) 4. おたんじょう<u>日</u>は <u>何月</u> <u>何日</u> ですか。(When is your birthday?) 5. ニュースを <u>見</u>ましたか。(Did you watch the news?)

❺ **More writing practice**

LESSON 36

PART 1

1. Read all of the notes for Lesson 36.

2. Learn the new vocabulary.

3. Complete Writing Practice ❷ Study, trace and write.

137

PART 2

1. Complete the remainder of the Writing Practice.

2. Preview the vocabulary and notes for Lesson 37.

WRITING PRACTICE

❶ **Dore desu-ka?**

1. <u>nen</u> 年　2. <u>gakkoo</u> 学校　3. <u>naka</u> 中 -ni　4. <u>mi</u> 見 te-imasu　5. <u>i</u> 行 kanai　6. o-<u>kane</u> 金　7. <u>taka</u> 高 ku-nai　8. <u>nan-nen</u> 何年　9. <u>kongetsu</u> 今月　10. furansu-<u>jin</u> 人　11. <u>nan-bon</u> 何本　12. <u>moku</u> 木 -yoo<u>bi</u> 日

❷ **Study, trace and write.**

❸ **Kakimashoo!**

1. お金　2. 今月　3. 行かない　4. 学校　5. 見ています　6. 年　7. 何本　8. フランス人　9. 高くない　10. 何年　11. 木よう日　12. 中 に

❹ **Dekimasu-ka?**

1. <u>今月</u> <u>中学校</u>の ともだちが <u>二人</u> <u>日本</u>に <u>行</u>きます。 (Two of my junior high school friends are going to Japan this month.)　2. <u>今日</u> デパートで <u>高校</u>の <u>日本</u>ごの せんせいを <u>見</u>ました。 (Today at the department store I saw my high school Japanese teacher.)

❺ **More writing practice**

LESSON 37

PART 1

1. Read all of the notes for Lesson 37.

2. Learn the new vocabulary.

3. Dekimasu-ka?

roomaji	plain form	*roomaji*	plain form
1. tabemasu	taberu たべる	6. kaimasu	kau かう
2. shimasu	suru する	7. nomimasu	nomu のむ
3. ikimasu	iku いく	8. kakimasu	kaku かく
4. yomimasu	yomu よむ	9. oshiemasu	oshieru おしえる
5. kimasu	kuru くる	10. moraimasu	morau もらう

PART 2

1. Dooshite kimasen-ka? [Sample answers]

1. Jugyoo-de tsukau-kara. じゅぎょうでつかうから。 (Because she will use it for a class.)
2. Amerika-ni iku-kara. アメリカに行くから。 (Because she'll go to the U.S.); Tesuto-ga aru-kara. テストがあるから。 (Because she has a test.); Tanoshii-kara. たのしいから。 (Because it's fun.)
3. Kutsu-ga iru-kara. くつがいるから。 (Because she needs shoes.); Purezento-o kau-kara. (Because she will buy a gift.)
4. Asa go-ji-ni okita-kara. あさごじにおきたから。 (Because he got up at 5:00.); Jugyoo-ga tsumaranai-kara. じゅぎょうがつまらないから。 (Because classes are boring.)
5. Isogashii-kara. いそがしいから。 (Because she is busy.); Shukudai-ga aru-kara. しゅくだいがある から。 (Because she has homework.)
6. Arubaito-ga aru-kara. アルバイトがあるから。 (Because she has a part-time job.); Juku-ni iku-kara. じゅくに行くから。 (Because she goes to cram school.)

2. Preview the vocabulary and notes for Lesson 38.

LESSON 38

PART 1

1. Read all of the notes for Lesson 38.

2. Learn the new vocabulary.

3. Dekimasu-ka?

2. itta	行った／いった	7. tabeta	たべた	12. kita	来た／きた
3. shita	した	8. nonda	のんだ	13. atta	あった
4. mita	見た／みた	9. miseta	見せた／みせた	14. tsukutta	つくった
5. hanashita	はなした	10. katta	かった	15. tsukatta	つかった
6. moratta	もらった	11. kaita	かいた	16. yonda	よんだ

1. Yomimashoo!

1. nan-no hon 2. ka-yoobi 3. o-kane 4. ima 5. tenki 6. mizu 7. watashi 8. nan-gatsu nan-nichi 9. sui-yoobi 10. kyoo 11. roku-juu-en 12. kimasen 13. genki 14. chiisai shoogakkoo 15. mimasu 16. kongetsu 17. kin-yoobi 18. nan-nin 19. ikimashita 20. do-yoobi 21. rainen 22. Ueda-san-to Yamashita-san

2. Preview the vocabulary and notes for Lesson 39.

LESSON 39

PART 1

1. Read all of the notes for Lesson 39.

2. Learn the new vocabulary.

3. Complete Writing Practice ❶ Study, trace and write.

PART 2

1. Complete the remainder of the Writing Practice.

2. Preview the vocabulary and notes for Lesson 40.

WRITING PRACTICE

❶ **Study, trace and write.**

❷ **Dore desu-ka?**

1. taka 高 i 2. i 行 kitai 3. en 円 4. kookoo 高校 5. chuugaku 中学 sei 6. mi 見 masen deshita 7. nan 何 -nen 年-sei 8. oo 大 kiku-nai 9. nihon-jin 日本人 10. kon-getsu 今月 11. kin 金 -yoobi 日 12. o-mizu 水

❸ **Kakimashoo!**

1. 見ませんでした 2. 金よう日 3. 日本人 4. 何年せい 5. 高い 6. 円 7. 行きたい 8. お水 9. 今月 10. 大きくない 11. 高校 12. 中学せい

❹ **Dekimasu-ka?**

1. 今月の 15日に ともだちの うちで 日本の えいがを 見ました。 (On the 15th of this month, I watched a Japanese movie at my friend's house.)

2. 来年の 8月 30 日に 日本に 行って、大学に はいって 日本ごの べんきょうを します。 (Next year on August 30th, I will go to Japan, enter a university and study Japanese.)

❺ **More writing practice**

LESSON 40

PART 1

1. Read all of the notes for Lesson 40.

2. Nyuu-yooku-ni itta-koto-ga arimasu. [Sample sentences]

1. Sushi-o tabeta-koto-ga arimasu. (I have eaten *sushi*.)
2. Sakkaa-o shita-koto-ga arimasu. (I have played soccer.)
3. Nihon-no manga-o yonda-koto-ga arimasu. (I have read Japanese *manga*/comics.)
4. Timu-sensei-ni atta-koto-ga arimasu. (I have met Tim-*sensei*.)
5. Furansu-ni itta-koto-ga arimasu. (I have been to France.)
6. Nihon-no eiga-o mita-koto-ga arimasu. (I have seen a Japanese movie.)

PART 2

1. Dooshite ikimasen-ka? [Sample answers]

1. Q. Dooshite ikimasen-ka? (Why won't you go?)
   A. いそがしい から。 Isogashii-kara. (Because I'm busy.); テストの べんきょうを する から。 Tesuto-no benkyoo-o suru-kara. (Because I'm going to study for a test.); うちに かえりたい から。 Uchi-ni kaeritai-kara. (Because I want to go home.)

2. Q. Dooshite sono nihongo-no hon-o kaimashita-ka? (Why did you buy that Japanese book?)
   A. やすかった から。 Yasukatta-kara. (Because it was cheap.); （日本ごの） じゅぎょうで よむ から。 (Nihongo-no) jugyoo-de yomu-kara. (Because we will read it for (Japanese) class.)

3. Q. Dooshite fuyu-yasumi-ni Hawai-ni ikimasu-ka? (Why are you going to Hawaii over winter break?)
   A. ハワイの うみを 見たい から。 Hawai-no umi-o mitai-kara. (Because I want to see the ocean in Hawaii.); しんせきが ハワイに いる から。 Shinseki-ga Hawai-ni iru-kara. (Because my relatives are in Hawaii.)

2. Dekimasu-ka?

1. いつ not a (an ordinal) number 2. たかい not related to taste 3. もらいました not a verb in plain past form 4. いち not a particle 5. が not a particle which comes at the end of a sentence 6. おとうさん not a humble family term 7. しずか not an *i*-adjective 8. あね not related to weather 9. やすみ not a season 10. しんぶん not a counter word

3. Preview the vocabulary and notes for Lesson 41.

LESSON 41

PART 1

1. Read all of the notes for Lesson 41.

2. Learn the new vocabulary.

3. Dekimasu-ka?

1. ¥ 71,600 2. ¥ 84,900 3. ¥ 93,600 4. ¥ 26,300 5. ¥ 52,100 6. ¥ 106,700 7. ¥ 17,800 8. ¥ 39,200 9. ¥ 65,400 10. ¥ 48,300

PART 2

1. Kakimashoo! [Sample drawing of T32X]

2. Preview the vocabulary and notes for Lesson 42.

LESSON 42

PART 1

1. Read all of the notes for Lesson 42.

2. Learn the new vocabulary.

3. Kanji review [Sample answers]

1. <u>watashi</u> (I) 2. ichi-<u>gatsu</u> (January) 3. <u>tenki</u> (weather) 4. <u>moku</u>-yoobi (Thursday) 5. ni<u>hongo</u> (Japanese) 6. san-<u>nin</u> (three people) 7. <u>tooka</u> (10th [of the month]) 8. <u>ichi</u>-nen-sei (freshman) 9. dai<u>gaku</u> (university) 10. <u>nan</u>-yoobi (what day) 11. o-<u>mizu</u> (water) 12. <u>sen</u>-en (1,000-yen) 13. <u>ka</u>-yoobi (Tuesday) 14. <u>shita</u> (under) 15. <u>hyaku</u>-nin (100 people) 16. <u>ue</u> (on, above) 17. <u>mi</u>mashita (saw, watched) 18. <u>ookii</u> (big) 19. go-juu-<u>en</u> (50-yen) 20. <u>has</u>-sai (8 years old) 21. <u>genki</u> (fine, healthy) 22. ichi-<u>man</u> (10,000) 23. <u>roku</u>-gatsu (June) 24. ikimasen (won't/don't/doesn't go) 25. ku-ji (9:00) 26. <u>yo</u>-nin (4 people) 27. <u>nana</u>-sen (7,000) 28. <u>Ya</u>mada (*family name*: Yamada) 29. <u>Ta</u>naka (*family name*: Tanaka) 30. <u>shoo</u>gakkoo (elementary school) 31. <u>koo</u>koo (high school) 32. <u>mittsu</u> (three *things*) 33. <u>kawa</u> (river) 34. gak<u>koo</u> (school) 35. go-<u>fun</u> (5 minutes) 36. <u>kin</u>-yoobi (Friday) 37. <u>rai</u>-shuu (next week) 38. <u>ni</u>-nen-sei (sophomore) 39. <u>ima</u> (now) 40. <u>chuu</u>gakkoo (junior high school) 41. ni-<u>nen</u> (two years) 42. ten<u>ki</u> (weather) 43. <u>do</u>-yoobi (Saturday) 44. <u>Ni</u>hon (Japan)

PART 2

1. Kakimashoo!

1. もしもし。 Moshi-moshi? 2. おはようございます。 Ohayoo gozaimasu. 3. 今、どこ ですか。 Ima, doko desu-ka? 4. うち です。 Uchi desu. 5. どう したん ですか。 Doo shita-n desu-ka? 6. は が いたいん です。 Ha-ga itai-n desu. 7. お大じに。 O-daiji-ni.

2. Preview the vocabulary and notes for Lesson 43.

LESSON 43

PART 1

1. Read all of the notes for Lesson 43.

2. Learn the new vocabulary.

3. Kanji review

4. Kakimashoo!

1. naka 中 2. kookoo 高校 3. en 円 4. ichi-nen-sei 一年せい 5. nan-nichi 何日 6. ikimashita 行きました 7. mimasen 見ません 8. sui-yoobi 水よう日 9. takai 高い 10. shoogakkoo 小学校

11. rainen 来年　12. chuugakusei 中学せい　13. gakkoo 学校　14. ookikunai 大きくない
15. kongetsu 今月

PART 2

1. **Kyoo-no nikki (Today's journal entry)** [Sample journal]

   [*Roomaji* version] shi-gatsu juu-hachi-nichi　ka-yoobi　tenki: ame
   Kyoo, ichi-nichi-juu kukkii-to keeki-o tabemashita. Totemo oishikatta desu. Demo, ima, onaka-ga itai kara, ashita kukkii-to keeki-wa tabemasen.
   (English translation) April 18th　Tuesday　Weather: rainy
   Today I ate cookies and cake all day. They were very delicious. But, now my stomach hurts, so I am not going to eat them tomorrow.

2. **Preview the vocabulary and notes for Lesson 44.**

LESSON 44

PART 1

1. **Read all of the notes for Lesson 44.**
2. **Learn the new vocabulary.**
3. **Time line** [Sample answers]

ASA-GOHAN
Asa-gohan-no ato-de (OR Jugyoo-*no mae-ni*) nihongo-no benkyoo-o shimashita. (After breakfast, / Before class, I studied Japanese.)
Jugyoo-no mae-ni tomodachi-to hanashimashita. (Before class, I talked with my friends.)
JUGYOO
HIRU-GOHAN
Hiru-gohan-no ato-de shukudai-o shimashita. (After lunch, I did homework.)
Miitingu-no mae-ni toshokan-ni ikimashita. (Before the meeting, I went to the library.)
MIITINGU
TENISU-NO SHIAI
Tenisu-no shiai-no ato-de uchi-ni kaerimashita. (After my tennis game, I went home.)
BAN-GOHAN
Ban-gohan-no ato-de kusuri-o nomimashita. (After dinner, I took my medicine.)
DEETO
Deeto-no ato-de uchi-ni kaette, terebi-o mite, nemashita. (After my date, I went home, watched TV and went to bed.)

PART 2

1. **Dekimasu-ka?**

   1. あした not a body part　2. 日 not a body part　3. て not a facial body part　4. がっこう not related to health　5. なに not a time-related phrase　6. かぜ not related to school　7. です not an action verb　8. あね not related to weather　9. 本 not a day-of the-week *kanji*　10. 万 not a time-of the-year *kanji*

2. **Non-stop talking exercise**
3. **Preview the vocabulary and notes for Lesson 45.**

LESSON 45

PART 1

1. **Read all of the notes for Lesson 45.**
2. **Lean the new vocabulary.**
3. **Kakimashoo!** [Sample answers]

   1. Honda-sensei-wa majime-de kibishii desu. (Professor Honda is serious and strict.)　2. Sono eiga-wa takakute tsumaranai desu. (That movie is expensive and boring.)　3. この ケーキは やすくて おいしい です。 Kono keeki-wa yasukute oishii desu. (This cake is cheap and delicious.)　4. 田中さんの コンピューターは あたらしくて はやい です。 Tanaka-san-no konpyuutaa-wa atarashikute hayai desu. (Mr./Ms. Tanaka's computer is new and fast.)　5. あの せんせいは やさしくて おもしろい です。 Ano sensei-wa yasashikute omoshiroi desu. (That teacher is kind and interesting.)　6. あきこさんは しずかで まじめ です。 Akiko-san-wa shizuka-de majime desu. (Akiko is quiet and serious.)　7. 高田せんせいの じゅぎょうは ながくて つまらない です。 Takada-sensei-no jugyoo-wa nagakute tsumaranai desu. (Mr./Ms. Takada's class is long and boring.)

PART 2

1. Kakimashoo! [Sample description]

[*Roomaji* version] Watashi-no eigo-no sensei-wa Sumisu-sensei desu. Sumisu-sensei-wa yon-jus-sai gurai desu. Genki-de akarui desu. Watashi-wa Sumisu-sensei-ga daisuki desu.

(English translation) My English teacher is Ms. Smith. Ms. Smth is about 40 years old. She is energetic and cheerful. I like her alot.

2. Preview the vocabulary and notes for Lesson 46.

LESSON 46

PART 1

1. Read all of the notes for Lesson 46.

2. Learn the new vocabulary.

3. Complete Writing Practice ❶ Study, trace and write.

PART 2

1. Complete the remainder of the Writing Practice.

2. Preview the vocabulary and notes for Lesson 47.

WRITING PRACTICE

❶ **Study, trace and write.**

❷ **Dore desu-ka?**

1. <u>nan</u> 何 -<u>nen</u> 年 2. <u>kotoshi</u> 今年 3. <u>mi</u> 見 tai 4. <u>chuugakkoo</u> 中学校 5. <u>nan</u> 何 -<u>sai</u> オ 6. 100-<u>en</u> 円

7. <u>taka</u> 高 ku-te 8. <u>i</u> 行 kitaku-nai 9. <u>kyoo</u> 今日 10. <u>Nihon</u> 日本 -<u>Daigaku</u> 大学 11. <u>do</u> 土 -<u>yoobi</u> 日

12. 15-<u>sai</u> オ

❸ **Kakimashoo!**

1. 中学校 2. 土よう日 3. 何オ 4. 今日 5. 何年 6. 行きたくない 7. 日本大学 8. 15 オ

9. 見たい 10. 高くて 11. 今年 12. 100円

❹ **Dekimasu-ka?**

1. おたんじょう<u>日</u>は <u>何月</u> <u>何日</u> ですか。(When is your birthday?) 2. <u>今年</u> <u>何才</u>に なりますか。(How old will you be this year?) 3. <u>今</u> <u>高校</u> <u>何年</u>せい ですか。(What year are you in in high school?)

❺ **More writing practice**

LESSON 47

PART 1

1. Read all of the notes for Lesson 47.

2. Learn the new vocabulary.

3. Change the dialogue. [Sample answers]

B: A, omawarisan! Kotchi desu. (Oh, policeman! This way.)

A: Dooshita-n desu-ka? (What happened?)

B: Doroboo desu. Mite kudasai. (It's a thief. Please look.)

A: Aa, doroboo-o mimashita-ka? (Did you see the thief?)

B: Hai, mimashita. (Yes, I did.)

A: Donna hito deshita-ka? (What kind of person was the thief?)

B: <u>せが たかい おとこ</u> でした。Se-ga takai otoko deshita. (He was a tall man.)

A: (writing) <u>せが たかい おとこ</u>。Se-ga takai otoko. (A tall man.)

B: それから、かみが <u>くろくて ながかった</u> です。Sorekara kami-ga kurokute, nagakatta desu. (And his hair was black and long.)

A: (writing) かみが <u>くろくて ながかったん</u> ですね。Kami-ga kurokute, nagakatta n desu-ne. (So, his hair was black and long.)

B: (nodding) Hai. (Yes.)

A: Nan-sai gurai deshita-ka? (About how old was he?)

B: (thinks hard) ええと、<u>五十オ</u> ぐらい でした。Eeto, go-jus-sai gurai deshita. (Um, about 50 years old.) それから、<u>あかい ジャケット</u>の 人でした。Sorekara, akai jaketto-no hito deshita. (And he was wearing a red jacket.)

PART 2

1. Yomimashoo!

1. Watashi-no kookoo-wa anmari ookikunai desu. わたし、こうこう、おお (My high school is not very big.) 2. Ano hito-wa chuugakkoo-no sensei desu. ひと、ちゅうがっこう、せんせい (That person is a

junior high school teacher.) 3. Tomodachi-no namae-wa Yamakawa-kun desu. なまえ、やまかわ (My friend's name is Yamakawa.) 4. Kotoshi-no san-gatsu-ni Tanaka-san-wa ni-juu-go-sai-ni narimasu. ことし さんがつ、たなか、にじゅうごさい (Ms. Tanaka will be 25 this March.) 5. Kin-yoobi-no tenki-wa yokatta desu. きん、び、てんき (Friday's weather was fine.) 6. Takada-san-kara nani-o moraimashita-ka? たかだ、なに (What did you receive from Mr./Ms. Takada?) 7. Saifu-no naka-ni okane-ga kyuu-man has-sen rop-pyaku nana-juu-en arimasu. なか、かね、きゅうまんはっせんろっぴゃくななじゅうえん (I have ¥98,670 in my wallet.)

2. **Preview the vocabulary and notes for Lesson 48.**

LESSON 48

PART 1

1. **Read all of the notes for Lesson 48.**
2. **Learn the new vocabulary.**
3. **Complete Writing Practice ❶ Study, trace and write.**

PART 2

1. **Complete the remainder of the Writing Practice.**
2. **Preview the vocabulary and notes for Lesson 49.**

WRITING PRACTICE

❶ **Study, trace and write.**

❷ **Dore desu-ka?**

1. <u>sengetsu</u> 先月 2. <u>nan</u> 何 -<u>sai</u> 才 3. 1,200-<u>en</u> 円 4. <u>daigaku</u> 大学 5. <u>mi</u> 見 taku-nai 6. <u>kyoo</u> 今日 7. <u>kongetsu</u> 今月 8. <u>kin</u> 金 -yoo<u>bi</u> 日 9. 59-<u>sai</u> 才 10. <u>sensei</u> 先生 11. <u>taka</u> 高 katta 12. <u>chuugakusei</u> 中学生 13. <u>oo</u> 大 kiku-nai 14. <u>i</u> 行 kimasen 15. <u>gakkoo</u> 学校 -no-<u>naka</u> 中 16. o-<u>mizu</u> 水 17. <u>Nihon</u> 日本 18. o-<u>kane</u> 金 19. <u>ka</u> 火 -yoo<u>bi</u> 日 20. <u>nan</u> 何 -<u>nin</u> 人

❸ **Kakimashoo!**

1. お金 2. 今月 3. 大きくない 4. 先生 5. 火よう日 6. 見たくない 7. 高かった 8. 学校の中 9. お水 10. 先月 11. 59才 12. 大学 13. 中学生 14. 何人 15. 金よう日 16. 日本 17. 今日 18. 行きません 19. 1,200円 20. 何才

❹ **Dekimasu-ka?**

1. Daigaku-no sensei-wa doko-de nihongo-no benkyoo-o shimashita-ka? <u>大学</u>の <u>先生</u>は どこで <u>日本</u>ごの べんきょうを しましたか。 (Where did the university professor studyJapanese?) 2. Kotoshi-no juu-gatsu-ni nan-sai-ni narimasu-ka? <u>今年</u>の <u>10月</u>に <u>何才</u>に なりますか。 (How old will you be this October?) 3. <u>日本</u>の えいがを <u>見</u>たことが ありますか。 (Have you ever seen a Japanese movie?) 4. その <u>小さい</u> <u>本</u>は とても <u>高かった</u> です。 (That little book was very expensive.)

❺ **More writing practice**

LESSON 49

PART 1

1. **Read all of the notes for Lesson 49.**
2. **Learn the new vocabulary.**
3. **Kakimashoo!** [Sample journal]

   [*Roomaji* version] go-gatsu tooka moku-yoobi tenki: hare
   Kyoo, totemo omoshiroi hito-ni aimashita. Namae-wa Tanaka-san desu. Tanaka-san-wa Tookyoo-de umaremashita. Kotoshi, nana-juu has-sai-ni narimasu. Kekkon shite-ite kodomo-san-ga roku-nin imasu. Tanaka-san-wa akarukute genki-na hito desu.
   (English translation) May 10th   Thursday   Weather: clear

   Today, I met an interesting person. His name is Mr. Tanaka. Mr. Tanaka was born in Tokyo. He will be 78 years old this year. He is married and has six children. Mr. Tanaka is a cheerful and energetic person.

PART 2

1. **Kakimashoo!**
2. **Preview the vocabulary and notes for Lesson 50.**

LESSON 50

PART 1

1. **Read all of the notes for Lesson 50.**

2. Learn the new vocabulary.

3. Dore desu-ka?

1. 学生 2. 大きくなかった 3. 今 4. お金 5. 小さくない 6. 3月 7. 9才 8. お水 9. 小学生
10. 100円 11. 何日 12. 今年 13. 中ごく人 14. 見ませんでした 15. 水よう日 16. 高校生
17. 今しゅう 18. 先生 19. 行かない 20. 何年生

PART 2

1. Kakimashoo!

1. 水よう日 2. 3月 3. 学生 4. 9才 5. 中ごく人 6. お水 7. 100円 8. 大きくなかった
9. 何年生 10. 行かない 11. 先生 12. 今しゅう 13. 今年 14. 何日 15. 高校生 16. お金
17. 小学生 18. 小さくない 19. 今 20. 見ませんでした

2. Dekimasu-ka?

1. 高校の 日本ごの 先生は やさしい ですか。 Kookoo-no nihongo-no sensei-wa yasashii desu-ka? (Is the high school Japanese teacher kind?) 2. 今 中学 何年生 ですか。 Ima, chuugaku nan-nen-sei desu-ka? (What grade of junior high are you in now?)

3. Preview the vocabulary and notes for Lesson 51.

<h2 style="text-align:center">LESSON 51</h2>

PART 1

1. Read all of the notes for Lesson 51.

2. Learn the new vocabulary.

3. Kakimashoo! [Sample answers]

Ex. 1. ともこさんは けんじさんと けっこん しています。 Tomoko-san-wa Kenji-san-to kekkon shite-imasu. (Tomoko is married to Kenji.) [false]

Ex. 2. ゆきおくんの おかあさんは 33才 です。 Yukio-kun-no okaasan-wa 33-sai desu. (Yukio's mother is 33 years old.) [true]

1. あきこさんの おとうさんは じろうさん です。 Akiko-san-no otoosan-wa Jiroo-san desu. (Akiko's father is Jiroo.) [true]

2. ひろふみくんの いもうとさんは みどりさん です。 Hirofumi-kun-no imooto-san-wa Midori-san desu. (Hirofumi's younger sister is Midori.) [false]

3. えりさんは おにいさんが います。 Eri-san-wa oniisan-ga imasu. (Eri has an older brother.) [true]

4. まきこさんの おかあさんは まゆみさん です。 Makiko-san-no okaasan-wa Mayumi-san desu. (Makiko's mother is Mayumi.) [true]

5. たけおさんの おじいさんは けんじさん です。 Takeo-san-no ojiisan-wa Kenji-san desu. (Takeo's grandfather is Kenji.) [false]

6. りえさんは としさんと けっこん しています。 Rie-san-wa Toshi-san-to kekkon shite-imasu. (Rie is married to Toshi.) [true]

PART 2

1. Yomimashoo!

1. nan-no-hon (what kind of book) 2. ka-yoobi-no mae-no hi (the day before Tuesday) 3. kodomo (child) 4. takai yama (tall mountain) 5. kyoo-no tenki (today's weather) 6. San-sai-ni narimashita. (He/she became three years old.) 7. Watashi-wa mizu-o nomimashita. (I drank water.) 8. nan-gatsu nan-nichi (what month, what day?) 9. chiisai shoogakkoo (small elementary school) 10. chichi-to haha (father and mother) 11. ichi-man san-zen yon-hyaku roku-juu-en (￥13,460) 12. Yamashita-san-wa kimasen. (Mr./Ms. Yamashita won't come.) 13. Genki ja nai desu. (He/she is not healthy/fine.) 14. mimasu (see, look at) 15. Yamashita-kun-ga itta. (Mr. Yamashita went.) 16. rainen-no sensei (next year's teacher)

2. Preview the vocabulary and notes for Lesson 52.

<h2 style="text-align:center">LESSON 52</h2>

PART 1

1. Read all of the notes for Lesson 52.

2. Learn the new vocabulary.

3. Kakimashoo! [Sample description]

[*Roomaji* version] Masayo-san-no ojiisan-no namae-wa Nakagawa Takeshi-san desu. Roku-juu go-sai desu. Gaka desu. Uchi-de hataraite-imasu. Mainichi osoku okite, asa-gohan-o tabete, juu-ji-kara yo-ji-made shigoto-o shimasu.

(English translation) Masayo's grandfather's name is Takeshi Nakagawa. He is 65 years old. He is an artist. He works at home. He gets up late, eats breakfast, and works from 10:00 to 4:00.

PART 2
1. **Kanji review**
2. **Kakimashoo!**

1. takai 高い (expensive) 2. kookoo 高校 (high school) 3. en 円 (yen) 4. kotoshi 今年 (this year)
5. nan-nen 何年 (what year) 6. sensei 先生 (teacher) 7. mimasen 見ません (won't/ don't/doesn't watch) 8. naka 中 (inside, middle) 9. sengetsu 先月 (last month) 10. chuugakkoo 中学校 (junior high school) 11. o-kane お金 (money) 12. shoogakusei 小学生 (elementary school student) 13. ikimashita 行きました (went) 14. san-juu yon-sai 34 才 (34 years old) 15. ima 今 (now)

3. **Preview the vocabulary and notes for Lesson 53.**

LESSON 53

PART 1
1. **Read all of the notes for Lesson 53.**
2. **Learn the new vocabulary.**
3. **Rirekisho (Résumé)** [Sample résumé]

Which job are you applying for? てんいん ten'in (shop clerk)

名前 namae (name)　パット・ジョーンズ (Pat Jones)		男 otoko (male)・⊘ onna (female)	
1990年 6月11日生　(Born on June 11, 1990)		18才 18-sai (18 years old)	
住所 juusho (address) 61996 Peartree Blvd., Atlanta, GA 33030		電話番号 denwa bangoo (phone number) (123) 456-7890	
連絡先 renrakusaki (contact person) Irasshai, 260 14th St., Atlanta, GA 30318		電話番号 denwa bangoo (phone number) (404) 685-2811	

年 nen (year)	月 gatsu (month)	学歴・職歴 gakureki・shokureki (educational and work history)
2002	8	アトランタノース中学校入学 (entered Atlanta North Middle School)
2004	5	アトランタノース中学校卒業 (graduated Atlanta North Middle School)
2004	8	アトランタメイン高校入学　(entered Atlanta Main High School)
2008	5	アトランタメイン高校卒業　(graduated Atlanta Main High School)
2008	8	フロリダ大学入学　(entered the University of Florida)

年 nen (year)	月 gatsu (month)	免許・習得・資格 menkyo・shuutoku・shikaku (licenses, certificates and qualifications)
2000	4	うんてんめんきょ　unten menkyo (driver's license)

得意な学科 tokui-na gakka (specialized subjects) 日本語 nihongo (Japanese) スペイン語 supeingo (Spanish)	健康状態 kenkoo jootai (state of health) 良好 ryookoo (good)
趣味 shumi (hobbies and interests) しゃしん shashin (photography)	志望の動機 shiboo-no dooki (reason for desiring this position)
スポーツ supootsu (sports) テニス、バレーボール tenisu, bareebooru (tennis, volleyball)	貴社のデザインがいいから Kisha-no dezain-ga ii kara (Because your company's designs are excellent)

(family)	名前 namae (name)	性別 seibetsu (gender)	年令 nenrei (age)
か ぞ く	トム Tomu (Tom)	男 otoko (male)	45 才
	ミッシェル Missheru (Michele)	女 onnna (female)	44 才
	マイケル Maikeru (Michael)	男 otoko (male)	20 才
	レイチェル Reicheru (Rachel)	女 onnna (female)	16 才

145

1. Yomimashoo!

1. O-namae-wa? (What's your name?) 2. Daigaku-sei desu. (I'm a college student.) 3. Ima, terebi-o mite-iru. (I'm watching TV now.) 4. Moo ichido itte kudasai. (Please say it one more time.) 5. kyoo-no tenki (today's weather) 6. juu-nana-sai (17 years old) 7. Denwa-to iimasu. (It's called a '*denwa*'.) 8. Ikimasen-deshita. (I didn't go.) 9. chiisai shoogakkoo (small elementary school) 10. otoosan-to okaasan (*someone's* father and mother) 11. hanashimasu (say/speak) 12. Yamashita-sensei (Professor Yamashita) 13. O-genki desu-ka? (How are you?) 14. Ueda-kun-ga kimasu. (Mr. Ueda will come.)

2. Preview the vocabulary and notes for Lesson 54.

LESSON 54

PART 1

1. Read all of the notes for Lesson 54.

2. Learn the new vocabulary.

3. Kakimashoo! Sample description

[*Roomaji* version] Watanabe-san-wa ima daigaku ni-nen-sei desu. Atama-ga ii hito desu. Mainichi toshokan-de go-jikan gurai benkyoo shimasu. Watanabe-san-wa ni-nen-go-ni sotsugyoo shimasu. Sono ato, me-isha-ni narimasu. Daigaku byooin-de hatarakimasu.

(English translation) Ms. Watanabe is now a sophomore. She is a smart person. She studies at the library for five hours every day. She will graduate in two years. After that, she will be an eye doctor. She'll work at a university hospital.

PART 2

1. Yomimashoo!

1. kuni (country) 2. hanashimasu (say/speak) 3. nihongo (Japanese language) 4. chuugoku (China) 5. iimashita (he/she said) 6. nani-go (what language?) 7. denwa (telephone) 8. chichi-to haha (my father and mother) 9. me (eye) 10. Yamaguchi-sensei (Professor Yamaguchi) 11. otoosan-no namae (*someone's* father's name) 12. kyuu-hyaku (900) 13. mimi (ear) 14. gairaigo (borrowed/loan words) 15. sengetsu-no tenki (last month's weather) 16. rainen-no sensei (next year's teacher)

2. Preview the vocabulary and notes for Lesson 55.

LESSON 55

PART 1

1. Read all of the notes for Lesson 55.

2. Learn the new vocabulary.

3. Kakimashoo! [Sample passage]

[*Roomaji* version] Watashi-no namae-wa Joonzu desu. Ima, kookoo san-nen-sei desu. Kodomo-no toki sensei-ni naritakatta desu. Demo, ima, isha-ni naritai desu. Shoorai, yasashikute atama-ga ii hito-to kekkon shitai desu. Kodomo-ga hitori hoshii desu. Onna-no-ko-ga hoshii desu. Montana-ni sumitai desu. Chiisakute shizuka-na machi-ni sumitai desu.

(English translation) My name is Jones. I'm in the third year of high school. When I was a child, I wanted to be a teacher. But now, I want to be a doctor. In the future, I want to marry a kind and smart person. I want one child. I want a girl. I want to live in Montana. I want to live in a small and quiet town.

PART 2

1. Kakimashoo! [Sample passage]

私の 名前は ポーター です。今、高校 三年生 です。子どもの とき いしゃに なりたかった です。でも、今、パイロットに なりたい です。けっこん したくない です。子どもも ほしくない です。しょう来、ニューヨークに すみたいです。

[*Roomaji* version] Watashi-no namae-wa Pootaa desu. Ima, kookoo san-nen-sei desu. Kodomo-no toki isha-ni naritakatta desu. Demo, ima, pairotto-ni naritai desu. Kekkon shitaku nai desu. Kodomo-mo hoshiku nai desu. Shoorai, Nyuu Yooku-ni sumitai desu.

(English translation) My name is Porter. I'm a high school senior. When I was a child, I wanted to be a doctor. But now, I want to be a pilot. I don't want to get married. I don't want kids either. In the future, I want to live in New York.

2. Preview the vocabulary and notes for Lesson 56.

LESSON 56

PART 1

1. **Read all of the notes for Lesson 56.**

2. **Kakimashoo!** [Sample journal]

[*Roomaji* version] shi-gatsu ni-juu-hachi-nichi   kin-yoobi   tenki: ame

Kyoo, totemo yasashikute omoshiroi hito-ni aimashita. Namae-wa Yamaguchi Toshio-san desu. Yamaguchi-san-wa Yokohama-de umaremashita. Ima, go-juu-nana-sai desu. Otanjoobi-wa san-gatsu juu-ku-nichi desu. Kodomo-no toki, Yokohama-ni sunde imashita. Chuugakusei-no toki, obaasan-to Tookyoo-ni sunde-imashita. Kookoosei-no toki, san-nen-kan Amerika-ni sunde-imashita. Sono toki, otoosan-wa Amerika-no kaisha-de hataraite-imashita. Daigakusei-no toki, Mekishiko-ni itte, supeingo-no benkyoo-o shimashita. Daigaku san-nen-sei-no toki, akarukute genki-na onna-no-hito-ni aimashita. Sotsugyoo-no ato, sono hito-to kekkon shimashita. Ima, Kariforunia-ni sunde-imasu. Kodomo-ga go-nin imasu. Yamaguchi-san-wa kookooo-de nihongo-to supeingo-o oshiete-imasu.

(English translation) April 28th Friday   Weather: rainy

Today, I met a very kind and interesting person. His name is Mr. Toshio Yamaguchi. Mr. Yamaguchi was born in Yokohama. He's 57 years old now. His birthday is March 19th. He lived in Yokohama when he was a child. When he was a middle school student, he lived with his grandmother in Tokyo. When he was a high school student, he lived for three years in the U.S. At that time, his father was working for an American company. When he was a college student, he went to Mexico and studied Spanish. When he was in his junior year, he met a cheerful and energetic woman. After graduation, he married that person. They have five children. Mr. Yamaguchi teaches Japanese and Spanish at a high school.

PART 2

1. **Yomimashoo!**

1. rainen (next year) 2. ka-yoobi (Tuesday) 3. kakimasu (write) 4. ima (now) 5. tenki (weather)
6. mizu (water) 7. chuugokugo (Chinese language) 8. iimashita (said) 9. sui-yoobi-to kin-yoobi
(Wednesday and Friday) 10. kyoo (today) 11. san-byaku roku-juu-go-en (365 yen) 12. hanashimasu
(speak/speaks, will speak) 13. genki (energetic, fine) 14. nan-nin (how many people?) 15. mimasu (see, look at) 16. kon-getsu (this month) 17. me-to mimi (eyes and ears) 18. do-yoobi (Saturday) 19. o-kane (money) 20. watashi (I) 21. yomimasen (don't/doesn't read, won't read) 22. hachi-man-nin (80,000 people) 23. kodomo (child) 24. nan-gatsu nan-nichi (what month? what day?) 25. nihongo-no hon (Japanese book) 26. Ueda-san-to Yamashita-san (Mr./Ms. Ueda and Mr./Ms. Yamashita) 27. kimasen (don't/doesn't come, won't come) 28. kotoshi (this year) 29. sensei (teacher) 30. ikimashita (went) 31. kyuu-juu-yon-sai (94 years old) 32. chiisai shoogakkoo (small elementary school) 33. kuchi (mouth) 34. namae (name)

2. **Preview the vocabulary and notes for Lesson 57.**

LESSON 57

PART 1

1. **Read all of the notes for Lesson 57.**

2. **Learn the new vocabulary.**

3. **Kakimashoo!** [Sample description]

[*Roomaji* version] Yamaguchi-san-wa pairotto desu. Kyonen-no aki, go-kazoku-to issho-ni Hawai-ni ikimashita. Hawai-ni is-shuu-kan gurai imashita. Hawai-no umi-de asobimashita. Saafin-to sukyuuba daibingu-o shimashita. Oishii painappuru-o takusan tabemashita.

(English translation) Mr. Yamaguchi is a pilot. He went to Hawaii with his family last fall. They stayed there for about a week. They played in the Hawaiian ocean. They went surfing and scuba-diving. They ate lots of delicious pineapples.

PART 2

1. **Yomimashoo!**

[*Roomaji* version] Watashi-no chuugokugo-no sensei-wa Sumisu-sensei desu. Sumisu-sensei-wa yon-jus-sai gurai desu. Genki-de akarui hito desu. Watashi-wa Sumisu-sensei-ga daisuki desu.

(English translation) My Chinese teacher is Professor Smith. He/she's about 40 years old. He/she's lively and cheerful. I like Professor Smith a lot.

1. Sensei-no o-namae-wa nan desu-ka. (What is the name of the teacher?) → スミス先生です。 Sumisu-sensei desu. (It's Professor Smith.)

2. Nan-sai gurai desu-ka. (About how old is he/she?) → 四十才ぐらいです。 Yon-jus-sai gurai desu. (He/She's about 40 years old.)

3. Donna hito desu-ka. (What kind of person is he/she?) → 元気であかるい人です。 Genki-de akarui hito desu. (He/She's lively and cheerful.)

[*Roomaji* version] Kyoo, totemo omoshiroi hito-ni aimashita. O-namae-wa Tanaka-san desu. Tanaka-san-wa Tookyoo-de umaremashita. Ni-juu-san-sai-no toki, kekkon shimashita. Kodomo-san-ga roku-nin imasu.
(English translation) I met a very interesting person today. His/her name is Mr./Ms. Tanaka. He/She was born in Tokyo. He/she got married when he/she was 23 years old. He/She has six children.

4. Tanaka-san-wa doko-de umaremashita-ka. (Where was Mr./Ms. Tanaka born?) → とうきょうで 生まれました Tookyoo-de umaremashita. (He/She was born in Tokyo.)

5. Itsu kekkon shimashita-ka. (When did he/she get married?) → 二十三オのとき、けっこんしました。 Ni-juu-san-sai-no toki, kekkon shimashita. (He/She got married when he/she was 23 years old.)

6. Kodomo-san-ga nan-nin imasu-ka. (How many children does he/she have?) → 六人います。 Roku-nin imasu. (He/She has six children.)

[*Roomaji* version] Rika-san-no obaasan-no o-namae-wa Nakagawa Chiyo-san desu. Roku-juu-go-sai desu. Gaka desu. Uchi-de hataraite-imasu. Mainichi hachi-ji-ni okite, asa-gohan-o tabete, juu-ji kara yo-ji-made e-o kakimasu. Hiru-gohan-wa tabemasen.
(English translation) Rika's grandmother's name is Chiyo Nakagawa. She is 65 years old. She is a painter. She works at home. Everyday she gets up at 8:00, eats breakfast, and paints pictures from 10:00 to 4:00. She does not eat lunch.

7. Nakagawa-san-no o-shigoto-wa nan desu-ka. (What is Ms. Nakagawa's job?) → がかです。 Gaka desu. (She is a painter.)

8. Nakagawa-san-wa mainichi nan-jikan gurai hatarakimasu-ka. (About how many hours does she work every day?) → 六じ間ぐらいはたらきます。 Roku-ji-kan gurai hatarakimasu. (She works about six hours.)

2. Preview the vocabulary and notes for Lesson 58.

LESSON 58

PART 1

1. Read all of the notes for Lesson 58.

2. Learn the new vocabulary.

3. Kakimashoo!

1. san-shuu-kan (three weeks) 2. ik-ka-getsu-kan (one month) 3. futsuka-kan (two days) 4. rok-ka-getsu-kan (six months) 5. go-nen-kan (five years) 6. tooka-kan (ten days) 7. kyuu-nen-kan (nine years) 8. mikka-kan (three days) 9. nan-nen-kan (how many years?) 10. yon-shuu-kan (four weeks) 11. juk-ka-getsu-kan (ten months) 12. ni-shuu-kan (two weeks) 13. ichinichi (one day) 14. yo-nen-kan (four years) 15. roku-shuu-kan (six weeks) 16. yokka-kan (four days) 17. ni-ka-getsu-kan (two months) 18. is-shuu-kan (one week)

PART 2

1. Kakimashoo!

[*Roomaji* version] Boku-wa shichi-gatsu-ni San Furanshisuko-ni ikimasu. Itsuka-kan-no tsuaa desu. Tookyoo-kara San Furanshisuko-made hikooki-de ikimasu. Hikooki-wa hatsuka-no gogo yo-ji go-fun-ni dete, hatsuka-no gozen ku-ji jup-pun-ni tsukimasu. Tsugi-no hi, basu-de Yosemite Kooen-ni ikimasu. Asa-no hachi-ji-ni dete, hiru-no juu-ni-ji-ni tsukimasu. Yosemite Kooen-de kirei-na yama-to mizuumi-o mitai desu. Sono hi-no yoru, San Furanshisuko-no hoteru-ni kaerimasu.
(English translation) I am going to San Francisco in July. It's a five-day tour. I am going there by airplane from Tokyo to San Francisco. The airplane will leave at 4:05 p.m. on the 20th and will arrive at 9:10 a.m. on the 20th. On the next day, I am going to Yosemite Park by bus. The bus will leave at 8:00 in the morning and arrive at noon. I want to see the beautiful mountains and lakes there. That night, I will go back to the hotel in San Francisco.

1. Ikeda-san-wa itsu San Furanshisuko-ni ikimasu-ka? (When will Mr. Ikeda go to San Francisco?) → 七月 に行きます。 Shichi-gatsu-ni ikimasu. (He will go there in July.)

2. Dore gurai San Furanshisuko-ni imasu-ka? (How long will he stay in San Francisco?) → 五日間います。 Itsuka-kan imasu. (He will stay five days.)

3. (a) Hikooki-wa nan-ji-ni demasu-ka? (What time will the airplane leave?) → ごご四時五分にでます。 Gogo yo-ji go-fun-ni demasu. (It will leave at 4:05 p.m.)

148

(b) Hikooki-wa nan-ji-ni tsukimasu-ka? (What time will the airplane arrive?) → ごぜん九時十分に つきます。 Gozen ku-ji jup-pun-ni tsukimasu. (It will arrive at 9:10 a.m.)

(c) Because the time in Tokyo is 17 hours ahead of the time in San Francisco. The traveling time is 11 hours and 5 minutes.

4. (a) Ikeda-san-wa San Furanshisuko-kara doko-ni ikimasu-ka? (Where will Mr. Ikeda go from San Francisco?)
→ ヨセミテこうえんに行きます。 Yosemite Kooen-ni ikimasu. (He will go to Yosemite Park.)

(b) Soko-made basu-de nan-jikan desu-ka? (How many hours by bus does it take to get there?) → 四時間です。 Yo-jikan desu. (It takes four hours.)

2. Preview the vocabulary and notes for Lesson 59.

LESSON 59

PART 1
1. Read all of the notes for Lesson 59.

2. Learn the new vocabulary.

3. Yomimashoo!

[*Roomaji* version] Watashi-wa roku-gatsu futsuka-kara arubaito-o shite-imasu. Ookii depaato-de hataraite-imasu. Depaato-wa watashi-no uchi-ni chikai desu. Shigoto-wa ka-yoobi-kara do-yoobi-made desu. Hachi-ji-kara go-ji-made desu. Ichi-jikan kyuu-doru desu. O-kane-ga ii kara, shigoto-ga daisuki desu.

(English translation) I've been working part-time since June 2nd. I work at a big department store. The department store is close to my home. My work days are from Tuesday through Saturday. My work hours are from 8:00 to 5:00. It pays nine dollars per hour. Because the money is good, I really like my job.

1. Doko-de hataraite-imasu-ka. (Where do you work?) → デパートではたらいています。 Depaato-de hataraite-imasu. (I work at a department store.)

2. Depaato-wa doko desu-ka. (Where is the department store?) → 私のうちにちかいです。 Watashi-no uchi-ni chikai desu. (It is near my house.)

3. Kin-yoobi-ni hatarakimasu-ka. (Do you work on Fridays?) → はい、はたらきます。 Hai, hatarakimasu. (Yes, I do.)

4. Dooshite shigoto-ga suki desu-ka. (Why do you like your job?) → お金がいいからです。 O-kane-ga ii kara desu. (Because the money is good.)

[*Roomaji* version] Kurisu-san-wa ima, daigaku san-nen-sei desu. Ongaku-no benkyoo-o shite-imasu. Rainen sotsugyoo shimasu. Sono ato, chuugakkoo-de ongaku-o oshiemasu.

(English translation) Chris is a college junior now. She is studying music. Next year, she will graduate. After that, she will teach music at a middle school.

5. Kurisu-san-wa itsu sotsugyoo shimasu-ka? (When will Chris graduate?) → 来年、そつぎょうします。 Rainen, sotsugyoo shimasu. (She will graduate next year.)

6. Nan-no kamoku-o oshiemasu-ka. (What subject will she teach?) → おんがくをおしえます。 Ongaku-o oshiemasu. (She will teach music.)

PART 2
1. Kakimashoo! [Sample description]

[*Roomaji* version] Go-gatsu san-juu-nichi-ni Nara-ni ikimashita. Gozen juu-ichi-ji-ni tsukimashita. Deer Park-ni itte, pikunikku-o shimashita. Sono ato, Toodaiji Temple-ni itte, shashin-o takusan torimashita. Nara-ni futsuka-kan imashita. Nara-kara Oosaka-made densha-de ikimashita. Soko-de nihon-jin-no tomodachi-ni atte, Osaka Castle-ni ikimashita. Oosaka-ni roku-gatsu yokka-made imashita.

(English translation) We went to Nara on May 30th. We arrived at 11:00 a.m. We went to Deer Park and had a picnic there. After that, we went to Toodaiji Temple and took a lot of pictures. We stayed in Nara for two days. From Nara to Osaka, we went by train. We met a Japanese friend there and went to Osaka Castle. We stayed in Osaka until June 4th.

2. Preview the vocabulary and notes for Lesson 60.

LESSON 60

PART 1
1. Read all of the notes for Lesson 60.

2. Learn the new vocabulary.

3. Kakimashoo!

1. 何月何日　なんがつなんにち　nan-gatsu nan-nichi　2. 小さい本　ちいさいほん　chiisai hon

3. そのお金を見ました。そのおかねをみました。Sono o-kane-o mimashita. 4. 十才 じゅっさい jus-sai 5. 日本人　にほんじん nihon-jin 6. 大きい大学　おおきいだいがく ookii daigaku 7. 水 みず mizu 8. 高校の先生　こうこうのせんせい kookoo-no sensei 9. 今　いま ima 10. 二年生 にねんせい ni-nen-sei 11. 木よう日と土よう日　もくようびと どようび moku-yoobi-to do-yoobi 12. 三十円　さんじゅうえん san-juu-en 13. 中学生　ちゅうがくせい chuugakusei 14. 今日 きょう kyoo 15. 行きました　いきました ikimashita

PART 2
1. Dekimasu-ka?

1. 火　not related to family　2. 万　not a single-digit number　3. 才　not a day-of-the-week　4. 駅　not a verb
5. 目　not related to time　6. 国　not a directional word　7. 元気　not related to weather　8. 百　not related to word, language　9. 日　not a body part
Sample Sentence: 火よう日に えきの 前で 百才の 元気な 女の 人に あいました。
Ka-yoobi-ni eki-no mae-de hyaku-sai-no genki-na onna-no-hito-ni aimashita. (On Tuesday, in front of the station, I met a lively 100-year old woman.)

2. Preview the vocabulary and notes for Lesson 61.

LESSON 61

PART 1
1. Read all of the notes for Lesson 61.
2. Learn the new voacabulary.
3. Change the dialogue. [Sample dialogue]

山口：すみません。<u>バックパック</u>がなくなりました。
中川：そうですか。どんな<u>バックパック</u>ですか。
山口：ええと、<u>小さくてあかいバックパックです。</u>
中川：<u>小さくてあかいバックパック</u>の中に何がはっていましたか。
山口：<u>パスポート</u>と<u>お金</u>です。
中川：<u>パスポート</u>と<u>お金</u>！それはたいへんですね。

[*Roomaji* version] Yamaguchi: Sumimasen. <u>Bakku-pakku</u>-ga naku narimashita.
Nakagawa:　Soo desu-ka. Donna <u>bakku-pakku</u> desu-ka?
Yamaguchi: Eeto, <u>chiisakute akai bakku-pakku</u> desu.
Nakagawa:　<u>Chiisakute akai bakku-pakku</u>-no naka-ni nani-ga haitte-imashita-ka?
Yamaguchi: <u>Pasupooto</u>-to <u>o-kane</u> desu.
Nakagawa:　<u>Pasupooto</u>-to <u>o-kane</u>! Sore-wa taihen desu-ne.
(English translation) Yamaguchi: Excuse me. I've lost my backpack.
Nakagawa:　Oh, really. What kind of backpack is it?
Yamaguchi: Umm, it's a small, red backpack.
Nakagawa:　What was inside the small, red backpack?
Yamaguchi: A passport and some money.
Nakagawa:　A passport and some money! Wow, that's too bad.

PART 2
1. Kakimashoo! [Sample description]

[*Roomaji* version] Watashi-no nihongo-no hon-ga naku-narimashita. Ookikute akai hon desu. Kyoo, tomodachi-to toshokan-ni itte, nihongo-no benkyoo-o shimashita. Sorekara, resutoran-ni ikimashita. Soko-ni hon-o wasuremashita.
(English translation) I lost my Japanese book. It is a big, red book. Today, I went to the library with a friend and studied Japanese. After that, we went to a restaurant. I left my book there.

2. Preview the vocabulary and notes for Lesson 62.

LESSON 62

PART 1
1. Read all of the notes for Lesson 62.
2. Yomimashoo!

1. Tanaka-san (Mr./Ms. Tanaka)　2. kakimasu (write/writes, will write)　3. me-to mimi (eyes and ears)
4. chuugokugo-to nihongo (Chinese language and Japanese language)　5. otoosan-no o-namae (*someone's* father's name)　6. ame-to yuki (rain and snow)　7. genki-na kodomo (lively child)　8. rainen-no shi-gatsu

mikka (April 3rd of next year) 9. Tookyoo Eki (Tokyo Station) 10. sen hyaku go-juu-ichi-en (1,851 yen) 11. watashi-no shoogakkoo (my elementary school) 12. ue-to shita (top and bottom) 13. yo-nen-sei (the fourth year student) 14. juu-man-nin (one/a hundred thousand people) 15. iimashita (said) 16. roku-nen-mae (six years ago) 17. haha-no o-kane (my mother's money) 18. yomimashita (read *past tense*) 19. kikimasu (listen/listens, will listen) 20. yattsu (eight *things*) 21. Nihon-no daigaku (Japanese universities) 22. kookoo-no sensei (high school teachers) 23. kyoo-no tenki (today's weather) 24. nan-ji nan-pun (what hour, what minute)

PART 2
Kakimashoo!

1. 今月中学校のともだちが二人日本に行きます。 2. 今日デパートで高校の日本語の先生を見ました。
3. 大学の先生はどこで日本語のべんきょうをしましたか。 4. 今年の 十月 に 何才になりますか。
5. その小さい本はとても高かったです。

LESSON 63

(This answer key is for the vocabulary review listed in the textbooks.)

VOCABULARY
TIME WORDS

	last	this	next
week	先しゅう senshuu	今しゅう konshuu	来しゅう raishuu
month	先月 sengetsu	今月 kongetsu	来月 raigetsu
year	きょ年 kyonen	今年 kotoshi	来年 rainen

SPORTING EVENTS
a. しあい shiai b. れんしゅう renshuu c. よわい yowai d. #たい# #-tai# e. だれがかちましたか。 Dare-ga kachimashita-ka? f. スコアはどうでしたか。 Sukoa-wa doo deshita-ka?

PARTS OF THE BODY
a. め me b. はな hana c. くち kuchi d. みみ mimi e. て te f. あし ashi g. は ha h. のど nodo

DESCRIBING PEOPLE
a. きびしい kibishii b. やさしい yasashii c. あかるい akarui d. まじめ majime e. かみ kami
f. みじかい mijikai g. きんぱつ kinpatsu h. せが高い se-ga takai i. せがひくい se-ga hikui

OCCUPATIONS AND GETTING A JOB
1. a. かいしゃ kaisha b. サラリーマン sarariiman c. じゅうしょ juusho d. おしごとは何ですか。 O-shigoto-wa nan desu-ka? e. 一時間いくらですか。 Ichi-jikan ikura desu-ka? f. くるまのうんてんが できますか。 Kuruma-no unten-ga dekimasu-ka?

GRADUATION AND PLANS FOR THE FUTURE
a. そつぎょう sotsugyoo b. そのあと sono ato c. 五年ごに go-nen-go-ni d. たぶん tabun e. 高校を そつぎょうする kookoo-o sotsugyoo suru f. しょうらい shoorai g. ゆうめい yuumei h. けっこん kekkon i. けっこんする kekkon suru j. あかちゃん akachan

OTHER VOCABULARY
1. かさ kasa 2. かぜ kaze 3. つよい tsuyoi 4. まど mado 5. きせつ kisetsu 6. どうぶつ doobutsu
7. どうぶつえん doobutsuen 8. おとな otona 9. こども kodomo 10. おなかがすいた／すきました。 Onaka-ga suita/sukimashita. 11. ひま hima 12. 私たち watashi-tachi 13. あそびに行く asobi-ni iku
14. あそびに来る asobi-ni kuru 15. おなじ onaji 16. ぜんぶで zenbu-de 17. どっち dotchi 18. こっち kotchi 19. そっち sotchi 20. あっち atchi 21. となり tonari 22. ちかく chikaku 23. となり tonari
24. くだもの kudamono 25. くだものや kudamono-ya 26. ほかに hoka-ni 27. もう moo 28. まだ mada
29. ちか chika 30. あまい amai 31. からい karai 32. つめたい tsumetai 33. めがね megane 34. しっている shitte-iru 35. しりません。 Shirimasen. 36. ひとりで hitori-de 37. おばあさん obaasan
38. おじいさん ojiisan 39. いちにち ichinichi 40. ごぜん gozen 41. ごご gogo 42. しゃしんをとる shashin-o toru 43. しんかんせん shinkansen

Volume 2 Particle Practice Answer Keys

Particle Practice 1 - (PL. 1-L. 5)
2. a) **ga** b) **kara, made** c) **ni** d) **ni, ga** e) **no** f) **ga** g) **o**
3. a) A: Supootsu-(**wa**) nani-(**ga**) suki-desu-ka?
      B: Gorufu-(**ga**) suki desu.
      A: Watashi-mo gorufu-(**ga**) suki desu-yo.
      B: Jaa, haru-yasumi-(**ni**) gorufu-(**o**) shimasen-ka?
      A: Ii desu-ne.
  b) A: Kenji-kun, petto-(**o**) katte-imasu-ka?
      B: Iie, katte-imasen.
      A: Petto-(**ga**) hoshii desu-ka?
      B: Hai, inu-(**ga**) hoshii desu.
  c) A: Rika-san, 6-gatsu-(**kara**) 8-gatsu-(**made**) Nihon-(**ni**) ikimashita-ne.
      B: Hai, soo desu.
      A: Nihon-(**de**) nani-(**o**) shimashita-ka?
      B: Nihonjin-no tomodachi-(**to**) Kyuushuu-(**ni**) ikimashita.
      A: Hee.

Particle Practice 2 - (L. 6-15)
2. a) A: **de, wa, o** B: **o** b) **no, kara** c) **no, ni** d) **de**
3. a) A: Yuka-san, kurabu-(**ni**) haitte imasu-ka?
      B: Iie, haitte-imasen. Mainichi, arubaito-(**o**) shimasu. Miki-san-wa?
      A: Watashi-wa basukettobooru-bu-(**ni**) haitte-imasu.
      B: Kurabu-wa doo desu-(**ka**)?
      A: Omoshiroi desu-yo.
  b) A: Jon-kun-wa nani-go-(**ga**) dekimasu-ka?
      B: Nihongo-(**to**) supeingo-(**ga**) dekimasu.
      A: Hee, sugoi desu-ne. Doko-(**de**) benkyoo-o shimashita-ka?
      B: Kookoo-(**de**) nihongo-no benkyoo-o shimashita. Supeingo-wa
        jibun-(**de**) benkyoo-o shimashita.
      A: Hee.
  c) A: Suisu-(**wa**) doko-ni arimasu-ka?
      B: Furansu-(**no**) higashi-(**ni**) arimasu.
      A: Suisu-(**de**)-(**wa**) nani-go-(**o**) hanashimasu-ka?
      B: Doitsugo-(**to**) furansugo-(**to**) itariago-(**o**) hanashimasu.
      A: Jaa, Suisu-(**de**) ichiban kireina yama-wa nan desu-ka?
      B: Mattaahorun desu.

Particle Practice 3 - (L. 16-23)
2. a) **e** b) **ni** c) **ni/e** d) **ni** e) **o**
3. a) A: Fuyu-yasumi-wa moo sugu desu-ne. Noriko-san-wa nani-(**o**) shimasu-ka?
      B: Amerika-ni itte, tomodachi-(**ni**) aimasu.
      A: Hee, ii desu-ne. Tomodachi-wa doko-(**ni**) imasu-ka?
      B: Furorida-(**ni**) imasu.
      A: Aa, soo desu-ka.
  b) A: Shumi-wa nan desu-ka?
      B: Ryokoo-(**o**) suru-koto-(**to**) shashin-(**o**) toru-koto desu.
      A: Natsu-(**ni**) doko-(**ni/e**) ikimashita-(**ka**)?
      B: Chuugoku-(**to**) Nihon-(**ni/e**) ikimashita.
  c) A: Senshuu-no nichi-yoobi-(**ni**) nani-(**o**) shimashita-ka?
      B: Nihonjin-no tomodachi-(**ni**) kaado [card]-(**o**) kakimashita
      A: Sorekara, nani-ka shimashita-ka?
      B: Ee, ane-no uchi-(**ni/e**) ikimashita.
      A: Oneesan-no uchi-wa doko-(**ni**) arimasu-ka?
      B: Atoranta-(**no**) minami-(**ni**) arimasu.

Particle Practice 4 - (L. 24-31)

2. a) **ni**, **ni** b) **wa**, **ni** c) **de**, **no** d) **no**, **ni** e) **no**, **ga**

3. a) (Person A is asking Person B for directions using a map.)

     A: Kono machi-(**ni**) niku-ya-(**ga**) arimasu-ka?

     B: Hai, arimasu.

     A: Doko-(**ni**) arimasu-ka?

     B: Kooen-(**no**) hidari-(**ni**) arimasu.

     A: Doomo.

  b) A: Moshi moshi? Irasshai Kookoo-(**no**) Timu desu kedo,

       Miki-san-(**wa**) irasshaimasu-(**ka**)?

     B: Aa, sumimasen. Ima rusu desu kedo.

     A: Aa, soo desu-ka. Nanji-goro okaeri desu-(**ka**)?

     B: Hachi-ji goro kaerimasu.

     A: Jaa, mata ato-(**de**) denwa shimasu.

     B: Hai, wakarimashita.

     A: Shitsurei shimasu.

  c) A: Makoto-kun, kongetsu-(**no**) 11-nichi, hima desu-ka?

     B: Hai, hima desu.

     A: Watashi-(**no**) uchi-(**de**) paatii-(**o**) shimasu kedo, asobi-(**ni**) kimasen-(**ka**)?

     B: Aa, ii desu-ne.

  d) A: Kinoo-(**no**) yakyuu-(**no**) shiai-wa doo deshita-(**ka**)?

     B: Yokatta desu-yo.

     A: Doko-(**ga**) kachimashita-(**ka**)?

     B: Raionzu-(**ga**) kachimashita.

     A: Sukoa-wa doo deshita-(**ka**)?

     B: 5 tai 3 deshita.

     A: Hee.

Particle Practice 5 - (L. 32-40)

2. a) **ga** b) **ni** c) **kara**   d) **ni**, **ga** e) **kara**, **no**, **o** f) **ni**, **kara**, **o** g) **ga** h) **ga**

3. a) A: Irasshaimase.

     B: Migi-(**kara**) 3-ban-me-(**no**) kamera-(**o**) misete kudasai.

     A: Hai, doozo.

     B: Ikura desu-ka?

     A: 25,000-en desu.

  b) A: Sumimasen. Kono chikaku-(**ni**) suupaa-(**ga**) arimasu-ka?

     B: Iie, arimasen.

     A: Soo desu-ka. Jaa, pan-ya-(**ga**) arimasu-ka?

     B: Hai, ano toshokan-(**no**) tonari-(**ni**) arimasu.

  c) A: Fuyu-yasumi-(**ni**) nani-(**o**) shimashita-ka?

     B: Kazoku-(**to**) sukii-(**ni**) ikimashita. A-san-wa sukii-(**o**) shita koto-(**ga**)

       arimasu-ka?

     A: Iie, arimasen. Sukii-(**wa**) doo deshita-ka?

     B: Totemo muzukashikatta desu.

  d) A: Kyoo sandoitchi-(**o**) tsukurimasu-kedo, nani-(**ga**) irimasu-ka?

     B: Tomato-(**ga**) 2-tsu-(**to**) pan-(**ga**) irimasu.

  e) A: Irasshaimase.

     [Person B is showing the store clerk, A, a catalogue of stereos.]

     B: Kono sutereo-(**ga**) arimasu-ka?

     A: Hai, kuro-(**to**) ao-(**ga**) arimasu-kedo, dotchi-(**ga**) ii desu-ka?

     B: Jaa, kuro, onegai shimasu.

     A: Hai, arigatoo gozaimasu.

  f) A: O-tanjoobi-(**wa**) doo deshita-ka?

     B: Yokatta desu-yo. Ani-(**kara**) purezento-(**o**) moraimashita.

     A: Nani-(**o**) moraimashita-ka?

     B: Kono kutsu-(**o**) moraimashita.

     A: A, kakkoii desu-ne.

Particle Practice 6 - (L. 41-48)

2. a) **ga** b) **no, ni** c) **no, de** d) **ga** e) **no** f) **o**
3. a)   A: Doo shita-n desu-ka?

        B: Onaka-(**ga**) itai-n desu.

        A: Itsu-(**kara**) desu-ka?

        B: Kyoo-(**no**) asa-(**kara**) desu.

        A: Soo desu-ka. Ja, kore-(**o**) nonde kudasai.

        B: Itsu kono kusuri-(**o**) nomimasu-ka?

        A: Gohan-(**no**) mae-(**ni**) nonde kudasai.

    b)   A: Eigo-(**no**) sensei-(**no**) o-namae-(**wa**) nan desu-ka?

        B: Tanaka-sensei desu.

        A: Tanaka-sensei-(**wa**) donna hito desu-ka?

        B: Se-(**ga**) takakute kami-(**ga**) nagai hito desu.

        A: Tanaka-sensei-(**wa**) megane-(**o**) shite-imasu-ka?

        B: Iie, shite-imasen.

        A: Tanaka-sensei-(**wa**) ano kuroi jaketto-(**no**) hito desu-ka?

        B: Hai, soo desu.

Particle Practice 7 - (L. 49-56)

2. a) **ni, de** b) **no, ni** c) **no, de** d) **ni, o** e) **de** f) **ni**
3. a)   A: Makoto-kun-(**wa**) doko-(**de**) umaremashita-ka?

        B: Tokyo-(**de**) umaremashita.

        A: Tokyo-(**ni**) dore gurai sunde-imashita-ka?

        B: 3-sai-(**no**) toki-made sunde-imashita.

    b)   A: Kyonen-(**no**) natsu yasumi-(**ni**) nani-(**o**) shimashita-ka?

        B: Hawai-(**ni**) ikimashita.

        A: Dare-(**to**) ikimashita-ka?

        B: Hitori-(**de**) ikimashita.

        A: Hawai-(**de**) nani-(**o**) shimashita-ka?

        B: Hoteru-(**de**) hatarakimashita.

    c)   A: Michiko-san-(**wa**) itsu daigaku-(**o**) sotsugyoo shimasu-ka?

        B: 2-nen-go-(**ni**) sotsugyoo shimasu.

        A: Sorekara, nani-(**o**) shimasu-ka?

        B: Gakkoo-(**no**) sensei-(**ni**) naritai desu.

Particle Practice 8 - (L. 57-63)

2. a) **ni** b) **ni, ni** c) **ni, o** d) **ga** e) **o** f) **made** g) **ga, o** h) **ni, ga** j) **ni, o**
3. a)   A: Sengetsu, Furansu-(**ni/e**) ikimashita.

        B: Hee, ii desu-ne. Itsu Amerika-(**o**) demashita-ka?

        A: 23-nichi-(**no**) gogo 8-ji-(**ni**) demashita.

        B: Soo desu-ka? Itsu Furansu-(**ni**) tsukimashita-ka?

        A: 24-ka-(**no**) gozen 10-ji-(**ni**) tsukimashita.

        B: Furansu-(**ni**) dore gurai imashita-ka?

        A: 6-ka-kan imashita.

    b)   A: Sensei, nihongo-(**no**) kyookasho-(**ga**) nakunarimashita.

        B: Soo desu-ka? Kyookasho-wa doko-(**ni**) arimashita-ka?

        A: Kaban-(**no**) naka-(**ni**) haitte imashita.

        B: Sono kaban-wa doko-(**ni**) arimasu-ka?

        A: A, wakarimashita. Tomodachi-no uchi-(**ni**) sono kaban-(**o**) wasuremashita.

Volume 2 Reading and Writing Practice Answer Keys

Topic: やすみの日 (Leisure Time)　　　　　　　**Reading and Writing Practice 1 (~ L. 5)**

Katakana **Review (all)**

A. Match the following activities and with their corresponding pictures.

   1. (d)　　　2. (a)　　　3. (b)　　　4. (c)

B. Write the following activities in *katakana*.

   1. ホームステイ　　2. ピクニック　　3. ドライブ　　4. パーティー

C. Fill in the blanks using the given cues. Write in *hiragana*. Write the corresponding *katakana* above the *roomaji*.

   1. たんじょうび、プールパーティー　　2. しゅうまつ、うち、テレビ、テニス、ゲーム

   3. ふゆやすみ、スノーボード、スノーボード、むずかしい

D. Read the following passage and answer the questions in English.

   1. a homestay in Japan　　　3. enjoyed driving (with his older host brother)　　5. They were fun.
   2. June 15, August 14　　　4. had a picnic

E. Write a similar passage about yourself. (sample passage)

   Watashi-wa <u>5-gatsu</u>-ni <u>kazoku</u>-to <u>Nyuu Orinzu</u>-ni ikimashita.
         (time word)　(person)　(the place you went)
   <u>2-ka</u>-kara　　　　<u>5-ka</u>-made ikimashita. <u>Jazu-o kikimashita</u>.
   (time word/date) (time word/date)　　　(activity you did there)
   <u>CD-o kaimashita</u>. Totemo ii ryokoo deshita.
   (another activity you did there)

> English translation:
> I went to New Orleans with my family in May. I went there from the 2nd until the 5th. I listened to jazz. I bought some CDs. It was a very good trip.

F. Now write it in *hiragana*. Write in *katakana* where appropriate. (sample passage)

   わたしは 5 がつに かぞくと ニューオリンズに いきました。2 か から 5 かまで
   いきました。ジャズを ききました。CD を かいました。とても いい りょこう でした。

Topic: くにとことば (Countries and Languages)　　　**Reading and Writing Practice 2 (~ L. 7)**

Katakana **Review (all)**

A. このくにはどこですか。 Do you know what countries these are? Write the English name of the country next to its *katakana* representation. Then match the famous item with each country from the pictures below.

   1. Germany (b)　　2. France (d)　　3. Australia (c)　　4. England (e)　　5. Italy (a)

B. Crossword Puzzle: Complete the puzzle in *katakana* based on the following clues.

Across		Down	
1. Italy	イタリア	a. Laos	ラオス
2. Poland	ポーランド	b. Vietnam	ベトナム
3. Sicily	シチリア	c. Lithuania	リトアニア
4. Australia	オーストラリア	d. Indonesia	インドネシア
5. Kenya	ケニア	e. Greece	ギリシャ

C. Read the following passage and answer the questions in English.

   1. east of Vietnam, north of Indonesia　　3. English and Tagalog
   2. bananas, mangos, and coconuts　　　4. the Philippines

D. Write a similar passage about a different country. (sample passage)

   Kono kuni-wa <u>chiisai</u> desu. <u>Nikaragua</u>-no　<u>minami</u>-ni arimasu.
       (descriptor)　(another country) (cardinal direction)
   Soshite, <u>Panama</u>-no　　<u>nishi</u>-ni arimasu.
     (another country) (cardinal direction)
   Kono kuni-wa <u>koohii</u>-to　　<u>banana</u>-de yuumei desu.
      (famous product) (famous product)
   Kono kuni-no hito-wa <u>supeingo-to eigo</u>-o hanashimasu.
        (language(s))
   Kono kuni-wa doko desu-ka?

> English translation:
> This country is small. It's south of Nicaragua. And it's west of Panama. It's famous for coffee and bananas. The people here speak Spanish and English. What is this country? [Costa Rica]

155

E. Now write it in *hiragana*. Write in *katakana* where appropriate. (sample passage)

このくには ちいさい です。ニカラグアの みなみに あります。そして [and] パナマの にしに あります。このくには コーヒーと バナナで ゆうめい です。この くにの ひとは スペインごと えいごを はなします。このくには どこ ですか。

Topic: ちり (Geography)　　　　　　　　　　　　　　**Reading and Writing Practice 3 (~ L. 11)**
Kanji Review

A. Fill in the chart by writing appropriate answers in *roomaji* and English in the parentheses.

	Kanji	Reading	Meaning
1.	月	GETSU, (GATSU)	(month), moon
2.	日	(NICHI); -bi, -ka	day, sun, counter for days of the month
3.	木	(MOKU); ki	(tree), wood
4.	本	(HON), BON, PON	(book), origin, source
5.	人	NIN, JIN; (hito), -ri	person, counter for (people)
6.	山	SAN; (yama)	(mountain)
7.	川	(kawa)	(river)
8.	大	DAI; (oo)-kii	(big), large, great
9.	小	(SHOO); chii-sai	(small), little

B. Choose the appropriate *kanji* from the chart above for the following words and copy the *kanji*.

1. 日本　　　2. 5人　　　3. 8月7日　　　4. 木よう日　　　5. 本をよむ

C. For the questions, fill in the blanks using the cues on the left. Then, complete the answers. Write in *hiragana* and *kanji*. Write the corresponding *katakana* above the *roomaji*.

1. 日本で、ふじ　　　2. きたアメリカ、ミシシッピー　　　3. せかい、ロシア

D. Read the following passage and answer the questions in English.

1. Alaska　　　3. Juneau　　　5. It's the longest river in Alaska.
2. west　　　4. Mt. McKinley　　　6. There are many lakes in Alaska.

E. Write a similar passage about your own town. (sample passage)

Boku-no machi-wa <u>Oregon</u>-shuu-ni arimasu.
　　　　　(name of your state)

<u>Oregon</u>-wa　<u>Washinton</u>-no　<u>minami</u>-ni arimasu.
(your state) (neighboring state) (cardinal direction)

<u>Oregon</u>-no shuuto-wa <u>Seiramu</u> desu.
(your state)　　　(capital of your state)

<u>Oregon</u>-ni <u>Kureetaa-ko</u>*-ga arimasu.
(your state)　(a landmark)

<u>Oregon</u>-de ichiban <u>takai</u>　　<u>yama</u>-wa　<u>Fuddo-san</u> desu.
(your state)　(high/long/big, etc.) (a natural feature) (feature's name)

> English translation:
> My town is in the state of Oregon. Oregon is located south of Washington. The state capital of Oregon is Salem. In Oregon, there is Crater Lake*. The highest mountain in Oregon is Mt. Hood.

F. Now write it in *hiragana* and *kanji*. Write in *katakana* where appropriate. (sample passage)

ぼくの まちは オレゴンしゅうに あります。オレゴンは ワシントンの みなみに あります。オレゴンの しゅうとは セイラム です。オレゴンに クレーターこ*が あります。オレゴンで いちばん たかい やま (山)は フッドさん (山) です。

Topic: がっこうせいかつ (School Life)　　　　　　　　**Reading and Writing Practice 4 (~ L. 14)**
Kanji Review

A. Fill in the chart by writing appropriate answers in *roomaji* and English in the parentheses.

	Kanji	Reading	Meaning
1.	月	(GETSU), GATSU	month, (moon)
2.	日	NICHI; -bi, (-ka)	day, sun, counter for days of the month
3.	小	SHOO; (chii)-sai	(small), little

4.	大	(DAI); (oo)-kii	big, large, great
5.	人	NIN, (JIN); hito, -ri	(person), counter for people
6.	学	(GAKU)	learning, science
7.	校	KOO	(school)
8.	中	CHUU; (naka)	(middle), inside, within
9.	高	KOO; (taka)-i	high, (expensive)

B. Choose the appropriate *kanji* from the chart above for the following words and copy the *kanji*.

1. 1 人   2. 中学せい   3. 小学校   4. 5月5日   5. まい日   6. 大すき

C. Fill in the blanks with the appropriate *kanji*. Write the appropriate readings for the underlined *kanji* in the parentheses.

1. 日よう日 (がっこう／gakkoo)   2. 日本ご   3. (こうこう／kookoo) 30人

D. Read the following excerpt of a letter and answer the questions in English. Mika, who lived in the U.S., has returned to Japan. She wrote a letter to Miriam who is studying Japanese.

1. Japanese high schools   4. Thursdays   6. It's busy, but she likes it very much.
2. the tennis club   5. English, history, and math   7. July 20th
3. 16

E. Write a similar passage about yourself. (sample passage)

<u>Getsu-yoobi</u>-kara   <u>kin-yoobi</u>-made gakkoo-ni ikimasu.
(day of the week)   (day of the week)
<u>Nihongo</u>-no jugyoo-wa <u>go</u>-jikan-me desu. <u>Nihongo</u>-wa
(name of the subject)   (period)   (name of the subject)
<u>muzukashii</u> desu.
(adjective to describe the subject)
<u>Nichi-yoobi</u>-ni gakkoo-de <u>sakkaa</u>-o shimasu.
(days of the week)   (name of the activity)
[If you belong to a club] Ima, <u>Nihongo</u>-bu-ni haitte-imasu.
                (name of the club)
Boku-no gakkoo-ga <u>daisuki</u> / -wa <u>tanoshii</u> desu.
        (adjective to describe your school)

English translation:
I go to school from Monday through Friday. Japanese class is 5th period. Japanese is difficult. On Sundays, I play soccer at school. I belong to the Japanese Club now. I like my school very much. / My school is fun.

F. Now write it in *hiragana* and *kanji*. Write in *katakana* where appropriate. (sample passage)

月よう日から きんよう日まで がっこう (学校) に いきます。日本ごの じゅぎょうは 5 じかんめ です。日本ごは むずかしい です。日よう日に がっこう (学校) で サッカーを します。いま、日本ごぶに はいって います。ぼくの がっこう (学校) が 大すき ／ は たのしい です。

Topic: わたしのへや (My Room)   **Reading and Writing Practice 5 (~ L. 17)**

Kanji **Review**

A. Fill in the chart by writing appropriate answers in *roomaji* and English in the parentheses.

	Kanji	Reading	Meaning
1.	何	nan, (nani)	(what?)
2.	大	(DAI); (oo)-kii	(big), large, (great)
3.	校	(KOO)	school
4.	本	HON, (PON), (BON)	book, (origin), source
5.	高	(KOO); taka-i	(expensive), high
6.	中	(CHUU); naka	middle, (inside), within
7.	学	GAKU	(learning), science
8.	人	(NIN) JIN; hito	(person), counter for people

B. Write the appropriate *kanji* for the following words.

1. 何人   2. 大学   3. 大きい本   4. 小さい人   5. 日本人

157

C. Fill in the blanks using the cues from the pictures. Write in *hiragana* and *kanji*. Write the corresponding *katakana* above the *roomaji*.

1. ざっし、よんでいます　　　2. 人、います　　　3. ステレオ、あります

D. Read the following passage and answer the questions in English.

1. a desk, a chair, a bookcase, a bed　　　　4. under the bed
2. The bookcase is to the left of the desk.　　5. small
3. in the bookcase　　　　　　　　　　　　6. It's dirty/messy but she likes it a lot.

E. Write a similar passage about your own room. (sample passage)

Watashi-no heya-ni <u>beddo</u>-to <u>teeburu</u>-to <u>isu</u>-ga arimasu.
　　　　　　　　(furniture)(furniture)(furniture)

<u>Beddo</u>-wa <u>teeburu</u>-no migi-ni arimasu. Heya-de yoku <u>terebi-o mimasu</u>.
(furniture) (furniture)　　　　　　　　　　(what you often do in your room)

Watashi-no heya-ga <u>daisuki</u> / -wa <u>suki janai desu.</u>
　　　　(description: clean, messy, you like it, you don't like it)

> English translation:
> In my room there is a bed, a table and a chair. The bed is to the right of the table. I often watch TV in my room. I like my room a lot.

F. Now write it in *hiragana* and *kanji*. Write in *katakana* where appropriate. (sample passage)

わたしの へやに ベッドと テーブルと いすが あります。ベッドは テーブルの みぎに あります。へやでよく テレビを みます。わたしの へやが 大すき／は すきじゃない です。

Topic: しゅみ (Hobbies and Interests)　　　　　**Reading and Writing Practice 6 (~ L. 20)**

Kanji Review

A. Fill in the chart by writing appropriate answers in *roomaji* and English in the parentheses.

	Kanji	Reading	Meaning
1.	今	KON, (ima)	(now), the present
2.	私	(watashi)	(I), privacy
3.	何	(nan); nani	(what), how many, *prefix to form questions*
4.	火	(KA)	(fire)
5.	水	SUI; (mizu)	(water)
6.	金	(KIN); kane	gold, (money)
7.	土	(DO)	(ground), soil

B. Write the appropriate *kanji* for the following words.

1. 今　　　2. 今日　　　3. 何月

C. Re-arrange the following days of the week from Sunday through Saturday. Start by putting the number 1 in the parenthesis under "Sunday."

水　　　金　　　月　　　日　　　木　　　土　　　火
(4)　　　(6)　　　(2)　　　(1)　　　(5)　　　(7)　　　(3)

D. Write answers by filling in the blanks using the cues on the left. Write in *hiragana*.

1. りょこう、する　　　2. きって、あつめる　　　3. え、かく

E. Read the following passage and answer the questions in English.

1. cooking　　　3. an apple pie　　　5. a strawberry shortcake
2. on weekends　　4. her mother　　　6. It is difficult but fun.

F. Write a similar passage about yourself. (sample passage)

Watashi-no shumi-wa <u>ongaku-o kiku koto</u> desu.
　　　　　　　　　　(your hobby)

<u>Mainichi, yoru,</u>　<u>ongaku-o kikimasu.</u>
　(time word)　(activity related to the hobby)

Kono aida, <u>tomodachi</u>-to　<u>konsaato-ni ikimashita.</u>
　　　　　(a person)　(specific thing regarding the hobby)

<u>Ongaku-o kiku-koto</u>-wa <u>totemo tanoshii desu.</u>
　(your hobby)　　(an adjective to describe the hobby)

> English translation:
> My hobby is listening to music. Every night, I listen to music. The other day, I went to a concert with my friend. Listening to music is very fun.

G. Now write it in *hiragana* and *kanji*. Write in *katakana* where appropriate. (sample passage)

わたしの しゅみは おんがくを きくこと です。まい日、よる、おんがくを ききます。
このあいだ、ともだちと コンサートに いきました。おんがくを きくことは とても
たのしい です。

Topic: きせつ (Seasons and Activities)

Kanji Review

A. Fill in the chart by writing appropriate answers in *roomaji* and English in the parentheses.

	Kanji	Reading	Meaning
1.	天	(TEN)	(sky), heaven
2.	元	(GEN); moto	beginning, (foundation)
3.	気	(KI), KE	(spirit), energy
4.	火	(KA); hi [bi]	(fire)
5.	水	(SUI); mizu	(water)
6.	木	(MOKU); ki [gi]	(tree), wood

B. Write the appropriate *kanji* for 1 through 3, and write the reading in *hiragana* for 4 and 5.

1. 水   2. 火よう日   3. 木よう日   4. てんき   5. げんき

C. Fill in the blanks using the cues on the left. Write the appropriate season in *hiragana* and the activities in *katakana*.

1. なつ、バーベキュー   3. あき、パンプキンパイ

2. ふゆ、クロスカントリースキー   4. はる、ピクニック

D. Read the following *shochuu-mimai* card and answer the questions in English.

1. Tuesday (August 10th)   4. fine
2. summer   5. played (beach) volleyball (with her friends)
3. very hot   6. It was fun.

E. Write a similar card. (sample card)

9-gatsu 15-nichi (sui-yoobi)
          (month)   (day) (day of the week)

Takuya-kun-e,
(name of your pen pal)
O-genki desu-ka? Kuriiburando-wa ima aki desu.   Suzushii desu.
          (name of your town) (current season) (adjective to describe the weather)
Senshuu-no shuumatsu-no tenki-wa hare deshita.
                    (last weekend's weather)
Boku-wa mizuumi-ni itte, haikingu-o shimashita.
          (activity you did last weekend)
Tanoshikatta desu.
(comment on the activity)
Takuya-kun-no ichiban suki-na kisetsu-wa nan desu-ka?
(name of your pen pal)
Takuya-kun, mata tegami-o kaite kudasai. Sayoonara.
(name of your pen pal)
                    Ken   (your name)

English translation: Sept. 15th (Wed.)
Dear Takuya,
How are you? It is now fall here in
Cleveland. It is cool. Last weekend's
weather was clear. I went to the lake and
hiked. It was fun. What is your favorite
season, Takuya? Please write me a letter
again. Good-bye.   Ken

F. Now write it in *hiragana* and *kanji*. Write in *katakana* where appropriate. (sample card)

9 月 (がつ) 15 日 (にち) (水よう日／すいようび)

たくやくんへ、
お元気 (げんき) ですか。クリーブランドは 今 (いま) あき です。
すずしいです。せんしゅうの しゅうまつの 天気 (てんき) は はれ でした。
ぼくは みずうみに いって、ハイキングを しました。たのしかった です。
たくやくんの いちばん すきな きせつは 何 (なん) ですか。
たくやくん、また てがみを かいて ください。さようなら。
                    ケン

Kanji Review

A. Fill in the chart by writing appropriate answers in *roomaji* and English in the parentheses.

	Kanji	Reading	Meaning
1.	田	DEN; (ta) [da]	(rice field)
2.	行	KOO, GYOO; (i)-ku	(go)
3.	見	KEN; (mi)-ru	see, (look at), (watch)
4.	金	KIN, KON; (kane)	gold, (money)
5.	土	(DO), TO; tsuchi	(earth), soil
6.	川	SEN; (kawa), [gawa]	(river)
7.	中	CHUU; (naka)	middle, (inside), within
8.	山	SAN; (yama)	(mountain)
9.	本	(HON); moto	book, (origin), source
10.	高	KOO; (taka)-i	(high), expensive

B. Match the family name in *kanji* with its *roomaji* equivalent below.
 1. (d)   2. (c)   3. (e)   4. (b)   5. (a)

C. Write the appropriate *kanji* for the following words.
 1. 金 よう 日   2. 土 よう 日

D. Fill in the blanks with appropriate words or expressions. Write in *hiragana*.
 (1) さん   (3) おかえり ですか   (5) しつれいします／さようなら
 (2) いらっしゃいます   (4) あとで

E. Read the following excerpt from Mayumi's letter and answer the questions in English.
 1. winter   2. went to Hokkaido / went skiing   3. wants to go to Tokyo
 4. wants to go to Disneyland, take a picture with Mickey Mouse and see the parade

F. Write a similar letter about your holiday plans. (sample letter)
 Moo sugu <u>haru</u> yasumi desu-ne. Boku-wa kyonen <u>Nyuu Yooku</u>-ni itte, <u>myuujikaru-o mimashita</u>.
        (season)   (place)   (activity)
 <u>Totemo yokatta desu.</u>   Kotoshi-wa <u>ani</u>-to <u>Bahama</u>-ni ikitai desu. <u>Daibingu-o shitai desu.</u>
 (adjective commenting on the trip or activity)   (person)   (place)   (activity you want to do there)
 <u>Kazuo</u>-kun-wa kotoshi-no <u>haru</u> yasumi-ni nani-o shitai desu-ka?
 (letter recipient's name)   (season)

G. Now write it in *hiragana* and *kanji*. Write in *katakana* where appropriate. (sample letter)

 もうすぐ はるやすみ ですね。ぼくは きょねん
 ニューヨークに 行 (い) って、 ミュージカルを
 見 (み) ました。 とても よかったです。 ことしは
 あにと バハマに いきたいです。 ダイビングを
 したいです。 かずおくんは ことしの
 はるやすみに 何 (なに) を したいですか。

> English translation:
> Spring break will soon be here. Last year
> I went to New York and saw a musical. It
> was great. This year I want to go to the
> Bahamas with my (older) brother. We
> want to go diving. Kazuo, what do you
> want to do this spring break?

Kanji Review

A. Fill in the chart by writing appropriate answers in *roomaji* and English in the parentheses.

	Kanji	Reading	Meaning
1.	見	(mi)-ru	(see), look at, watch
2.	行	(i)-ku	(go)
3.	来	(RAI); (ku)-ru	(come)
4.	年	(NEN); toshi	(year)

B. Write the following *kanji* in Arabic numbers.
 1. 四 (4)   2. 六 (6)   3. 九 (9)   4. 八 (8)   5. 二十三 (23)   6. 五十七 (57)

C. Write the appropriate *kanji* for 1 and 2, and write the reading in *hiragana* for 3 and 4.

1. 見る   2. 行く   3. こ と し   4. ら い し ゅ う

D. Fill in the blanks using the cues on the left. Write in *hiragana* and *kanji*. Write the corresponding *katakana* above the *roomaji*.

1. カ ラ オ ケ 、 行 き ま し た   3. バ ー ス デ ー ケ ー キ 、 つ く り ま し た

2. ハ ロ ウ ィ ー ン 、 ド ラ キ ュ ラ 、 見 ま し た

E. Read the following invitation and answer the questions in English.

1. Sachiko's   3. Friday   5. sandwiches and pasta salad

2. Saturday this week   4. 7:00 p.m.   6. their favorite drinks

F. Write a similar invitation for your own party. (sample letter)

<u>Raishuu-no nichi-yoobi</u>-wa <u>Harowiin</u> desu. <u>Yoru-no 6-ji</u>-kara <u>Akutibitii Sentaa</u>-de paatii-o shimasu.
   (specific day)   (special occasion)   (specific time)   (place)

Mina-san, tomodachi-to issho-ni kite kudasai. Tabemono-wa <u>piza</u>-to <u>chokoreeto keeki</u>-o tsukurimasu.
                                      (food item)   (food item)

Mina-san-wa suki-na nomimono-o motte kite kudasai.

G. Now write it in *hiragana* and *kanji*. Write in *katakana* where appropriate. (sample letter)

来 (らい) し ゅ う の 日 よ う 日 (にちようび) は
ハ ロ ウ ィ ー ン で す 。 よ る の 六 (ろく) じ か ら
ア ク テ ィ ビ テ ィ ー セ ン タ ー で パ ー テ ィ ー を し ま す 。
み な さ ん 、 と も だ ち と い っ し ょ に 来 (き) て
く だ さ い 。 た べ も の は ピ ザ と チ ョ コ レ ー ト ケ ー キ を
つ く り ま す 。 み な さ ん は す き な の み も の を も っ て
来 (き) て く だ さ い 。

> English translation:
> Next Sunday is Halloween. We will have a party at the Activity Center from 6:00 p.m. Everyone, please come with your friends. We will make pizza and chocolate cake. Please bring your favorite drink.

Topic: スポーツ (Sports)   **Reading and Writing Practice 10 (~ L. 33)**

Kanji **Review**

A. Fill in the chart by writing appropriate answers in *roomaji* and English in the parentheses.

	Kanji	Reading	Meaning
1.	来	(RAI); (ku)-ru	come
2.	私	(watashi)	(I), privacy
3.	天	(TEN)	sky, (heaven)
4.	見	(mi)-ru	see, (look at), watch
5.	水	SUI; (mizu)	water
6.	年	NEN; (toshi)	(year)

B. Write the appropriate *kanji* for the following words.

1. 見る   2. 行く   3. 今 し ゅ う

C. What counter words do you use in the following? Write the Arabic number in the parentheses and the counter word in *kanji* (where possible) on the line.

1. 九 人 : (9) people   3. 四年 かん : for (4) years   5. 六 本 : (6) pens

2. 八 さい : (8) years old   4. 七 まい : (7) sheets of paper

D. Fill in the blanks using the given cues. Write in *hiragana* and *kanji*. Write the corresponding *katakana* above the *roomaji*.

1. 今 、 チ ー ム 、 人   3. テ ニ ス 、 チ ケ ッ ト 、 ま い 、 行 き た い

2. フ ッ ト ボ ー ル 、 し あ い 、 見 ま し た

E. Read the following excerpt from Tsuyoshi's letter and answer the questions in English.

1. older brother   4. very good

2. last Saturday   5. Kyooto Middle School

3. with his father   6. three

F. Write a similar letter about a school sports event you went to. (sample passage)

Watashi-no <u>ane</u>-wa   <u>Nishi Kookoo</u>-no <u>tenisu-bu</u>-ni haitte-imasu. Senshuu-no <u>kin-yoobi</u>-ni
    (friend/family member) (school name) (sports club/team)   (day of the week)

watashi-wa <u>haha</u>-to   <u>Nishi Kookoo</u>-to   <u>Higashi Kookoo</u>-no
(friend's name or family member) (friend/family member's school name) (another school's name)

shiai-ni ikimashita. Tenki-wa <u>yokatta desu</u>. Shiai-wa <u>amari yokunakatta desu</u>.
               (adjective)   (adjective)

<u>Nishi Kookoo</u>-wa   <u>makemashita</u> Sukoa-wa <u>san</u> tai <u>ni</u> deshita.
(friend/family member's school name) (won/lost)   (score) (score)

G. Now write it in *hiragana* and *kanji*. Write in *katakana* where
   appropriate. (sample passage)

<u>私</u>（わたし）の あねは にし<u>高校</u>（こうこう）のテニスぶに
はいっています。せんしゅうの <u>金</u>よう<u>日</u>（きんようび）に
<u>私</u>（わたし）は ははと にし<u>高校</u>（こうこう）と ひがし<u>高校</u>
（こうこう）の しあいに <u>行</u>（い）きました。<u>天気</u>（てんき）は
よかったです。しあいは あまりよくなかったです。にし
<u>高校</u>（こうこう）は まけました。スコアは <u>三</u>（さん）たい
<u>二</u>（に）でした。

> English translation: My older sister is in the tennis club at Nishi High School. Last Friday, I went with my mom to the match between Nishi High School and Higashi High School. The weather was good. The match was not so good. Nishi High School lost. The score was 3 to 2.

Topic: かいもの (Shopping 1)   **Reading and Writing Practice 11 (~ L. 37)**

Kanji Review

A. Fill in the chart by writing appropriate answers in *roomaji* and English in the parentheses.

	Kanji	Reading	Meaning
1.	学	(GAKU); mana-bu	(learning); science
2.	校	(KOO)	(school)
3.	中	CHUU; (naka)	(middle), inside, within
4.	高	KOO; (taka)-i	high, (expensive)
5.	年	(NEN); toshi	(year)
6.	上	(ue)	(top), up, above, over
7.	下	(shita)	(below), down, under

B. Write the appropriate *kanji* for the following words.

  1.<u>中学校</u>   2.<u>高校</u>せい   3.<u>四年</u>まえ

C. Write the *kanji* for the size of the T-shirts below. 大 、 中 、 小

（ 小 ）   （ 中 ）   （ 大 ）

D. Fill in the blanks using the given cues. Write in *hiragana* and *kanji*. Write in *katakana* where appropriate.
   Write the prices in Arabic numbers.

  1. 6,800 えん   2,900 えん   2. 何、 いります   トマト、 ミルク、 いります

E. Read the following passage and answer the questions in English.

  1. today   3. five sweaters   5. two pairs of jeans
  2. at a department store   4. because they were cheap

F. Write a similar passage about yourself. (sample passage)

Boku-wa <u>ani</u>-to   <u>Kuroogaa</u>-de <u>kaimono-o shimashita</u>.
   (a person) (name of the store)   (shopped)

<u>Chokoreeto keeki</u>-o   <u>hitotsu</u>-to
(name of one item that you bought) (number + counter)

<u>koora</u>-o   <u>juu-ni-hon</u> kaimashita.
(name of the other item)   (number + counter)

> English translation:
> I shopped at Croger with my older brother. We bought one chocolate cake and 12 colas. We bought (these) because we will have a birthday party.

<u>Tanjoobi paatii-o suru</u>-kara kaimashita.
(reason for buying these items)

G. Now write it in *hiragana* and *kanji*. Write in *katakana* where appropriate. (sample passage)
ぼくは あにと クローガーで かいものを しました。チョコレートケーキを 一 (ひと) つと
コーラを 十二本 (じゅうにほん) かいました。たんじょう旦 (び) パーティーを するから
かいました。

Topic: かいもの (Shopping 2)　　　　　　　　　　　**Reading and Writing Practice 12 (~ L. 40)**

Kanji Review

A. Fill in the chart by writing appropriate answers in *roomaji* and English in the parentheses.

	Kanji	Reading	Meaning
1.	円	(EN)	(yen), circle
2.	百	(HYAKU) [BYAKU, PYAKU]	(hundred)
3.	千	(SEN) [ZEN]	(thousand)
4.	高	(KOO); taka-i	expensive, (high)
5.	見	(mi)-ru	see, (look at), watch
6.	金	KIN; (kane)	gold, (money)

B. Read the following price tags written in *kanji* and write the price in Arabic numbers below.
　　1. (7,200 yen)　　　　2. (4,300 yen)　　　　3. (6,150 yen)

C. Write the appropriate readings of these *kanji* in *roomaji*.
　　1. 八百 (hap-pyaku)　　　　　　3. 三千 (san-zen)
　　2. 九百 (kyuu-hyaku)　　　　　　4. 八千 (has-sen)

D. Fill in the blanks using the given cues. Write in *hiragana* and *kanji*. Write the corresponding *katakana* above the *roomaji*.
　　1. バレンタイン、何、もらいました　　　チョコレート、もらいました
　　2. すみません、何かいです

E. Read the following passage and answer the questions in English.
　　1. (Japanese) department stores　　　3. often eats Italian gelato　　　5. post office and bookstore
　　2. underground / basement　　　　　4. seventh floor

F. Write a similar passage about your favorite section of a department store or shopping mall.
　　(sample passage)
　　Watashi-no machi-ni <u>Derakkusu Mooru</u>-ga arimasu.
　　　　　　　(name of a department store/mall)
　　<u>Derakkusu Mooru</u>-ni o-mise-ga takusan arimasu.
　　(name of a department store/mall)
　　Watashi-wa <u>Nyuu Neebii</u>-ga <u>ichiban suki</u> desu.
　　　　　　(name of the store)　(like the best)
　　<u>Nyuu Neebii</u>-wa　　<u>ik-kai</u>-ni arimasu.
　　(name of the store) (floor level)
　　Soko-de <u>T-shatsu</u>-o kaimasu. Watashi-wa <u>eigakan</u>-mo
　　　　(name of the item)　　　　　　(name of another store)
　　suki desu. <u>Eigakan</u>-wa　　<u>ni-kai</u>-ni arimasu.　　<u>Amerika-no mooru-ni itta koto-ga arimasu-ka.</u>
　　(name of another store) (floor level)　　　　(Have you ever been to an American department store or mall?)

> English translation:
> Deluxe Mall is in my town. There are many stores in Deluxe Mall. I like NEW NAVY the best. NEW NAVY is located on the first floor. I buy T-shirts there. I like the movie theater, too. The movie theater is located on the second floor. Have you ever been to an American shopping mall?

G. Now write it in *hiragana* and *kanji*. Write in *katakana* where appropriate. (sample passage)
私 (わたし) のまちに デラックスモール が あります。デラックスモールに おみせが
たくさんあります。私 (わたし) は NEW NAVY が 一 (いち) ばん すきです。NEW NAVYは
一 (いっ) かいに あります。そこで Tシャツを かいます。私 (わたし) は えいがかんも
すきです。えいがかんは 二 (に) かいに あります。アメリカの モールに 行 (い) ったこと
が ありますか。

Kanji **Review**

A. Fill in the chart by writing appropriate answers in *roomaji* and English in the parentheses.

	Kanji	Reading	Meaning
1.	口	(kuchi) [guchi]	(mouth), opening
2.	目	(me)	(eye); *ordinal suffix*
3.	耳	(mimi)	(ear)
4.	天	(TEN)	(sky), heaven
5.	元	(GEN)	(beginning), foundation
6.	気	(KI)	(spirit), energy, attention

B. Match the following words with the pictures.

1. 口　(g)　　　3. はな　(b)　　　5. 耳　(a)　　　7. 目　(e)

2. て　(c)　　　4. あし　(d)　　　6. は　(f)

C. Change the given sentences to sentences in the past tense as if you were writing about what happened to you. Write in *hiragana*.

1. いたかったです　　　　2. ありました

D. Complete the following dialogue using the cues on the left. Write in *hiragana*.

A: くすり　　　　　　　B: ごはん、 あとで のんで

E. Read the following excerpt from a letter and answer the questions in English.

1. fine, but windy　　　　　　3. Saturday　　　　　　5. if Miyuki is all right

2. She had a cold.　　　　　　4. a fever and sore throat

F. Imagine that you were sick last week, and write a similar letter to sharing your experience. (sample letter)

O-genki desu-ka? <u>Daburin</u>-no kyoo-no tenki-wa <u>ame</u> desu.
　　　　　(name of your town)　　　　　(description of weather)
<u>45-do gurai desu. Samui desu.</u>
(additional information about the weather: temperature, wind, etc.)
Watashi-wa senshuu byooki deshita. <u>Kaze deshita. Onaka-ga itakatta desu.</u>
　　　　　　　　　　　　　　　　　　(symptoms of the illness)
<u>Yuuki</u>-kun-wa daijoobu desu-ka? Karada-ni ki-o tsukete kudasai-ne.
(pen pal's name)

G. Now write it in *hiragana* and *kanji*. Write in *katakana* where appropriate. (sample letter)

お元気 (げん き) ですか。
ダブリンの 今日 (きょう) の 天気 (てん き) は
あめです。四十五 (45) ど ぐらいです。 さむいです。
私 (わたし) は せんしゅう びょう気 (き) でした。
かぜでした。 おなかが いたかったです。
ゆうきくんは 大 (だい) じょうぶですか。
からだに 気 (き) を つけてくださいね。

English translation: How are you? Today's weather in Dublin is rainy. It is about 45 degrees. It is cold. I was sick last week. I had a cold. (And) I had a stomachache. Are you all right, Yuuki? Please take care of yourself.

Kanji **Review**

A. Fill in the chart by writing appropriate answers in *roomaji* and English in the parentheses.

	Kanji	Reading	Meaning
1.	名	(na)	(name)
2.	前	(mae)	(before), front
3.	才	(SAI)	talent; *suffix for counting* (age)
4.	高	KOO; (taka)-i	(tall), expensive
5.	金	(KIN); kane	gold; (money)
6.	気	(KI)	spirit, (energy), attention

B. Write the appropriate *kanji* for 1 through 3, and write the English meaning for 4 and 5.

1. 一 才   2. せが<u>高</u>い   3. <u>金</u>ぱつ   4. <u>impatient</u>   5. <u>name</u>

C. Complete the answers to the question below using the cues on the left. Write in *hiragana* and *kanji*.

1. やさしく、あかるい   3. せ、ひくくて、かみ、ちゃいろい

2. しずか、まじめな   4. せ、高くて、かみ、みじかい

D. Read the following passage and answer the questions in English.

1. Yamada, Kenji   4. energetic and interesting
2. 21 years old   5. at her birthday party (last year)
3. tall and has short black hair

E. Write a similar passage to describe someone. (sample passage)

Kono hito-no namae-wa <u>Kimu Buraun-san</u> desu.   <u>Kimu</u>-san-wa   <u>18-sai</u> desu.
                 (name of the person) (name of the person)   (age of the person)
<u>Kimu</u>-san-wa se-ga   <u>hikukute,</u>   kami-ga <u>akakute</u>   <u>nagai</u> desu.
(name of the person) (height: tall or short)   (color of the hair) (hair: long or short)
<u>Nigiyaka-de okashii</u> hito desu.   <u>Rekishi-no jugyoo</u>-de <u>Kimu</u>-san-ni aimashita.
(description of his/her personality: Use two adjectives.) (place/event where you met this person)

F. Now write it in *hiragana* and *kanji*. Write in *katakana* where appropriate. (sample passage)

この<u>人</u>（ひと）の <u>名前</u>（なまえ）は キム・ブラウン
さんです。キムさんは <u>十八才</u>（じゅうはっさい）
です。キムさんは せが ひくくて、かみが あかくて
ながいです。にぎやかで おかしい<u>人</u>（ひと）です。
れきしの じゅぎょうで キムさんに あいました。

> English translation:
> This person's name is Kim Brown. She is 18 years old. She is short and has long, red hair. She is a lively and funny person. I met her in history class.

Topic: 人生 (Life Events)   **Reading and Writing Practice 15 (~ L. 52)**

Kanji **Review**

A. Fill in the chart by writing appropriate answers in *roomaji* and English in the parentheses.

	Kanji	Reading	Meaning
1.	才	(sai)	talent; *suffix for counting* (age)
2.	先	(sen); saki	(previous), ahead
3.	生	(SEI); (u)-mareru	birth, (life), be born
4.	母	(haha), o-(kaa)-san	(mother)
5.	父	(chichi), o-(too)-san	(father)
6.	子	(ko) [go]	(child)

B. Write the readings in *hiragana* for the 1 and 2, and write appropriate *kanji* for 3 and 4.

1. <u>ちちと はは</u>   2. <u>こどもの なまえ</u>   3. 十八<u>才</u>   4. <u>先生</u>

C. Fill in the blanks using the cues on the left to complete sentences about Tim-*sensei*. Write in *hiragana* and *kanji*. Write the corresponding *katakana* above the *roomaji*.

1. 先生、月、日、ミシガン、生   3. 日本、えいご、おしえました

2. ワシントン、すんでいました   4. ハワイ、けっこんしました

D. Read the following passage and answer the questions in English.

1. 29 years old   5. Tokyo
2. Canadian   6. Seattle
3. tall and cheerful   7. in May of next year
4. Vancouver   8. a Japanese woman

E. Write a similar passage about a real or imaginary person. (sample passage)

<u>Lopez</u>-san-wa   <u>28-sai</u>-no <u>Mekishiko</u>-jin desu. <u>Kami-to me-ga chairokute,</u> <u>omoshiroi</u> hito desu.
(person's name) (age)   (nationality)   (physical description)   (personality description)
<u>Lopez</u>-san-wa   <u>Mekishiko</u>-de umaremashita. Kodomo-no toki <u>San Diego</u>-ni sunde-imashita.
(person's name) (place of birth)   (place s/he lived as a child)
Ima-wa <u>Rosanzerusu</u>-ni sunde-imasu. <u>Kekkon shite-imasu.</u>   <u>Ichi-gatsu</u>-ni <u>kekkon shimashita</u>.
(place s/he lives now)   (whether s/he is married or not)   (time word)   (will marry/got married)

F. Now write it in *hiragana* and *kanji*. Write in *katakana* where appropriate. (sample passage)

ロペスさんは 二十八才 (にじゅうはっさい) の
メキシコ人 (じん) です。かみと 目 (め) が
ちゃいろくて、おもしろい人 (ひと) です。
ロペスさんは メキシコで 生 (う) まれました。
子 (こ) どものとき サンディエゴに すんで
いました。今 (いま) は ロサンゼルスに すんで
います。けっこんしています。一月 (いちがつ)
に けっこんしました。

English translation:
Ms. Lopez is a 28-yr. old Mexican. She has brown hair and brown eyes and is an interesting person. Ms. Lopez was born in Mexico. When she was a child, she lived in San Diego. Now she lives in Los Angeles. She is married. She got married in January.

Topic: しょうらい **(Future Plans)**   **Reading and Writing Practice 16 (~ L. 55)**
Kanji **Review**

A. Fill in the chart by writing appropriate answers in *roomaji* and English in the parentheses.

	Kanji	Reading	Meaning
1.	言	(i)-u	(say)
2.	話	(hana)-su	(speak)
3.	読	(yo)-mu	(read)
4.	国	KOKU [GOKU]; (kuni)	(country)
5.	語	(GO)	(word), speech
6.	子	(ko) [go]	(child)

B. Choose the direct object that the following verbs take and write its letter in the parentheses.
1. 読む (a)   2. 話す (d)   3. きく (b)   4. 見る (c)

C. Answer the question below using the cues on the left. Write in *hiragana* and *kanji*. Write the corresponding *katakana* above the *roomaji*.
1. ピアノ、先生、なりたい   3. 大きい ぎんこう、はたらきたい
2. イタリア、すみたい   4. けっこん したい

D. Read the following excerpt from a letter and answer the questions in English.
1. in two years   4. She wants to get married.
2. travel to Paris and Nice   5. two
3. become an elementary school French teacher

E. Write a similar passage about yourself. (sample passage)
Watashi-wa kookoo 3-nen-sei desu.   Kotoshi sotsugyoo shimasu. Sono ato, daigaku-de suugaku-o
        (grade)   (when you will graduate)   (what you will do after
benkyoo shimasu. Shoorai, kookoo-no sensei-ni naritai desu.   Soshite, kekkon shitai desu.
you graduate)   (what you want to do/be in the future)   (whether you want to marry or not)
Kodomo-ga hitori hoshii desu.
        (number)

F. Now write it in *hiragana* and *kanji*. Write in *katakana* where appropriate. (sample passage)

私 (わたし) は 高校 (こうこう) 三年生 (さんねんせ
い) です。今年 (ことし) そつぎょうします。そのあ
と、大学 (だいがく) で すう学 (がく) を べんきょう
します。しょう来 (らい)、高校 (こうこう) の 先生
(せんせい) に なりたいです。そして、けっこんした
いです。子 (こ) どもが 一人 (ひとり) ほしいです。

English translation:
I am a high school senior. I will graduate this year. After that, I'll study math in college. In the future, I want to be a high school teacher. And I want to get married. I want one child.

166

Kanji **Review**

A. Fill in the chart by writing appropriate answers in *roomaji* and English in the parentheses.

	Kanji	Reading	Meaning
1.	書	(ka)-ku	(write)
2.	聞	(ki)-ku	(hear), listen to, ask
3.	間	(KAN)	space, (interval)
4.	時	(JI); toki [doki]	(time), *counter for clock hours*
5.	分	(FUN) [PUN]; wa-karu	(minute), *counter for minutes*; understand
6.	雨	(ame)	(rain)
7.	雪	(yuki)	(snow)

B. Read the following phrases and choose the appropriate situation when you would most likely use the phrase. Write the letter in the parentheses.

1. (b)　　　2. (c)

C. Complete the answers below using the cues on the left. Write in *hiragana* and *kanji*.

1. 十二 (12) 日間 (かん)

2. しんかんせんで　一 (1) 時間 (じかん) 四十五 (45) 分 (ふん)

3. [六 (6) 月二十二 (22) 日の]ごご十二 (12) 時 (じ) 七 (7) 分 (ふん) に

D. Read the following post card and answer the questions in English.

1. on winter vacation　　　3. It is snowing today.　　　5. 750 years old
2. Japan　　　4. very cold　　　6. for six days

E. Imagine that you are traveling. Write a postcard to your Japanese teacher or friend. (sample letter)

Konnichi-wa.　　　Ima, haru yasumi-de,　　　Furansu-ni kimashita. O-tenki-wa ame-de,
(opening greeting) (name of the holiday or vacation) (name of the place)　　　(weather)

sukoshi samui desu.　　　Kyoo, Machisu-no e-o mimashita.
(comment on the temperature)　(time word)　(activity that you did)

E-wa　　　iro-ga totemo kirei de, romanchikku deshita.
(activity/object) (description of the activity/object. Use adjective(s).)

Sui-yoobi-kara　Maruseiyu-ni ikimasu. Maruseiyu-de　　　oishii sakana-o takusan tabetai desu.
(time word)　(name of the place)　　　(place)　　　(activity that you want to do. Use the *-tai* form.)

Nichi-yoobi-ni　　　Atoranta-ni kaerimasu. Sayoonara.
(time word)　　(name of the place)　　　(closing greeting)

F. Now write it in *hiragana* and *kanji*. Write in *katakana* where appropriate. (sample letter)

今日(こんにち)は。今(いま)はるやすみで
フランスに来(き)ました。お天気(てんき)は
雨(あめ)で、すこしさむいです。今日(きょう)、
マチスの えを見(み)ました。えは いろが とても
きれいで ロマンチックでした。水(すい)よう日(び)
から マルセイユにいきます。マルセイユで
おいしい さかなを たくさん たべたいです。
日(にち)よう日(び)に アトランタに かえります。
さようなら。

> English translation:
> Hello. It is now Spring Break and I came to France. It is raining and a little cold. Today, I saw Matisse's paintings. The paintings had very pretty colors and were romantic. I am going to Marseille from Wednesday. I want to eat lots of delicious fish in Marseille. I am going back to Atlanta on Sunday. See you!

Kanji Review

A. Fill in the chart by writing appropriate answers in *roomaji* and English in the parentheses.

	Kanji	Reading	Meaning
1.	東	(TOO), higashi	(east)
2.	京	(KYOO), KEI	(capital)
3.	駅	(eki)	(station)
4.	百	(HYAKU) [BYAKU, PYAKU]	(hundred)
5.	千	(SEN) [ZEN]	(thousand)

B. Write the following in Arabic numbers. Then match the number with the fact listed below, and write its letter in the parentheses.

1. 7,830,000 (c)   2. 1,863 (a)   3. 850 (b)

C. Read the sentences below and in Japanese write the names of the buildings described on the line. (If you need help, re-read the textbook, Culture Notes in Lesson 59.)

1. とちょう   2. こうきょ   3. めいじじんぐう

D. Read the following passage and answer the questions in English.

1. She will arrive at Tokyo Station.   3. She wants boots.   5. You can find it on the 10th floor.

2. She will shop (at Roppongi Hills).   4. It has 60 floors.

E. Research Tokyo's sight-seeing spots. Then write a brief passage about your plans in Tokyo. (sample passage)

<u>Getsu-yoobi</u>-ni   <u>hikooki</u>-de,   <u>Narita</u>-ni tsukimasu. Sono ato, <u>Dizunii Rizooto</u>-de
  (time word)   (means of transportation)   (a place)   (another place)

<u>pareedo-o mimasu.</u>   <u>Dizunii Rizooto</u>-wa <u>ookikute omoshiroi desu.</u>
(activity that you will do)   (the place)   (description of the place)

<u>Harajuku</u>-de   <u>sutoriito pafoomaa-o mitai desu.</u>   Sorekara, <u>Asakusa</u>-ni   <u>ikitai desu.</u>
(another place) (activity that you want to do: Use *-tai* form.)   (another place) (want to go: Use *-tai* form.)

F. Now write it in *hiragana* and *kanji*. Write in *katakana* where appropriate. (sample passage)

月 (げつ) よう日 (び) に ひこうきで なりたに
つきます。そのあと、ディズニーリゾートで
パレードを 見 (み) ます。ディズニーリゾートは
大 (おお) きくて おもしろいです。はらじゅくで
ストリートパフォーマーを 見 (み) たいです。
それから、あさくさに 行 (い) きたいです。

> English translation:
> On Monday, I will arrive in Narita by
> airplane. Later, I will see the parade at
> Disney Resort. Disney Resort is big
> and fun. I (also) want to see the street
> performers in Harajuku. Then, I want
> to go to Asakusa.

月	日	木
本	人	山
川	大	小
学	校	中

R: L8 W: L11
MOKU

木

木よう日　moku yoo bi

tree, wood

R: L7 W: L10
NICHI; bi, ka

日

日よう日　nichi yoo bi
十一日　juu ichi nichi
二日　futsu ka

day, sun; *counter for days of the month*

R: L7 W: L10
GETSU, GATSU

月

月よう日　getsu yoo bi
一月　ichi gatsu

month, moon

R: L8
SAN [ZAN];
yama

山

山　yama
ふじ山　Fuji san

mountain

R: L8 W: L11
NIN, JIN; hito,
~ri

人

人　hito
一人　hito ri
六人　roku nin
日本人　ni hon jin

person; *counter for people*

R: L8 W: L11
HON [BON,
PON]

本

本　hon
一本　ip pon
三本　san bon

book, origin, source; *counter for long, narrow objects*

R: L9 W: L12
SHOO; chii(sai)

小

小さい　chii sai
小学校　shoo gak koo
小人　kodomo

small, little

R: L9 W: L12
DAI; oo(kii)

大

大きい　oo kii
大学　dai gaku
大人　otona

big, large, great

R: L8
kawa [gawa]

川

川　kawa
山川　Yama kawa
中川　Naka gawa

river

R: L14 W: L35
CHUU; naka

中

中学校　chuu gak koo
中　naka

middle, inside, within

R: L13 W: L34
KOO

校

学校　gak koo

school

R: L13 W: L34
GAKU

学

学生　gaku sei
学校　gak koo

learning, science

高	何	今
私	火	水
金	土	天
元	気	田

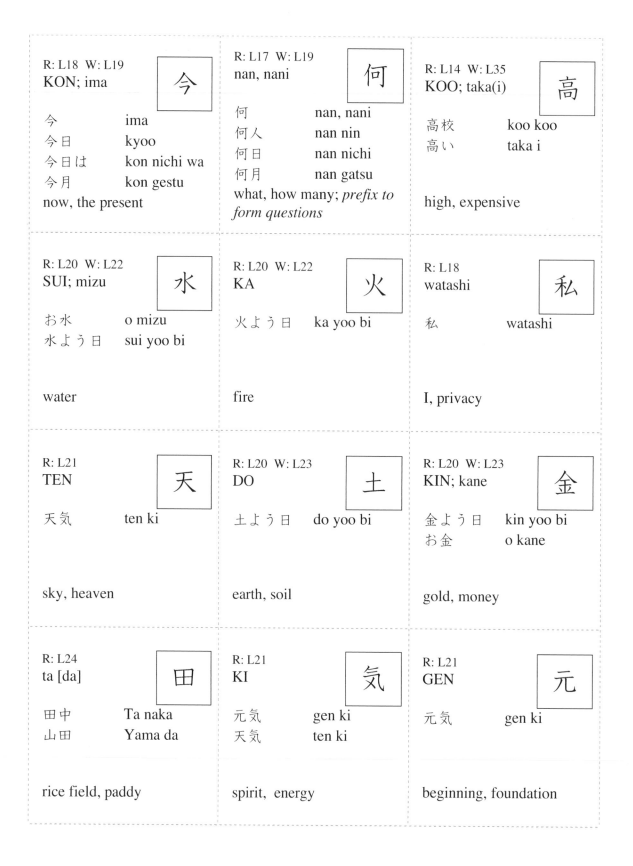

R: L18 W: L19
KON; ima

今 | ima
今日 | kyoo
今日は | kon nichi wa
今月 | kon gestu

now, the present

R: L17 W: L19
nan, nani

何 | nan, nani
何人 | nan nin
何日 | nan nichi
何月 | nan gatsu

what, how many; *prefix to form questions*

R: L14 W: L35
KOO; taka(i)

高校 | koo koo
高い | taka i

high, expensive

R: L20 W: L22
SUI; mizu

お水 | o mizu
水よう日 | sui yoo bi

water

R: L20 W: L22
KA

火よう日 | ka yoo bi

fire

R: L18
watashi

私 | watashi

I, privacy

R: L21
TEN

天気 | ten ki

sky, heaven

R: L20 W: L23
DO

土よう日 | do yoo bi

earth, soil

R: L20 W: L23
KIN; kane

金よう日 | kin yoo bi
お金 | o kane

gold, money

R: L24
ta [da]

田中 | Ta naka
山田 | Yama da

rice field, paddy

R: L21
KI

元気 | gen ki
天気 | ten ki

spirit, energy

R: L21
GEN

元気 | gen ki

beginning, foundation

172

見	行	来
年	一	二
三	四	五
六	七	八

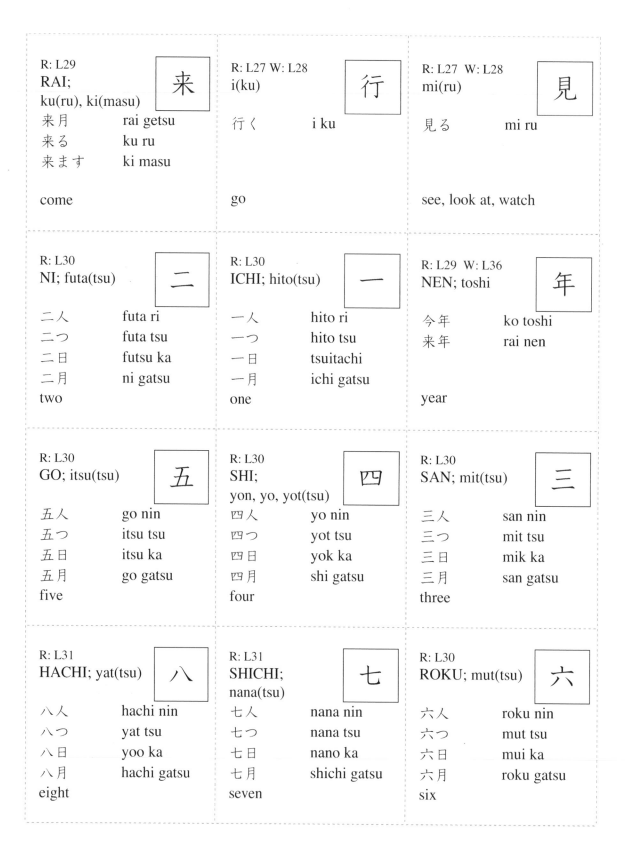

R: L29
RAI;
ku(ru), ki(masu)

来

来月　　　rai getsu
来る　　　ku ru
来ます　　ki masu

come

R: L27 W: L28
i(ku)

行

行く　　　　i ku

go

R: L27 W: L28
mi(ru)

見

見る　　　　mi ru

see, look at, watch

R: L30
NI; futa(tsu)

二

二人　　　futa ri
二つ　　　futa tsu
二日　　　futsu ka
二月　　　ni gatsu

two

R: L30
ICHI; hito(tsu)

一

一人　　　　hito ri
一つ　　　　hito tsu
一日　　　　tsuitachi
一月　　　　ichi gatsu

one

R: L29 W: L36
NEN; toshi

年

今年　　　　ko toshi
来年　　　　rai nen

year

R: L30
GO; itsu(tsu)

五

五人　　　go nin
五つ　　　itsu tsu
五日　　　itsu ka
五月　　　go gatsu

five

R: L30
SHI;
yon, yo, yot(tsu)

四

四人　　　　yo nin
四つ　　　　yot tsu
四日　　　　yok ka
四月　　　　shi gatsu

four

R: L30
SAN; mit(tsu)

三

三人　　　san nin
三つ　　　mit tsu
三日　　　mik ka
三月　　　san gatsu

three

R: L31
HACHI; yat(tsu)

八

八人　　　hachi nin
八つ　　　yat tsu
八日　　　yoo ka
八月　　　hachi gatsu

eight

R: L31
SHICHI;
nana(tsu)

七

七人　　　　nana nin
七つ　　　　nana tsu
七日　　　　nano ka
七月　　　　shichi gatsu

seven

R: L30
ROKU; mut(tsu)

六

六人　　　roku nin
六つ　　　mut tsu
六日　　　mui ka
六月　　　roku gatsu

six

九	十	上
下	円	百
千	万	口
目	耳	名

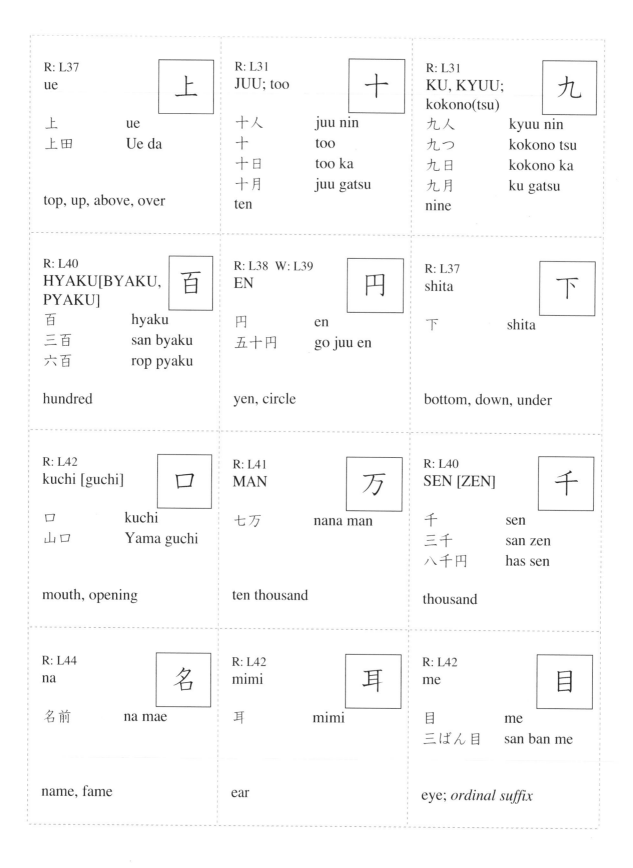

R: L37
ue

上　　　　　ue
上田　　　Ue da

top, up, above, over

R: L31
JUU; too

十人　　　juu nin
十　　　　too
十日　　　too ka
十月　　　juu gatsu

ten

R: L31
KU, KYUU;
kokono(tsu)

九人　　　kyuu nin
九つ　　　kokono tsu
九日　　　kokono ka
九月　　　ku gatsu

nine

R: L40
HYAKU[BYAKU,
PYAKU]

百　　　　hyaku
三百　　　san byaku
六百　　　rop pyaku

hundred

R: L38 W: L39
EN

円　　　　en
五十円　　go juu en

yen, circle

R: L37
shita

下　　　　shita

bottom, down, under

R: L42
kuchi [guchi]

口　　　　kuchi
山口　　　Yama guchi

mouth, opening

R: L41
MAN

七万　　　nana man

ten thousand

R: L40
SEN [ZEN]

千　　　　sen
三千　　　san zen
八千円　　has sen

thousand

R: L44
na

名前　　　na mae

name, fame

R: L42
mimi

耳　　　　mimi

ear

R: L42
me

目　　　　me
三ばん目　san ban me

eye; *ordinal suffix*

前	才	先
生	父	母
子	言	話
国	語	読

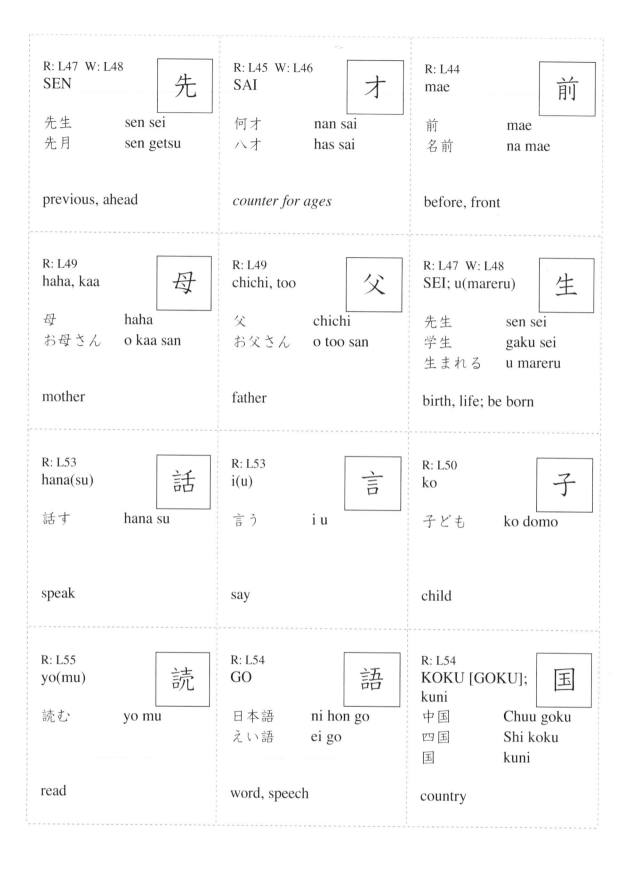

R: L47 W: L48 先	R: L45 W: L46 才	R: L44 前
SEN	SAI	mae
先生 sen sei 先月 sen getsu	何才 nan sai ハ才 has sai	前 mae 名前 na mae
previous, ahead	*counter for ages*	before, front

R: L49 母	R: L49 父	R: L47 W: L48 生
haha, kaa	chichi, too	SEI; u(mareru)
母 haha お母さん o kaa san	父 chichi お父さん o too san	先生 sen sei 学生 gaku sei 生まれる u mareru
mother	father	birth, life; be born

R: L53 話	R: L53 言	R: L50 子
hana(su)	i(u)	ko
話す hana su	言う i u	子ども ko domo
speak	say	child

R: L55 読	R: L54 語	R: L54 国
yo(mu)	GO	KOKU [GOKU]; kuni
読む yo mu	日本語 ni hon go えい語 ei go	中国 Chuu goku 四国 Shi koku 国 kuni
read	word, speech	country

書	聞	間
時	分	雨
雪	東	京
駅		

R: L57 **KAN** 三日間　　mik ka kan interval, space	間	R: L57 **ki(ku)** 聞く　　　ki ku listen to, hear, ask	聞	R: L56 **ka(ku)** 書く　　　ka ku write	書
R: L59 **ame** 雨　　　　ame rain	雨	R: L58 **FUN [PUN]** 二分　　　ni fun 八分　　　hap pun minute, *counter for minutes*	分	R: L58 **JI; toki** 何時　　　nan ji 学生の時　gaku sei no toki 四時間　　yo ji kan time, *counter for clock hours*	時
R: L60 **KYOO** 東京　　　Too kyoo capital	京	R: L60 **TOO; higashi** 東　　　　higashi 東京　　　Too kyoo east	東	R: L59 **yuki** 雪　　　　yuki snow	雪
				R: L60 **EKI** 駅　　　　eki 東京駅　　Too kyoo eki station	駅

Culture Matrix - Volume 2 (L. 1~63)

L.	Topics Covered in Lesson	Culture Notes in Lesson	*Irasshai* Website www.gpb.org/irasshai - for students Student Notebook (SN) **Online Resources** (OR) Use various search engines to look up the following topics	*i-irasshai* **Culture Topics and Activities** Look under "Guidebook (Index)" and click on the following key words
1	Homestay 1		(SN) Writing Practice Sheet: *katakana a-o* *ka-ko* (OR) Japanese homestay	- etiquette – gift - etiquette – sitting - gift (quiz) - greetings (activity) - house – removing shoes (activity) - nameplate - *hyoosatsu* - welcome
2	Homestay 2		(SN) Writing Practice Sheet: *katakana sa-so* *ta-to* Choose Your Lesson: *Nihon Isshuu Tsuaa* (OR) Exchange student in Japan	- alcove (2) - chair – *zaisu* - curtains – *noren* (house) - cushion – *zabuton* - *fusuma* doors - scrolls – *kakejiku* - table (2) - *tatami* (5) - wood carving - *ranma*
3	Homestay 3	- Summer greeting cards	(SN) Writing Practice Sheet: *katakana na-no* *ha-ho* Choose Your Lesson: *Nihon Isshuu Tsuaa* (OR) Japanese summer greeting cards *Shochu mimai*	- bamboo curtains – wind bells - baths (6) - bed (2) - etiquette – bathtub - hair care - hot springs (2) - kimono – *yukata* - pillow - toilets - wash bowl
4	Homestay 4		(SN) Writing Practice Sheet: *katakana ma-mo* *ya, yu, yo, wa, o* Choose Your Lesson: *Nihon Isshuu Tsuaa* (OR) Japanese pets Japanese pet animals	- house cleaning - laundry - recycling items - tissue box (quiz) - washing machine

L.	Topics Covered in Lesson	Culture Notes in Lesson	Irasshai Website / Online Resources	i-irasshai
5	Homestay 5		(SN) Choose Your Lesson: *Nan-to iimasu-ka?* / *Nihon Isshuu Tsuaa*	- gas stove - kitchen - microwave – *denshi renji* and *oobun renji* - oven - refrigerator - rice cooker - sink - thermos – *dendoo jaa potto* - toaster and breakfast
6	Countries and Languages	- Japanese world map - *Kanji* notes The origin and use of *kanji*	(SN) Writing Practice Sheet: *katakana ra-ro* / Choose Your Lesson: *Nihon Isshuu Tsuaa* / (OR) Japanese maps / Japanese world map / Japanese *kanji* history / origin	
7	Locations and Cardinal Directions	- *Kanji* notes Reading Japanese Reading *kanji*	(SN) Choose Your Lesson: *Nihon Isshuu Tsuaa* / (OR) Reading Japanese / Reading Japanese *kanji*	
8	Geography	- Japan – an island nation - *Fuji-san* - *Biwa-ko*	(SN) Writing Practice Sheet: *kanji – yama, kawa* / Choose Your Lesson: *Nihon Isshuu Tsuaa* / (OR) Islands of Japan / Mount Fuji / Lake Biwa	- bonsai - garden (2) - geology classroom - maple tree - mountains (2) - ocean - port
9	Describing with Superlatives		(SN) Choose Your Lesson: *Nihon Isshuu Tsuaa*	
10	Telling How Long One Has Done Something	- Compliments - *Kanji* notes Writing *kanji*	(SN) Writing Practice Sheet: *kanji – getsu, nichi* / Choose Your Lesson: *Nihon Isshuu Tsuaa* / (OR) Japanese compliments / Writing Japanese *kanji*	
11	Current Activities		(SN) Writing Practice Sheet: *kanji – moku, hon, jin* / Choose Your Lesson: *Nihon Isshuu Tsuaa* / (OR) Japanese *kanji* stroke order	
12	Talk about What Someone Was Doing		(SN) Writing Practice Sheet: *kanji – ookii, chiisai* / Choose Your Lesson: *Nihon Isshuu Tsuaa*	

L.	Topics Covered in Lesson	Culture Notes in Lesson	Irasshai Website / Online Resources	i-irasshai
13	Daily School Life	- School cleaning	(SN) Choose Your Lesson: *Nihon Isshuu Tsuaa* (OR) Japanese school cleaning *Soji / sooji* school cleaning	- education – overview - English class (2) - gymnasium - school - school cleaning (video) - school sink (quiz) - school transportation
14	School Clubs	- Japanese boxed lunches	(SN) Choose Your Lesson: *Nihon Isshuu Tsuaa* (OR) Japanese boxed lunches *Obento* *Bukatsudo* school clubs	- after school activities and field day – *undookai* - broadcasting room - etiquette room - school lunch (optional video) - swimming - volleyball
15	Asking for and Giving Permission	- *Kanji* notes The Importance of Review	(SN) Choose Your Lesson: *Nan-to iimasu-ka?* (OR) Japanese *kanji* review	
16	More Spatial Relationships		(SN) Choose Your Lesson: *Nihon Isshuu Tsuaa*	
17	Sequences of Daily Activities		(SN) Choose Your Lesson: *Nihon Isshuu Tsuaa* (OR) *Tadaima* *Okaeri*	
18	Weekend Activities		(SN) Writing Practice Sheet: *kanji – watashi* Choose Your Lesson: *Nihon Isshuu Tsuaa*	
19	Hobbies and Interests	- *Shumi*	(SN) Writing Practice Sheet: *kanji – nan, ima* Choose Your Lesson: *Nihon Isshuu Tsuaa*	- air mail (quiz) - bonsai - calligraphy - coffee - comic books – *manga* - dolls (quiz) - e-mail (activity) - flower arrangement – *ikebana* - karaoke machine - library

L.	Topics Covered in Lesson	Culture Notes in Lesson	Irasshai Website / Online Resources	i-irasshai
20	Writing to a Pen Pal	- Shumi	(SN) Choose Your Lesson: Nihon Isshuu Tsuaa (OR) Japanese hobbies shumi	- mail - movies - music – hoogaku and yoogaku - newspapers - novels - pachinko - paper folding – origami - radio - sushi – what is it? (video) - sword fighting – kendo - tea ceremony - television – terebi
21	Writing a Letter to a Friend	- Seasonal references in letters - Four seasons in Japan	(SN) Writing Practice Sheet: kanji – ten, gen, ki Choose Your Lesson: Nihon Isshuu Tsuaa (OR) Expressions used in Japanese letters Japanese seasons Japanese winter / spring / summer / fall	- bamboo curtains – wind bells - flowers - kimono – yukata - maple tree
22	Seasons and Activities		(SN) Writing Practice Sheet: kanji – ka, sui Choose Your Lesson: Nihon Isshuu Tsuaa (OR) Japanese seasonal events	
23	Talking about a Trip		(SN) Writing Practice Sheet: kanji – kin, do Choose Your Lesson: Nan-to iimasu-ka? Nihon Isshuu Tsuaa	
24	Telephoning	- Important Japanese telephone numbers - Kanji notes Japanese family names	(SN) Writing Practice Sheet: kanji – ta Choose Your Lesson: Nihon Isshuu Tsuaa (OR) Japanese telephone 110 / 119 / 117 / 177 Japanese family name kanji	- telephone (activity) - telephone directories - telephone numbers (activity)
25	Expressing Wants		(SN) Choose Your Lesson: Nihon Isshuu Tsuaa	
26	Admission Prices	- Admission prices for adults and children	(SN) Choose Your Lesson: Nihon Isshuu Tsuaa	- bullet train – buy tickets (activity) - commuter train – buy tickets (activity)
27	Sporting Events		(SN) Choose Your Lesson: Nihon Isshuu Tsuaa (OR) Japanese sports news	
28	Leisure Time		(SN) Writing Practice Sheet: kanji – miru, iku Choose Your Lesson: Nihon Isshuu Tsuaa	
29	Having a Party	- Personal pronouns	(SN) Writing Practice Sheet: kanji – kuru Choose Your Lesson: Nihon Isshuu Tsuaa (OR) Japanese personal pronouns	

L.	Topics Covered in Lesson	Culture Notes in Lesson	*Irasshai* Website / Online Resources	i-*irasshai*
30	Review	- *Kanji* notes *Kanji* and Arabic numbers	(SN) Writing Practice Sheet: *kanji* – 1~6 Choose Your Lesson: *Nihon Isshuu Tsuaa* (OR) Japanese Arabic numbers	
31	Review		(SN) Writing Practice Sheet: *kanji* – 7~10 Choose Your Lesson: *Nan-to iimasu-ka?* *Nihon Isshuu Tsuaa*	
32	Reviewing Counting and Prices		(SN) Choose Your Lesson: *Nihon Isshuu Tsuaa* (OR) Counting in Japanese	- fish market – buy shrimp (activity) - fruit stand – buy fruit (activity) - money - pay cashier (activity) - vegetable market – buy bamboo shoots (activity)
33	Nearby Locations	- Addressing an envelope Japanese style	(SN) Choose Your Lesson: *Nihon Isshuu Tsuaa* (OR) Addressing a Japanese envelope	- air mail - mail - mail – addressing postcard (activity)
34	More Spatial Relationships	- Japanese Vending Machines	(SN) Writing Practice Sheet: *kanji* – *gaku, koo* Choose Your Lesson: *Nihon Isshuu Tsuaa* (OR) Japanese vending machines	- stamp vending machine (activity)
35	Numbers up to 100,000	- *O-chuugen* and *o-seibo*	(SN) Writing Practice Sheet: *kanji* – *naka, takai* Choose Your Lesson: *Nihon Isshuu Tsuaa* (OR) *Oseibo* *Ochuugen*	
36	Expressing Needs	- Fruit as a gift	(SN) Writing Practice Sheet: *kanji* – *nen* Choose Your Lesson: *Nihon Isshuu Tsuaa* (OR) Japanese gift fruit	- fruits - gift (quiz)
37	Asking For and Giving Reasons		(SN) Writing Practice Sheet: *kanji* – *ue, shita* Choose Your Lesson: *Nihon Isshuu Tsuaa*	
38	Locating Items in a Department Store		(SN) Choose Your Lesson: *Nihon Isshuu Tsuaa* (OR) Japanese department stores	
39	Past Experiences		(SN) Writing Practice Sheet: *kanji* – *en* Choose Your Lesson: *Nihon Isshuu Tsuaa*	
40	Review	- Valentine's Day (*Barentain-dee*)	(SN) Writing Practice Sheet: *kanji* – 100, 1000 Choose Your Lesson: *Nan-to iimasu-ka?* *Nihon Isshuu Tsuaa* (OR) Japanese Valentine's Day Japanese White Day	

L.	Topics Covered in Lesson	Culture Notes in Lesson	Irasshai Website / Online Resources	i-irasshai
41	Parts of the Body	- Common expressions related to body parts	(SN) Writing Practice Sheet: *kanji* – 10,000 Choose Your Lesson: *Nihon Isshuu Tsuaa* (OR) Japanese parts of the body Body part expressions in Japanese	
42	Asking About and Describing Health Conditions	- Japanese medicine	(SN) Writing Practice Sheet: *kanji – kuchi, me, mimi* Choose Your Lesson: *Nihon Isshuu Tsuaa* (OR) Japanese medicine Medicine in Japan	- height and weight
43	Asking About and Describing Health Conditions	- Giving Flowers to a Sick Person	(SN) Choose Your Lesson: *Nihon Isshuu Tsuaa* (OR) Japanese gift giving mistakes	- flowers
44	Taking Medicine		(SN) Writing Practice Sheet: *kanji – na, mae* Choose Your Lesson: *Nihon Isshuu Tsuaa* (OR) *Kampo* medicine	
45	Describing People (Personality)		(SN) Choose Your Lesson: *Nihon Isshuu Tsuaa*	
46	Describing People (Physical Characteristics)		(SN) Writing Practice Sheet: *kanji – sai* Choose Your Lesson: *Nihon Isshuu Tsuaa*	
47	Describing People (Clothing)		(SN) Choose Your Lesson: *Nihon Isshuu Tsuaa* (OR) Japanese clothing Japanese accessories	- kimono - kimono – *yukata* - uniforms (activity)
48	Knowing People and Things		(SN) Writing Practice Sheet: *kanji – sen, sei* Choose Your Lesson: *Nan-to iimasu-ka?* *Nihon Isshuu Tsuaa*	
49	Life Events (Birth and Marriage)	- O-Miai	(SN) Writing Practice Sheet: *kanji – chichi, haha* Choose Your Lesson: *Nihon Isshuu Tsuaa* (OR) Japanese *omiai* Japanese weddings	- Buddhist temple room - *hondoo* - cemetery (quiz) - cemetery rituals - funerals - wedding
50	Where People Live	- Choosing a name for a child in Japan	(SN) Writing Practice Sheet: *kanji – kodomo* Choose Your Lesson: *Nihon Isshuu Tsuaa* (OR) Japanese baby names Japanese baby name *kanji*	- housing situation - housing types
51	Relatives	- Traditional Japanese Calendar	(SN) Choose Your Lesson: *Nihon Isshuu Tsuaa* (OR) Japanese traditional calendar Japanese horoscope / zodiac	

L.	Topics Covered in Lesson	Culture Notes in Lesson	*Irasshai* Website / Online Resources	i-*irasshai*
52	Occupations		(SN) Choose Your Lesson: *Nihon Isshuu Tsuaa* (OR) Japanese salaryman	- bakery - banks - English class - gas station – service person (quiz) - mail carrier - police officer (quiz) - sushi chef – *itamae* - taxi - teachers - wait staff
53	Getting a Job	- Japanese resumes (*rirekisho*) - Owning and driving a car in Japan	(SN) Writing Practice Sheet: *kanji – iu, hanasu* Choose Your Lesson: *Nihon Isshuu Tsuaa* (OR) Japanese resumes *Rirekisho* Owning / driving a car in Japan	- automobile - car blessing ceremony - car wash - gas station (3) - transportation
54	After Graduation		(SN) Writing Practice Sheet: *kanji – koku, go* Choose Your Lesson: *Nihon Isshuu Tsuaa* (OR) Japanese graduation ceremonies Japanese graduation	- graduating class gifts
55	Dreams for the Future		(SN) Writing Practice Sheet: *kanji – yomu* Choose Your Lesson: *Nihon Isshuu Tsuaa* (OR) Japanese fortune telling / *uranai*	- *omikuji* (activity) - shrine – fortune telling
56	Review	- Religion in Japan	(SN) Writing Practice Sheet: *kanji – kaku* Choose Your Lesson: *Nan-to iimasu-ka?* *Nihon Isshuu Tsuaa* (OR) Religion in Japan Japanese Buddhism Japanese temples *Shinto* Japanese shrines	- Buddhist or Shinto - gardens - good luck items – *omamori* - mountains – spiritual significance - New Year celebration - *oshoogatsu* Buddhism - Buddha - flowers - Buddhism - lanterns - Buddhist (9) - monk doll – *daruma* - coin box - pagoda Shinto - donor board - *shimenawa* - *omikuji* (activity) - Shinto (5) - purification - shrine (3) - sake barrels - *torii*
57	Length of Events		(SN) Writing Practice Sheet: *kanji – kiku, kan* Choose Your Lesson: *Nihon Isshuu Tsuaa*	

L.	Topics Covered in Lesson	Culture Notes in Lesson	Irasshai Website / Online Resources	i-irasshai
58	Travel Schedules		(SN) Writing Practice Sheet: *kanji – ji, fun* Choose Your Lesson: *Nihon Isshuu Tsuaa* (OR) Japanese travel / itinerary Japanese train schedules	- bullet train - *shinkansen* - kiosk - public transportation - trains (5)
59	Famous Tourist Sites in Japan	- Famous tourist sites in Japan - TOKYO - *Tochoo* (Tokyo City Hall) - *Tookyoo Tawaa* (Tokyo Tower) - *Kookyo* (Imperial Palace) - *Kokkai-gijidoo* (National Parliament Building) - *Meiji-jinguu* (Meiji-jinguu Shrine) - KYOTO - *Kinkakuji* (Temple of the Golden Pavilion) - *Heian-jinguu* (Heian-jinguu Shrine) - *Kiyomizu-dera* (Kiyomizu-dera Temple) - *Ryooanji* (Ryooan-ji Temple)	(SN) Writing Practice Sheet: *kanji – ame, yuki* Choose Your Lesson: *Nihon Isshuu Tsuaa* (OR) Japanese tourist attractions Tokyo City Hall Tokyo Tower Tokyo Imperial Palace National Diet Building *Meiji Jingu Shrine* Edo-Tokyo Museum Asakusa Tokyo, Shinjuku Tokyo Akihabara Tokyo, Ginza Tokyo Harajuku Tokyo, Shibuya Tokyo *Kinkakuji* / Golden Pavilion *Ginkakuji* / Silver Pavilion *Heian Jingu Shrine* *Kiyomizudera* *Ryoanji* Kyoto National Museum Nijo Castle Gion Kyoto, Arashiyama Kyoto	
60	Transportation Arrangements	- Japan's international airports	(SN) Writing Practice Sheet: *kanji – too, kyoo, eki* (SN) Choose Your Lesson: *Nihon Isshuu Tsuaa* (OR) Narita International Airport Kansai International Airport Central Japan International Airport Centrair New Chitose Airport Bullet train / *shinkansen*	- commuter train (2) - passport - bullet train (3) - time zones (activity)
61	Describing Lost Items		(SN) Choose Your Lesson: *Nihon Isshuu Tsuaa*	
62	Review		(SN) Choose Your Lesson: *Nihon Isshuu Tsuaa*	
63	Review	- Culture Notes review	(SN) Choose Your Lesson: *Nan-to iimasu-ka?* *Nihon Isshuu Tsuaa*	

13274291R00110

Made in the USA
San Bernardino, CA
15 July 2014